IN FULL FLIGHT

IN FULL FLIGHT

A STORY OF AFRICA AND ATONEMENT

JOHN HEMINWAY

ALFRED A. KNOPF · NEW YORK · 2018

Grateful acknowledgment is made to the following for permission to reprint previously published material:

New Directions Publishing Corp. and David Higham Associates Limited: Excerpt of "Do Not Go Gentle into That Good Night" by Dylan Thomas from *The Poems of Dylan Thomas,* copyright © 1952 by Dylan Thomas. Reprinted by permission of New Directions Publishing Corp. and David Higham Associates Limited.

Sony/ATV Music Publishing LLC: Excerpt of "Guilty" written by Gus Kahn, Harry Akst, and Richard Whiting. Copyright © 1931 by EMI Feist Catalog Inc. All rights administered by Sony/ATV Music Publishing LLC, 424 Church Street, Suite 1200, Nashville, TN 37219. All rights reserved. Reprinted by Sony/ATV Music Publishing LLC.

LIBRARY OF CONGRESS CATALOGING-IN-PUBLICATION DATA
Names: Heminway, John Hylan, 1944—author.
Title: In full flight : a story of Africa and atonement / by John Heminway.
Description: New York : Alfred A. Knopf, 2018.
Identifiers: LCCN 2017021058 | ISBN 9781524732974 (hardcover)R692 | ISBN 9781524732981 (ebook)
Subjects: LCSH: Spoerry, Anne, 1918–1999. | Women physicians—Africa—Biography. | Aeronautics in medicine—Africa. | Humanitarian assistance—Africa. | BISAC: BIOGRAPHY & AUTOBIOGRAPHY / Women. | TRAVEL / Africa / General. | HISTORY / Holocaust.
Classification: LCC R507.S64 H46 2018 | DDC 610.92 [B]—DC23
LC record available at https://lccn.loc.gov/2017021058

Jacket design by Janet Hansen

For Kathryn and Lucia

Going up that river was like travelling back to the earliest beginnings of the world, when vegetation rioted on the earth and the big trees were kings. An empty stream, a great silence, an impenetrable forest. The air was warm, thick, heavy, sluggish. There was no joy in the brilliance of sunshine. The long stretches of the waterway ran on, deserted, into the gloom of overshadowed distances. On silvery sandbanks hippos and alligators sunned themselves side by side. The broadening waters flowed through a mob of wooded islands; you lost your way on that river as you would in a desert, and butted all day long against shoals, trying to find the channel, till you thought yourself bewitched and cut off forever from everything you had known once—somewhere—far away in another existence perhaps. There were moments when one's past came back to one, as it will sometimes when you have not a moment to spare to yourself; but it came in the shape of an unrestful and noisy dream, remembered with wonder amongst the overwhelming realities of this strange world of plants, and water, and silence. And this stillness of life did not in the least resemble a peace. It was the stillness of an implacable force brooding over an inscrutable intention. It looked at you with a vengeful aspect.

—JOSEPH CONRAD, *HEART OF DARKNESS*

CONTENTS

◄◦►◄◦►◄◦►

Anne's 1948 journal: One week after escaping from France as she prepares to land in Beirut.

IN FULL FLIGHT

THE END

On February 6, 1999, a mob of yellow-billed kites circled Wilson Airport in Kenya, the busiest civil aviation hub in all Africa. The carrion birds had just left the nearby Nairobi slum of Kibera and were exploiting an uncommon void in the airspace over the runways. They might have been honor guards as they circled above a cortege of Land Cruisers, sedans, and buses out of which poured mourners: women in dated frocks and men stiff in regimental blazers, shiny at the elbow from age. Here and there, Ismaili and Sikh women, exiting minivans, arranged their saris. The great majority of arrivals were African, dressed in clothes reserved for church, weddings, and death.

Within the hangar only a few found seats; otherwise, it was

standing room only. None could recall Wilson Airport so hushed, with all airplanes tied down, as a mark of respect.

East Africa was in mourning for its celebrated flying doctor Anne Spoerry (pronounced Shpeuri), felled by a stroke four days previously at age eighty, still in harness to her life's calling, helping the rural poor. Over a thousand people found space in the Flying Doctors' hangar to pay last respects. The ceremony rang with the solemnity of a state funeral. Many had traveled from overseas, and no sector of Kenyan society was lacking. Infants strapped to their mothers' backs, creaky-limbed elders, a colorful array of tribes, Asian merchants, Europeans, Americans, government ministers, the diplomatic corps, and unattended children all jostled for sight lines in the echoing metal building.

Dr. Anne Spoerry had spent nearly fifty years in Africa, tending to the health of over a million patients, drawn mostly from the far corners of Kenya. It was said no other physician could match her industry, tenacity, and productivity in the cause of Africa's well-being. As a sole lifeline for the poor, it was not uncommon for patients to declare her a saint.

In the hangar the mourners were a study in devotion, stifling coughs, eyes flickering from emotion, minds reliving the triumphs of her life. The sight of Spoerry's Piper Lance PA-32 plane, known throughout Kenya as "Zulu Tango" from its call sign, 5Y-AZT, drew many to reach for handkerchiefs. Positioned front and center, both coffin and airplane were draped in tropical garlands. For those who once awaited Anne on ribbon-thin airstrips, this Africa-scarred machine spoke of endurance and courage. Zulu Tango had been their sole glimmer of hope in a land begging for miracles.

Over the course of Spoerry's long career, no place had been too far, no airstrip too risky, no patient beyond caring. Inside the echoing hangar, eulogies ran long, with every speaker heaping praise on the doctor for her no-nonsense style, strength, and compassion. An elderly woman whose broken arm Dr. Spoerry had set years before likened her to Mother Teresa. Another called her "an angel from heaven." Wherever she landed, she was greeted as "Mama Daktari," Mother Doctor—a sobriquet that met with Anne's hearty approval. When an unscheduled speaker, footsore from travel, rushed the podium, mourners checked their programs to see if they had missed something. He was a tall, dignified farmer, dressed in his one suit, confected with the red dust of Africa, and a tie that was black and borrowed. All leaned forward to hear his love sonnet. In linen-soft words, he declared that Dr. Spoerry had saved not just him but entire villages. He was here at the urging of his community to reassure all Dr. Spoerry would never be forgotten—not in the far corners of Africa, in this generation or the next. When he finished with a barely audible "God bless you, Mama Daktari," the Kenya Boys' Choir burst into Ave Maria. Soon the chanting bridged into a song of old Africa with one lone alto, repeating *"kaa maisho marefu,"* live forever, against an alto chorus and the beating aorta of a drum. The finale cued six strong men to lever open the hangar doors. As they did, a laser beam of noonday sun formed a corona over Zulu Tango, prompting a woman to confide, "The doors of heaven just opened."

Pallbearers hoisted the casket into the hold, then jockeyed the plane onto the apron. Outside, a throng of Wilson Airport personnel, most in coveralls, bowed their heads to honor the woman who, for over thirty-five years, they had guided safely home.

Dispensing with preflight checks, the Flying Doctors' chief pilot, Jim Heather-Hayes, fired up Zulu Tango's engine and was soon airborne. Almost immediately, he dropped a wing and banked hard. He had one last time-honored African ritual to perform before setting off for an Indian Ocean island, 290 miles to the east. Leaning into the controls, he drove Zulu Tango at the hangar, scattering the kites and missing the roof by mere feet. Later he recalled that as he rocketed over the heads of the mourners, the fluttering white hand-kerchiefs evoked a white-capped sea.

Once he had burst through equatorial clouds, Heather-Hayes set a course for the coast. From the ground, even when Zulu Tango was a mere pinprick, a few mourners continued to wave, as if trying to will Anne Spoerry back, for one last farewell. Many viewed her final flight as a death knell of individualism, a paean to an older Africa of boundless dreams and extravagant passions.

But Africa has a gift for concealment. This funeral was not only a tribute to a much-loved caregiver but also a triumph of trans-formation. In 1948, when Anne Spoerry set foot in Africa for the first time, she was consumed by two dreams: one was to disappear, the other to start over. Admittedly, she was not the first to use the continent for cover. With great spaces and laws begging to be bro-ken, Africa lends itself to secrets. In Anne's case, it rearranged a past of staggering complexity into a future of endless possibilities. Even now after half a century, her secrets were still safe. Among those who loved her—I include myself—no one knew what plights she once faced, how she had survived them, or the miraculous way she reinvented herself on this continent of endless beginnings.

At the time of Anne's death, I, like the rest, believed her decades in Africa was the only narrative that counted. So overcome was I by Africa's loving farewell and my own fresh memories of her I would set out to write her biography. In it I would showcase the exponen-tial power of the individual—how one astonishing soul can bring hope to the world's forgotten, on a colossal scale. Mine would be a tribute to Anne's indefatigable will to better the lives of the down-trodden, an affectionate memoir of a blazing career, propelled by idealism on the greatest stage of all—Africa.

Then I learned the truth.

CHAPTER 1

THAT'S ALL I'LL SAY

I first began chasing down Anne Spoerry long ago, in 1979. At the time I knew only headlines, with dozens of questions left unanswered. Was she French or Swiss? Was it conceivable she had only learned to fly in her mid-forties? What drove her to risk her life for a cause virtually of her own creation? Why had she never married? Was it true the desert nomads of northern Kenya know exactly the hour and by which thorn tree to gather to await the sound of her approaching plane? Whom did she answer to? Why did she conceal her past? Why had she really come to Africa?

Friends resorted to generalities, painting Anne Spoerry with the broadest of brushes: skilled aviator, gifted doctor, and rousing character. As a freelance journalist, I was regularly on the lookout for heroes and originals, and Anne Spoerry seemed to tick off all the right boxes: a bigger-than-life personality, exceedingly self-reliant, and driven to fulfill a remarkable African calling, on her own terms.

I began with a formal letter requesting an interview. No response. I wrote again, and again she did not answer. Finally, in February 1980, I called. The exchange was brief. Dr. Spoerry said she had no time for journalists and nothing to contribute to an article. Her terseness put me off. Was this a show of modesty or bad temper? Did she really believe her life was of no interest? In March, I called again. This time she answered straightaway and sounded a different note: she was curious and faintly warm and, best of all, had five minutes to spare that afternoon. The date was March 10, 1980.

With thunderheads heaped above the Ngong Hills, I drove to her office, closeted in a prewar bungalow beside Nairobi's Wilson Airport. She greeted me in mechanical monosyllables that cut through the high-octane rev of a country in love with aviation. Her firm handshake hinted that she had done her share of rotating props on bush strips and winching Land Rovers out of swollen rivers. As I settled into a straight-backed chair and jimmied my notebook from my bush jacket, I followed her scalpel eyes and did my best to affect an air of calm.

With Dr. Spoerry I hoped to discover a common core—a shared passion for Africa. Should we become friends one day, I would tell her my Africa tale: how, as a sixteen-year-old, I set sail along with three other schoolboys and a self-proclaimed explorer for Cape Town on the *Winchester Castle,* a refurbished Liberty ship; how from the moment the ship's horn sounded in Southampton, the word "Africa" became a fixation, tantalizing me with freedom I lacked at home. My fellow passengers appeared to have stepped out of a Somerset Maugham short story. A freshly minted missionary was bound for an outpost in Northern Rhodesia; a breakfast beer drinker, having failed as a prizefighter, was returning to Natal to take up sugar farming. One Lancashire family sought its fortune in the mines of Southern Rhodesia; a saucy girl, disappointed by Britain, was returning to Piketberg to grow apples and to break up with her tiresome boyfriend. By the makeshift pool, and in a dark-paneled saloon, I threw liars' dice, drank Pimm's Cups, listened to tales of the veld, and tapped my foot in time to songs of the Great Trek. I had staked everything that in Africa, I, all of sixteen, would find my way.

Braced for transformation, I spent the last night of the two-week passage lying on hemp ropes in the bow. When dawn mists cleared, Cape Town's perimeter landmark, Table Mountain, all lavender, towered to port. Soon, Malay stevedores jousted us to the dock. The gangplank was barely in place when I took my first African footstep. Straightaway I crossed a threshold into the epic.

It only got better. In South-West Africa we climbed into a cave with a two-thousand-year-old petroglyph of a warrior, in the Kala-hari Bushmen fled from our Land Rover, and at night herds of elephants ghosted past our cots under the stars. When I fished the Zambezi, crocodile eyes cut the river's surface and ghosted toward my knobby knees. Stunned and seduced by Africa's ferocity, gener-osity, and primal heart, I barely slept for two months.

Now in Anne Spoerry's office, after twenty years of knocking about the continent, I was ready to acknowledge a kindred spirit. Surely, she too must be a victim of *le mal d'Afrique,* the Africa passion. As she organized the clutter on her desk, my eyes ranged around the room. On a shelf lay a model of a dhow, the wooden ships that traded along the East African coast for well over two thousand years. To the right were Makonde carvings of stylized, emaciated women, propped against thick medical tomes. She had not yet bothered to frame a munificent commendation honor-ing her "ten years of service to the Foundation," signed by "His Excellency Hon. Daniel arap Moi, The President of the Republic of Kenya and Commander in Chief of the Kenya Armed Forces." Notebooks were stacked willy-nilly on her desk and at her feet lay two *kikapus,* sisal baskets, bursting with the bouquet of fresh fruits and vegetables. The moment I began my pitch, Dr. Spoerry interrupted: "Okay, meet me tomorrow morning at eight. Sharp. Otherwise I leave."

—◦—

So it was that on Tuesday, March 11, 1980, I waited beside 5Y-AZT just after dawn. When Dr. Spoerry arrived, she found me circling the plane to keep warm. She was all baskets, flight plan, and Gladstone bag. Her only remarks were one-word commands as she unlocked the passenger door and indicated where I was to sit as she conducted her preflight check. Once airborne, the doctor set a course for the north. For three hours, traversing two-thirds of Kenya, she said not a word, preferring to study instruments, charts, and landmarks. Every few minutes, I stole a glance. Her sculpted face—no hard edges but well-lived arcs—seemed right for the job. Hers was a reassuring look, especially the silver hair, cropped short, hinting at efficiency and scorn of convention. Laugh lines around her mouth fed into ridges circling her eyes, more hazel than blue, agitating back and forth across the instruments. It was a wonder that a sixty-one-year-old woman could be such a confident pilot, having only learned to fly in her mid-forties.

There was more to this lady. Already I had heard that since joining the Flying Doctors, she annually attended to as many as twenty thousand patients and inoculated over a hundred thousand—mostly children. One fellow doctor said Dr. Spoerry's productivity was "beyond comprehension." Another claimed she had personally saved more lives in Africa than any one human. Even without means of judging all the hyperbole, I considered myself privileged beyond measure to be flying with her. I glanced her way, seeking affirmation that I was in the company of greatness. Her eyes told me nothing.

An hour into our flight, hills flattened and forest green bleached to tin gray. Soon we were flying over an eroded desert, interrupted by narrow strokes of green where underground watercourses coaxed grass out of stone. Through Dr. Spoerry's side window, a perfectly round caldera appeared. It formed the southern edge of a vast soda lake that cut a furrow as far north as Ethiopia. Named a century before after Crown Prince Rudolf, heir apparent to the Austro-Hungarian Empire, this "Jade Sea" was renamed Lake Tur-kana, to honor the tribe inhabiting its western flank. Here, since the mid-1960s the Leakey family team had uncovered some of the earth's earliest humans. The name Turkana was now uttered in the same breath with other legendary sites, like the Olduvai Gorge in Tanzania and Taung in South Africa.

Today Dr. Spoerry was in no mood for pointing out landmarks. After nearly four hundred miles, she lowered the undercarriage and pulled on flaps. Leaning heavily into the controls, she set herself up for a carrier landing. "Illeret," she explained, needlessly referencing the sunbaked mission station, as she slammed on brakes. "Bloody awful surface."

After unloading, she pointed a finger at her Gladstone—her signal for me to pick it up and follow. I did so at a trot, reaching the clinic seconds after her. Standing a little over five feet, Dr. Spoerry appeared to compensate for size with a voice fit for a giant. It was so persuasive a six-foot, buck-naked warrior clicked bare heels and stood to attention, as if for regimental inspection. The doctor was only casually amused, reserving her smiles for children. As we cir-culated, she scribbled notes, checking off each patient with a num-ber, whenever a name was lacking.

At first, Dr. Spoerry seemed disposed to abstractions. "Soon" was any time ranging from five minutes to five months. She divided her thoughts into paragraphs, often punctuated by a clearing of the throat or a jingling of keys in a pocket. Alternately warm and remote, she had little time for introspection. Praise—giving or getting—was pointless. When one Illeret missionary called her a "godsend," she clinked loose shillings in her pocket, then studied her watch impatiently.

The doctor's first patient was a man so old that when asked his age, the nurses stretched their arms to describe infinity. That morning he had dragged himself over five miles to reach the clinic, and now, as he lay on a rubber bed cover, he appeared to be giving up the ghost. His skin was a shade of eggplant and taut like beaten tin. Over his rib cage, it flickered with each heartbeat as he clung to the bed frame, coughing and fighting the headwinds of death.

During her examination, Dr. Spoerry accidently dropped her stethoscope. Another was produced. That too proved useless. "Maybe this man has no heartbeat." Dr. Spoerry grasped his forearm for a second and, feeling little pulse, studied his eyes for a sign. She asked whether any family members were going to attend him in his last hours. The Sister shook her head. Dr. Spoerry paused to reflect, then stretched, placing her hand on his cheek. She kept it there as long as his eyes remained open. When she saw my smile, she scowled, snapped shut her bag, and followed the sound of wailing coming from another ward.

On the floor sat a young woman, bare above the waist except for a Maria Theresa thaler attached to a whirlpool of copper, encircling her neck, framing her breasts. As her eyes circled the room, she drummed her feet on the ground and hummed off-key. For the last few weeks, according to the nurse, she had ceased doing chores in her village. All her time was spent engaged in an incomprehensible internal dialogue. When Dr. Spoerry questioned her, she said, "Cha cha . . . ata"—meaningless words.

"Is she supposed to get married and does not want to?" the

doctor asked. The nurse shook her head. "What's wrong with the thumb?" The Sister removed dirty dressings to reveal a gash. Dr. Spoerry studied it and shook her head. She would have none of the girl's mother's explanation—that she had engaged in *hyana*—devil worship. "A brain tumor?" She shook her head. "Not with that pulse." In quick succession Dr. Spoerry discounted a brain ulcer, typhoid, and snakebite. The woman was now swaying, on the edge of a fall. Seizing her shoulder, the doctor gave her a sharp nudge. She remained standing.

"Just what I thought. You can feel her muscles tightening. She still knows enough not to let herself fall over." The doctor was already on her way to another patient. "Give her fifty milligrams of BD [bipolar medication], then if she does not recover, send her down to the hospital in Marsabit." Dr. Spoerry was convinced the girl was faking. "Maybe she does not want to work . . . or get married. Who knows?" Dr. Spoerry moved on.

Rendille, Daasanach, and Hamar patients had been waiting in the shade for hours. With babies jimmied to their breasts, women braced against the wind, hooding their eyes from plumes of dust. Dr. Spoerry scanned the sea of faces and immediately pointed out to the nurse the three she deemed the neediest. These she examined with some care, prescribing drugs and, in one case, cleaning and suturing an ugly wound. The rest she studied at a clipped pace, calling out each diagnosis to the attending Sister, as if she were sounding the roll call.

Once rounds were complete and the missionaries could catch their breaths around a table, Dr. Spoerry presented them with a *kikapu*, overflowing with fruits and vegetables from her farm. Having survived on canned food for the last month, they looked at the basket with reverence, thanking Dr. Spoerry over and over. "Enough of me," she broke in. "How have you been?" With solemn faces, they described a lamentable month of hardships. When one slipped "the Lord" into her list of happenings, Spoerry smartly set her glass back on the table and rose to leave. Missionaries, she later explained, were in Africa to do a job. Preaching was secondary. "Right," she said, turning to the door. "We'll be flying in the dark if we don't leave now." As she exited, she gathered up a packet of letters for posting: "That's all I am—the postman."

Back at Zulu Tango, juddering in the desert wind, the doctor reached into the plane's hold and presented the lay priests with another present—a month's supply of drugs and dressings. She then hoisted herself onto the plane's wing, snapped the seat belt, locked the door, and fired up the engine, scattering a herd of goats.

As Dr. Spoerry and 5Y-AZT flew out of the missionaries' lives, they stood absently, with all the sadness of a final farewell, as if they had lost a link to earth. Seen through scratched glass, they faded, stick figures one moment, dust devils the next.

—◦—

I flew with the doctor for three more days to destinations with charmed names—Laisamis, Loiyangalani, Illeret, Moyale, Saborei, Maikona, and Marsabit. At each, medics had consigned Dr. Spoerry's schedule to memory. Sometimes only warriors, wives, and toddlers, casting sundial shadows in the long grass, met us. By the end of our Northern Frontier tour, the doctor complained that she had attended to a mere 120 patients. "That's what happens when I have a journalist like you . . . Normally, I see double."

Examples of Dr. Spoerry's fearlessness abounded, especially when we landed in Moyale, in bandit country close to the Ethiopian border. As she treated multiple rifle and spear wounds in the makeshift clinic, the newly appointed resident doctor and his wife studied her in bewilderment, gobsmacked at her irreverent approach to danger. These two were polar opposites, they confided, living every moment braced for imminent death. At night they even slept together in the narrow bathtub as precaution against rifle fire. Dr. Spoerry said nothing. I even thought I heard a harrumph of disdain. Bush doctors, she later explained, have no right to complain. This was the life they chose.

On our penultimate evening, we landed at Loiyangalani on Lake Turkana's barren east shore. Dr. Spoerry thought nothing of touching down on an ill-marked and unlit strip just after sunset, with no margin for error. Her only comment was "I could use a beer." The fishing lodge where we were to stay was a collection of untidy huts, with no other guests, no manager, and a fetid swimming pool. Triumphantly applauding our arrival, the staff turned out in full livery and wide smiles. After showering, Dr. Spoerry and I joined each other on the terrace and immediately ordered a round of cold Tuskers as I readied my notebook for the interview. I had every intention of focusing on Africa, but for some unaccountable reason I began with a question about the war.

"You must have been twenty when the Germans invaded Paris?"

"No," she said, exploding. "I'm not going to talk about those times." Gripping her glass, she glared at me. "Yes, I watched those Panzer divisions move into Paris. The only way we could put up with it was with a bottle of cognac a day. We did our work and fortified ourselves with liquor. That was how demoralized we were. And when there was no more point being a medical student, I traveled south with all of France, along the roads, skirting the roadblocks. Yes, I was in the underground, and then I was taken a prisoner. That's all I'll say. Those days have no bearing on me today, or on the Flying Doctors. Absolutely nothing."

For a while, I sat immobile, hearing only the piping of bats. Occasionally, I stole glances at Dr. Spoerry, polishing off her beer, glowering at the palms, whipsawing against the stars. I should have known.

A week later back in Nairobi, I would interview Dr. Spoerry's boss, Dr. Michael Wood (later, Sir Michael Wood), director general of AMREF (African Medical and Research Foundation), and try to make sense of her tantrum. Wagging bushy eyebrows, he explained, "I don't blame her for not wanting to talk about the war. She was one of the few who survived. There's no doubt she's seen the seamy side of life. Why have to relive it now? I can tell you one thing, though: she has been made tough by it."

While Wood and Spoerry had worked together for well on fifteen years, he knew nothing of her past and seemed little to care. "It's almost too simple," he explained. "She just does her job. Others must evaluate, consider, weigh, before action. I call it paralysis by analysis. Modern people, it seems to me, are desperately analytical because they have no faith in what they are doing. It's easy, therefore, to talk yourself out of an act of courage. That, of course, is not Anne. She thinks by jumping in."

During that evening at Loiyangalani, Dr. Spoerry remained a puzzle. With banshee winds shrieking off the lake, her caftan snapping, silver hair shimmering under a pitching hurricane lantern, she continued to fulminate over my indiscretion. It was clear she had willed her life into chapters, with one resolutely sealed off as "classified."

Dr. Spoerry ordered the Nile perch ("the goat is deplorable") for the two of us. I willed myself to resume my interview and began with a simple question: Why had she come to Africa in the first place? Sawing on her Nile perch, she explained she had been inspired by the writings of the buccaneer traveler Henry de Monfreid. So transported was she, she traveled in his footsteps to Aden, then Ethiopia, and finally Kenya. Africa was love at first sight. By now, Dr. Spoerry was warming to the subject.

"So what is it about Africa?" I jumped in.

I expected her to conjure a moonlit night, a savanna alive with migrating wildebeest, or an infant's cherubic smile, but she abruptly changed the subject. "Look down there," she commanded. I turned and saw a row of *bandas,* or guest cabins. "*Banda* number six," she pronounced. "There it is." She gesticulated into the darkness. "At Christmas one year, I flew in here, and there were the lodge manager, Guy Poole, a missionary father, and an Italian lorry driver—all pumped full of lead, murdered by *shiftas,* bandits out of Ethiopia."

Disregarding my astonished look, the doctor now hit her stride: "We put the bodies in bags, and that was that." She slapped her hands to dramatic effect. "*Banda* number six. After it was repainted and the bullet holes in the walls filled in, I stayed there often. Take my word, there aren't any ghosts."

Emboldened by the fun of a brutal African tale, Dr. Spoerry called over the waiter, dressed in a ragged white mess jacket, and ordered the only white wine on the menu. "Probably turned to vinegar in the heat," she said to no one in particular. The man returned at a run, and as we swigged the syrupy confection, Dr. Spoerry's face softened. Her Africa was not a philosophical idea but a string of adventures: "There are strips, like Ngasume and Nabarera in the Masai Steppe, that make me scared out of my skin every time I have to land." The worst experience happened at Lobakat, a remote village on the west of the lake. "The strip was short and narrow, and—back in 1965—I came in very low, holding the nose high. Suddenly all went to hell as I got caught in a dust devil and could see nothing. The plane stalled out and dropped to the ground with a crash—so hard, in fact, it sheared off a wheel. We slid on the undercarriage and spun like a top. I stepped out to the most terrifying silence. Hell of a job getting help, since the place was known only to a few of us. One was Michael Wood. I strung out an antenna and called on the single-sideband radio. By sheer good luck, Michael answered and immediately dispatched help and spare parts." Dr. Spoerry beamed with Flying Doctor glory.

"What about the satisfaction?" I interrupted.

"Satisfaction." Her eyes cast about, weighing the question. In no time the answer came to her: "When I flew a pregnant woman to Nairobi Hospital, and one month later brought her back to her village with triplets. We sat them in the backseat of the plane, one dressed in blue, the other in pink, another in yellow." The light from the swinging lantern illuminated Dr. Spoerry's broad smile.

"Isn't birth control of concern to you?" Dr. Spoerry frowned as she banged down her wineglass. "Handing out birth-control information doesn't do any good at all. Anyway, that's not my job. The bulk of Africa won't ever respond to prodding. They'll have as many babies as they can." Her face softened. "Listen: I'm both a doctor and a farmer, and I've kept my eyes open. Personally, I believe we need better farmers more than we need less reproduction." She clapped her hands, subject closed.

—◇—

During the night my *banda* seemed to rock from the force of lake winds. Even the cot pitched, and there was a time when I felt I would be upended. In the morning, the wind died to a whisper, leaving the floor covered in red dust. I stumbled outside and called for Dr. Spoerry. Finding her *banda* empty, I ran down to the Loiyangalani mission clinic, by the lake, now all innocence. Dr. Spoerry was sitting at a makeshift desk on the porch, deep into morning rounds. Beside her, a hunchbacked Italian Sister announced each patient's ailments at full pitch. The first patient had a case of corneal ulcers, the second suspected tuberculosis, and the third, an old warrior, was diagnosed with "a bad tooth and a bad chest." Dr. Spoerry gave remedies for all except the old man, whom she waved away, having considered his condition more psychosomatic than real. Fourth on her list was a pregnant El Molo girl, who said her baby "is playing in my stomach." Dr. Spoerry tenderly rubbed it, then sent her off with an aspirin. Turning her attention to a man with amoebic colitis, she listened briefly, then handed him eight pills. Work on these four patients was complete in ten minutes and announced by the clinking of keys in her pocket.

En route to Zulu Tango, Dr. Spoerry detoured to the village. She had learned the El Molo were beset by an intestinal parasite. Studying a green film of slime covering a water hole, she concluded, "It's very simple. Everybody drinks from the same source, including camels and donkeys. Last time I was here, there was a crocodile in the pool. Either the water hole is to be cleaned and a fence erected, or everyone will have to start boiling water or live with diarrhea."

By our fourth and final day, Dr. Spoerry had yet to divulge anything personal. I still could not account for the career achievements that made her colleagues gasp in admiration. I knew only basics: she practiced her own brand of community medicine, with no time for lengthy diagnoses or expressions of sentimentality. Her genius lay in snap battlefield judgments. Whether she had acquired these instincts during the war was still a mystery. She may be the most efficient doctor in the world, but with no bedside manner she would never make it in a smart Western practice, say, on Park Avenue or Harley Street. In Africa, among the earth's poorest, she thrived.

Our final stop was a diocesan mission called Maikona, a settlement clinging to the hem of a sand dune, beside abandoned Gabbra *manyattas,* compounds. On the airstrip, we were met by Father Pelerino and Father Tablino, pale and off plumb in the howling wind. They led us to the hospital's examining room, where Dr. Spoerry barked at the mob to wait outside. When a warrior stood his ground, she leaned her shoulder into his waist until he stumbled away. Closing the door on another, she growled, "I can only see one patient at a time." "Now," she said in quite a different tone, fixing her eyes on an eight-year-old girl, with copper-colored skin, glossy hair, and a thin straight nose.

This triumph of desert beauty went by the name Kabala. At first, her body seemed as graceful as a ballerina's. "What a bonny little thing," Dr. Spoerry concurred. But when Kabala balanced herself on her right foot, she trembled from pain. Only by flailing her arms was she able to steady herself on her bent legs. Her mother, so desert worn she could pass for a granny, stood off to one side, her face stolid as stone. Naked, the girl performed a pirouette for Anne. Her right leg was three inches shorter than the left.

A Catholic Sister lifted Kabala onto the examining table. When the girl was asked to straighten the arch in her back, she strained until tears welled in her eyes. "Her hip is anchored in an awful position." Pointing to an open sore on one of Kabala's legs, Dr. Spoerry exclaimed, "Osteomyelitis." Generally introduced by an exterior agent, she said, the infection would spread. It had already affected Kabala's hips and spine. If not addressed, it would prove fatal. "Fancy surviving," Dr. Spoerry marveled.

Dr. Spoerry had a plan. She would fly Kabala and her mother a hundred miles to Marsabit hospital for X-rays. Then she would transport her to Sololo for orthopedic surgery. Her procedure would be phased over two operations: the first, to remove the infected bone; the second, to replace it with metal alloys. "She can also go to school in Sololo, and she will not be very far from home . . . Someday she might be able to walk normally." Through an interpreter, the proposal was put to the child's mother. The cost of flights, operation, and six months of hospital care came to the princely sum of two dollars. "I'll fly them both to Marsabit this afternoon," said the doctor, clapping her hands with finality.

Kabala's mother glowered. Addressing the interpreter, she gave her verdict: Airplanes were certain to fall from the sky, Marsabit was too far, and the child's father needed to be consulted. When she pronounced "Sololo," her manner turned to defiance. Her daughter would never go to school with children of the Boran, sworn enemies of the Gabbra. Kabala would not have the operation.

Dr. Spoerry snapped shut her notebook and headed for the next patient. One moment afire with the transforming power of medicine, now defeated by habits as old as the desert, she resumed rounds. Looking straight ahead she said, "Ask me first why she wasn't brought in a year ago before her condition became chronic. Ask me why her parents didn't care enough until now, and then I'll explain why I can't argue with the mother about Sololo. This is Africa. Let's go."

As Zulu Tango's shadow crossed a sand river, I picked out the forms of hobbled camels only from their petroglyph shadows. Once above the clouds, Dr. Spoerry, clinging to silence, set a course for Nairobi.

A month later I learned that Dr. Spoerry returned to Maikona to try to win over Kabala's mother. After an hour, the aged lady capitulated, and with Kabala they boarded a plane for the first time in their lives. Dr. Spoerry paid for everything—travel, surgery, food, and even the girl's interim education. Because of Dr. Spoerry's persistence, the surgery promised Kabala a long life.

Yet during my desert safari, Dr. Spoerry preferred me to see her commitment to community health alone; she affected little interest in individual cases, however dire or dramatic. But there were inconsistencies in the image she tried to portray. Especially telling was a moment in Loiyangalani when, just before leaving the clinic, Dr. Spoerry was approached by a woman, with teeth sharpened to points and her breast glistening from the suck of her child, now fast asleep on her back. The woman was not the only beggar in the throng, but she was the only one with a newborn. "My child is sick."

"What kind of sickness?" Dr. Spoerry responded.

"He suffers from *njaa*" (hunger), replied the mother. Dr. Spoerry looked carefully at the tubby boy, fast asleep and dressed only in an ostrich shell necklace. He seemed as healthy as other El Molo children.

"There is only one medicine for this disease of *njaa*," Dr. Spoerry told the mother. "And I happen to have it here." She dug into her pocket and presented the woman with all the shillings she had. I would easily have missed this moment if Dr. Spoerry had her way. As soon as she saw my admiring smile, she snapped shut her case and said, "Let's go."

CHAPTER 2

IF

Anne Spoerry possessed a narrative style all her own. At Loiyangalani when she recounted how she came to Africa, her past was a scattershot affair, one incident tripping over another in cockeyed chronology. With wind whistling through palms and our wine warm and sweet, she made the ocean voyage out to be a giant caper in a life of grand adventure.

It was not until after her death, when Anne's illustrated handwritten journal and other documents fell into my hands, that I learned her departure from Europe was anything but a breeze—much more than what she described as an "escape from bloody conflicts to a more peaceful world." In fact, when Anne, aged thirty, embarked from Marseille harbor, she was on the run.

While Anne's journal peters out after seven months, it represents her life's most meticulously illustrated and robust account of daily happenings. In it, she never missed an opportunity to celebrate moments of discovery and daring. But try as she might, she could not disguise a deep brooding frame of mind, an unsettling discomfort with Europe, and a compulsion to mask the past.

—◦—

"Leaving Marseille. Sunday, October 10, 1948, at noon": Anne Marie Spoerry began the story of her voyage like a bulletin. Today, in this gutted harbor, she boarded *El Hak,* a fifteen-hundred-ton rusting cargo ship, veteran of several identities and carrier of more than one flag. Her staccato sentences gave no hint that at the time Mademoiselle Spoerry, possessing two passports, one Swiss, one French, was alone, conflicted, and battling a troubling past.

None of *El Hak*'s other fourteen passengers knew anything of the thirty-year-old single woman. If she drew stares, it would have been for the intensity of her grip on the railing. Some might have defined her features as Germanic, but when, in time, she spoke, her public school English, tinged by a Gallic lisp, would have comforted them, mostly British civil servants returning from leave.

With black-headed gulls wheeling past the stanchions, Mademoiselle Spoerry invited little attention to herself. The clothes she wore made her look older than her years—lace-up shoes, brown skirt, and mackintosh. Her prematurely silvering hair, cut short, framed a strong face—the sort that refused to wear makeup. Nettled by the ship's slow progress leaving the harbor, she sought out a figure on the shore. At last, when the ship's bell rang for the last, she waved. The gesture brought a gentleman on the quay back to life. Here was the revered and sometimes feared head of the Spoerry family and guardian of its fortunes. For as long as she remembered, she had addressed her father as "Papo." In his company, she was still a child. From him, she had learned the art and science of the well-kept secret.

As the ship's Yemeni crew coiled the hemp lines, she saw Papo raise his arm in a discreet wave. She strained to hear words across the widening divide, with the ship's horn sounding. She noted the handkerchief dab at his eyes and painfully watched him avert his gaze. Was this theatricality, or was Papo truly in pain? She could not be certain. This Calvinist family was expert at concealing the workings of the heart. With similar restraint, Anne Spoerry responded with a wan smile and a hurried wave.

Anne Spoerry had dreamed of an eventless farewell while fearing the worst—gendarmes hurtling along the quay, demanding the gangplank be lowered, and hauling her off in front of startled passengers. But as the battered ship worked its way out from the quay, she grew more confident. With the gap widening, her nerves steadied, and in the space of a few minutes her grip relaxed as she gazed upon the last of France.

When the ship drew away, the legacy of war was written all over the shuttered storefronts and warehouses of Marseille harbor. The oiled sea, slate sky, and splintered docks mirrored the temper of postwar France, and even on deck memories of war were raw, three years after Adolf Hitler committed suicide and Germany capitulated.

With the *El Hak* churning muck and oil from the harbor, two storm petrels hurtled past the stanchions. The sight of these wanderers bucked up Mademoiselle Spoerry, yearning to fly away as well. As the sight of her father's fedora vanished, she hoisted two oversize suitcases, turned, and headed down a flight of narrow stairs to a small, airless cabin.

—<o>—

After Anne Spoerry took in the cabin's bunk, washstand, and open wardrobe, she had time to ponder the circumstances that had brought her here. A month before, her father had sat with his neighbor, friend, and in-law, Antonin "Anto" Besse, and decided her future. With little time to waste, decisions were made, absent her opinion.

Monsieur Besse owned *El Hak;* on it, he could do as he pleased. The cargo vessel flew under a red and green company flag, circling his monogram, AB. All *El Hak* bathrooms were stocked with bars of soap stamped with an identical moniker. As shipowner, he possessed rights that dwarfed even those of the captain. One was the right to appoint the ship's doctor. Who would know that Anne, a mere medical student, lacked any certification and, according to maritime law, was not qualified to serve on board?

Hilda and Antonin Besse were returning to their base in Aden, after an idyll of a summer at Le Paradou, their farm in the hills above the Spoerry estate in the South of France. The two families were old friends, and with the marriage of Anne's brother, François, to Anto's daughter that friendship became a dynastic coalition.

On her first night at sea, as she passed the Château d'If and Monte-Cristo and later Toulon, the wind picked up, and by midnight it grew to a force five gale. The Spoerrys, accomplished yachtsmen, prided themselves on their seafaring legs. A rolling ship was pure adventure for Anne Spoerry. But for Mademoiselle Taillarde, one of her fellow passengers, the night was pure misery. The captain directed "Dr." Spoerry to attend to her. She carefully determined her symptoms, administered two sedatives, and watched her eyes close. Once she was asleep, Anne stole away to her own berth. Sleep was intermittent, for reasons she never divulged. Was she deliberating over events of her past or weighing the future? After midnight, Anne swept off the sheets, tossing.

For the next four nights, Anne slept fitfully. In a previous time, she might have been exhilarated, slipping through the Strait of Messina, rounding Brindisi, skirting Crete. Like her father and brother, she worshipped the Mediterranean and its mythology. When they sailed, the men manned the helm, while she ruled over the foredeck, trimming jib and spinnaker. Papo always struck a memorable pose, with his trilby pulled down over his bald spot, as he steered the gaff-rigged sloop through "wine dark seas" into coves, he claimed, where Odysseus might once have slipped anchor.

Monsieur Besse was cut from a different cloth than her father. She knew the legends—Aden's most prominent trader, with interests ranging from the manufacture of soap to trade in leopard skins, Maria Theresa thalers, and gold bullion. Anyone planning business in Yemen, the Hadramawt, and the Horn of Africa needed Monsieur Besse, for in addition to *El Hak* he owned another steel-hulled vessel, as well as a fleet of motorized wooden dhows that plied the Red Sea and the Indian Ocean. Wandering ships, foreign soils, mysterious cargoes—Anne had dreamed of this swashbuckling life since childhood. Now she would live it, sailing tropical seas, venturing where few Frenchwomen dared.

Forty-one years Mr. Besse's junior, Anne belonged to a generation given to addressing their parents' friends formally. "Monsieur Besse" was not merely her elder; he was her patron and savior, coming to her rescue with this conveniently timed job on the high seas. Now she needed to reward his trust in every way—no great problem because Anne held him in high esteem, for his independent spirit and unlimited supply of yarns about exotic ports and shadowy consignments. Every time he began with "that reminds me" she felt airborne, free from the torment of history.

On day four, Monsieur Besse showed her a letter he intended to send to a certain unidentified "SE" in her defense on an undisclosed matter. She thought his argument too forceful and that it might not have the desired effect. He brushed aside her concerns and sealed the envelope. Anne thereupon returned to her journal and banished from her mind his heavy-handed intervention. A brush and palette served up necessary distractions. She began by illustrating Mount Etna in all its drabness, and when a pigeon landed on deck, she added a blush of pink to its chest. On a high deck, she could delight in the sight of fulmars cresting swells and of a three-master under full sail, beating for the great beyond. *El Hak* and Anne's destiny now lay on a heading of 120 degrees.

Nearing Lebanon, Anne began to find the equipoise that had eluded her so far. Monsieur Besse, devotee of vigorous exercise, encouraged her to join him on his power circuits of the ship. With France now well below the horizon, Anne looked to Suez, the Red Sea, and the future. On their invigorating tramps, Monsieur Besse reminisced about friends, such as explorers St. John Philby and Freya Stark; he enchanted Anne with tales of the vast Empty Quarter of Saudi Arabia, its wanderers, and its secret oases.

On Saturday, October 16, Monsieur Besse gave Anne a lifetime gift, when he recited Rudyard Kipling's "If—" in French. She called it extremely beautiful, *fort belle*. For both, its verses captured prized battlefield virtues—tenacity, modesty, and self-confidence. When she heard the lines

> *If you can meet with triumph and disaster*
> *And treat those two impostors just the same,*

she felt a frisson of hope she had not known since before the war. With each verse—brief, positive, and steady as gunfire—a veil parted, and she saw the future with metronomic clarity. It little mattered that Kipling was addressing a boy. With scant effort, Anne could read herself into the stanzas of "If—," willing her enemies in France to vaporize, the swirl of old passions to ebb, and a new future to rise from the far shore ahead.

Since her teens, Anne had been drawn to medicine. Once she had intended to take up a village practice in France or Switzerland. She was analytic, cool in emergencies, and driven to repay the world for the good fortune of her birth. Now shut out of Europe, Anne had readjusted her sights. Somewhere far from home, in a remote and exotic landscape, she would start over. She pictured herself in the desert surrounding Palmyra. There, Bedouins, squatting on haunches, would await her signal. With syringe and forceps, suture and antibiotic, she would regain the esteem denied her at home and save nomads, one at a time.

—◦—

As *El Hak* left France far behind, Anne's journal became more assured, with drawings increasingly colorful and descriptions more detailed. In Beirut, she walked backstreets, admiring desert chiefs in long robes and nomads, dressed in kaffiyehs, just arrived from the Bekaa valley. When she returned to her cabin on her last evening in Beirut, she discovered yet another gift. Monsieur Besse had pinned to her door a sign reading, DR. SPOERRY: SHIP'S SURGEON. With four words he presented her with a future. She was now the first physician in the Spoerry family. If only Papo could see the sign for himself. She could imagine his glee at the shock written across the face of a passenger, scandalized that the ship's doctor was a woman. When Anne opened the green cover of her journal that evening, her handwriting was bold and triumphant. The next morning, when *El Hak* steamed out of Beirut harbor, plunging into the Mediterranean, she wrote that she enjoyed her first good sleep since leaving Marseille.

Where once the sea had roiled like mercury, today, beneath a pale pink sky, it turned mother of pearl. The next evening Anne retired early in order to be on hand for the ship's arrival in Port Said at 23:30. Once in the Suez Canal, she positioned herself on deck, experimenting with one watercolor after another—cobalt seas, ocher dunes, and bloodred fires above the petrol fields of Djebel Gharib. Her best works were simple—a lone lighthouse, a crest of hills, a monument at Ismailia, at the mouth of the canal.

During scalding days in the Red Sea, Anne completed Papo's reading list—art historian Élie Faure's biography of Napoleon and Salomon Reinach's history of religions. She packed both books up as *El Hak* landed in Jeddah to drop four Mecca-bound pilgrims and take on a hundred more, each paying Monsieur Besse the princely sum of twenty gold sovereigns for the privilege of deck passage to Aden. Anne joined them on deck, so determined was she not to miss the phosphorescence of the Red Sea or her first view of what she called "Arabie."

While watching a school of porpoises cresting *El Hak*'s bow wave, Anne admitted that she felt better rested than she had in years. Now she was free to perform medical duties without the corrosive oversight she found so toxic in France, and each night on the bridge she reveled in the sight of the Southern Cross, a few degrees to starboard of *El Hak*'s course.

By now, the small knot of fellow passengers had begun to pay more attention to this mysterious woman of dual nationality. She undoubtedly came from a family of means. Why did she always insist on sitting at Monsieur and Madame Besse's table with the captain and chief engineer? Why was she agitated when others posed questions? Mr. and Mrs. Jackson made that mistake when they asked her where she had been during the war. Anne's eyes narrowed, the table went quiet, and Monsieur Besse gallantly changed the subject. It came as no great surprise that in Beirut the Jacksons disembarked, in favor of sailing on the much faster *Pace*. Anne would not miss them.

Anne's reluctance to discuss the war in the early postwar years was nothing exceptional. Indeed, she might not have been the only *El Hak* passenger escaping Europe. Many, living with difficult memories, had perfected similar stratagems to dodge inquiries. Even Anne's journal studiously banned memories. Long ago she had learned from her father to camouflage matters of the heart in banalities and displays of modesty. On matters related to the war, her steely glare was sufficient to keep the inquisitive at bay.

Before she reached Aden, a glow returned to Anne's face, and at meals she took to wearing her one tropical blouse. On Friday, October 29, she asked Monsieur Besse, four decades her senior, to hold her legs as she dangled upside down—to film with her color Keystone 8 mm movie camera nine porpoises cresting the bow wave. As the rusted plates of the ship sliced the indigo water inches away, she felt airborne. She was Rudyard Kipling's boy hero—brash, daring, like a "son." Cheating death at the convergence of rusted steel and blue sea was her tonic. The stunt might have been a trifling conquest, but for her levitating upside down in the bow wave heralded a new beginning. That night she slept on the deck, vowing not to miss anything.

On November 1, Anne awoke to the sight of eroded volcanic hills plunging into angry surf. In the afternoon, *El Hak* rounded a headland to berth in its home port of Aden. Soon Anne's journal rhapsodized about sunsets, rustling palms, and cumin-scented air. After one special night, she painted a falling comet so bright it dimmed the stars. Cerulean, crimson, and magenta had become Anne's new palette.

◂◦▸

In Aden, Anne signed on once again under Captain Dennis Welch for her second *El Hak* tour, this time ferrying pilgrims between Jeddah and Aden. Twice daily she conducted her surgery. Even though she did not understand the Somali deck passengers, she had no difficulty diagnosing their many wounds, resulting from their violent lifestyle with cousins cutting up brothers, and brothers other brothers, all with long knives. So stoic were they that Anne sutured their muscles and scalps without anesthesia.

Captain Welch held Mademoiselle Spoerry in such high esteem

for her medical efficiency that when *El Hak* returned to its berth in its home port of Aden on November 5, he signed her certificate of discharge with a "V.G." (very good). When she countersigned it, she preceded her name with a forceful "Dr."

Back in Aden, Anne stayed in Monsieur Besse's house. She called him the perfect host and the house "princely." She admired his knack of engaging and charming every member of society, whatever the class or the means. In Aden he lived by his own rules, never answering to others. Anne called him *"le grand patron"* as well as "a true MAN" (Anne's capitals), referencing Kipling. "AB" (for Antonin Besse), she wrote, was everything she admired—"gentleman scholar, merchant, and psychologist."

As much as possible, Anne steered clear of introspection in her journal. Something unspoken appeared to drive her, filling her with anxiety and doubt and leaving her in hope that "Arabie" would offer her what she could not find at home. Thanks to Monsieur Besse, she had become fixated on Kipling's "man," seemingly her new ideal.

In the fortresslike Besse villa (whose floor plan Anne rendered with great exactitude in her journal), she settled into a spacious room on the second floor not far from her hosts' apartment. She was not to linger long. On November 21, 1948, she again set to sea as ship's doctor, this time on another pilgrim trip to Red Sea ports of call that included Djibouti, Asmara, Port Sudan, and Hodeida. As soon as she returned to Aden on the twenty-ninth, Monsieur Besse announced his intention of sending her to a favorite destination—Al Mukalla, 125 miles east of Aden. He was certain she would find it as enchanting as he.

On December 1, from the deck of *El Hak* Anne watched the blistered volcanic Hadramawt shore give way to a narrow defile that led to a harbor unlike any she had ever seen. With the exception of a "Mrs. Sargent," the local doctor, and the British political adviser,

Anne was the only European in medieval Al Mukalla at the time, and she adored the distinction. Framed by low ocher volcanoes, white filigreed mud-bricked "skyscrapers," and tall minarets, Al Mukalla rose above the waterfront. The leaning masts of ocean-going dhows left a hatch work of reflections in still waters, and at dusk the most consistent sounds along the harbor front were ropes chafing and muezzins calling the faithful to prayer. In alleys, black-robed captains, or nakhodas, bargained for cargoes, and veiled women, shunning eye contact, seemed to fly past, like bats, as they hurried to rejoin the harem. Crowds followed Anne, no doubt agape at the sight of a white woman, hair cut short and sporting a khaki jacket with epaulets. Out of the desert dust came a swirl of Bedouins. "Chameleons, all blue," she called them, "their skin indigo," and around their pencil-thin waists clattered silver belts. The people, the architecture: this was why she had come to Arabie. She called Al Mukalla "one of the most beautiful places in the world."

In the harbor Anne saw her first *boom,* a large wooden ship out of Kuwait, awaiting the *kuzi,* the northeast monsoon that for nearly two thousand years had wafted dhows to Africa. On the open deck rested a pair of arctic terns, regaining strength for the migration south. One deck below, a thousand baskets of Basra dates were stored. After bartering in Al Mukalla, the *boom*'s nakhoda would set course for the eastern headland of Socotra, then sail before the wind down the coast of Somaliland, to Lamu and Mombasa, before tacking into the harbor of Zanzibar. There he would exchange his cargo for mangrove poles, elephant ivory, and perhaps (lips sealed) slaves.

Entranced, Anne returned to Aden and for ten days worked in the hospital, studied Arabic, and rode horseback. On December 11, Monsieur Besse sent her to Djibouti, where she conducted medical rounds before flying to Addis Ababa to await final preparations for what Monsieur Besse had described as the perfect journey—a thousand-mile safari across Ethiopia, in his splendid Plymouth "woody" station wagon, driven by his chauffeur, Haillié. Joining her was Mr. Davies, Monsieur Besse's Addis Ababa office agent, and Bon Patia, his Hindu accountant, to pay the bills.

Anne's safari through this feudal land—almost all of it on rough roads—took forty-five days. It was the fulfillment of a dream, born two years after the war. She had always viewed Aden as a port of call en route to a final destination. Africa might well be that final destination.

-◄o►-

Anne's excitement, reflected in her journal, was notable on her first day in Ethiopia. Where once her journal illustrations had reflected the grays of war-shadowed Bordeaux, now the pages shone with reds and blues, verging on the garish. On two occasions, she dedicated eight pages of writing to a single day, descriptions tumbling over each other, extolling geology, birds she found near mythic, and ancient ways of life straight from scripture. Her sole guidebook was a much-thumbed paperback titled *En Abyssinie,* by Hermann Norden, published in 1930.

Anne's diary bears the hallmark of a classic traveler's journal, with maps and architectural renderings crafted with a nineteenth-century explorer's precision. Little is left to the imagination. All noteworthy features were illustrated—gray rocky outcrop, reed beehive, and hand-hewn culvert. Whenever she told Haillié to brake the Plymouth, she leaped into the bush with her journal to capture the extravagance of carmine bee-eaters, ground hornbills, banded barbets, stilts, and louries. Donkey herders, dressed in cloaks, waving shepherds' crooks, reminded her of the New Testament, and when she painted the African sky, her renderings were electric. Dessie, Batie, Lake Haik, Jimma, Agaro, the Blue Nile, Diré Daoua, Harar, were all way stations on the road to transformation.

In Ethiopia, Anne, about to turn thirty-one, discarded the past and embraced everything that was remote and foreign.

Anne's ardor for Africa peaked a few days before Christmas 1948. Miles from comfort, at the foot of a giant euphorbia, local herders lit a fire, illuminating a broad, grisaille landscape. Around the fire clustered men and women, chattering and laughing as if there had never been a war. Hobbled donkeys brayed. The star-drenched sky lit up an entire mountainside and turned the sand at her feet into eggplant purple. At this wide remove from the twentieth century, Anne lay alone, drugged by the plainsong of Amharic laughter. Even without understanding one word, she gloried in the sound of their language. When the herders drifted off, she stretched out on the hard ground. From time to time opening her eyes as voices rose and fell, she experienced an explosion of pure joy that she had not known in almost a decade.

Some fifty years later, Anne described this very place to me, matching word for word her journal account. Even in old age, she said, she could still feel the hard ground, see the diamond sky, and thrill to the impenetrable laughter. Recounting the story of that evening, framed by euphorbia and unshackled people, made her eyes glisten. For her, that evening would always encapsulate Africa in all its purity and innocence.

Oddly, Anne never made lasting friends in Ethiopia—not even with Mr. and Mrs. Davies, with whom she stayed in Addis Ababa. While she found them *"très aimables,"* one senses unease, perhaps brought on by her concern that Monsieur Besse had divulged more than necessary about her past. After Anne celebrated Christmas in Addis with a French family, spoiling their small daughter with toys, she never spoke of them again. At this time in her life, she seemed little interested in friendships. She grilled every expat she met for information about life in Ethiopia. It would appear she was trying to imagine how she would fit in. A Swiss couple, resident in

Ethiopia for three years, felt inert in the grip of Ethiopia's ancient customs. Now they were planning to leave for Kenya, to the south. Anne took note.

When Anne applied to Ethiopia's general consul of the Ministry of Health for a job as a medical officer, her application was rejected. In her journal, one detects relief. "So much still has to be done." In Harar, Anne took a special interest in its leprosarium. She interrogated its doctor about the cost of care and the contributions of government to the welfare of its patients, some with elephantiasis.

By the end of January 1949, Anne had accepted defeat. The magnitude of Ethiopia's epidemics, plagues, locusts, and poverty was simply overwhelming. Even the largest health-care center in Ethiopia—the government hospital in Addis—lacked essential medicines. In 1949 Ethiopia, with fifteen million people, there were only twenty-nine Western-trained doctors. Even more concerning, the great majority of these were American Seventh-Day Adventists, devoutly practicing vegetarianism and temperance—unsavory restrictions for Anne, who saw nothing amiss in satisfying her hunger and slaking her thirst with beer and wine, as every French-woman should.

Another reality weighed heavily on Anne: Ethiopia was remote. While she was no stranger to isolation, in Ethiopia she would have to accept life as a hermit. Anne needed the company of other Europeans, as much for friendship as for solidarity. She believed she was best suited to a colony with disciplined workers and pukka clubs with jolly members.

Throughout her Ethiopian account, there is little trace of inner turmoil. When a Monsieur and Madame de Blascon told her they were going to France on holiday, she wrote, "I think they must regret leaving this beautiful life, even temporarily." Anne's transformation also was expressed by her appetite. She wrote rapturously about jam, butter, goat, and berries. In Africa, she would never starve again.

On Thursday, January 27, 1949, after a month and a half, she returned to Aden. There she reconnected with a mysterious woman called "I.O." whose identity she would not disclose to her journal. I.O. was not only her driving instructor but also a regular companion. On January 31, she met with Mrs. Cochrane at the hospital and signed a six-month contract to work in the women's ward. For the moment, she felt content working on a fixed schedule, galloping across the desert in the afternoons and socializing with other expats at the club each evening. Like her father and Monsieur Besse, Anne was an ardent Anglophile. She loved Aden's imperial pomp, class system, and quaint colonial eccentricities and found nothing awkward in the presumption that a few European civil servants could impose their wills and biases upon a large population of "the great unwashed." But while her politics might have embraced privilege, her medical ethics were rigorously egalitarian, with a fair shake for all. Once she accepted never being free to practice medicine in Europe, she had set herself a goal of helping the less fortunate in other regions. In Yemen, that ambition was easily met. The locals were compliant, trusting, and grateful, unlike the French she had left behind.

In Aden, loneliness never afflicted Anne. Whenever she sought fellowship, there was a pool of agreeable men and women, regularly resupplied out of the British Isles. Most were of a mind that Aden was a staging post to a more permanent assignment in some other colony.

Anne's daily routine began with morning hospital rounds, often followed by afternoons studying Arabic or learning to drive an automobile. When not sailing, she played polo or, with Monsieur Besse, explored on horseback the surrounding *djebels,* cantering back to the stables just before dusk. Anne rarely turned down an invitation to the club. Several times a week, she dined with the Besses and never tired of A.B.'s erudite conversation. Whenever she was alone in her room, she wrote letters, most to her father in Mulhouse, the site of the Spoerry family seat in eastern France. None have survived, because Henry Spoerry was habitually discreet about family matters.

On Sunday, March 6, 1949, Anne wrote in her journal, "I went to the hospital to assist with Cochrane's visit. He told me that I have the government's approval for my hospital work, but Dr. Jones who previously held my position is probably my enemy." Anne hinted that Dr. Jones had been casting aspersions on her qualifications as a doctor as a means of regaining his foothold. Perhaps he had heard rumors of her past. But Anne seemed little worried because she knew, when the chips were down, Monsieur Besse would come to her defense. That afternoon, Anne went sailing with friends, and the following morning she purchased an automobile. Her boldness was rewarded. A week later, Dr. Jones gave up and left Aden for good. Anne celebrated with a morning sail. Ten days later, she was appointed head of the women's ward.

Even in her new position, Anne's workday began at seven, ended with lunch at one, with an afternoon of sport, followed by dinners under the stars. Colonial Aden in 1949 could not have been jollier or more accommodating for a young woman with a troubled European past.

Anne wrote her last entry in her journal on April 10, just after posing for a photograph with her team of Yemeni nurses, all wearing ankle-length dresses and head scarves. While Anne was more comfortable in trousers, hospital rules mandated a strict dress code for women. Anne wore a matronly white skirt, reaching just below her knees—bare minimum for Europeans living in this strict Muslim society.

In the group photograph, Anne's sunny smile conveyed more than job security. Previously, on January 25, 1949, thirty-five hundred miles away in Paris, a long, painful ordeal had been resolved in Anne's favor. Months passed before a clerk legitimized the ruling and her father sat down to write her with the news that her life's great burden had been lifted. She received his letter a few days before happily posing for her photograph with her team of Yemeni nurses.

While Henry's letter gave Anne a second chance in life, it cautioned her that others might not be of the same mind. After reading the letter, Anne Spoerry reapplied herself to her life's calling. Now she could devote the rest of her life to ministering to the needy. With this hushed victory came one lingering concern: no matter how far from France she settled, she would always live in dread that someone with a long memory would come calling.

CHAPTER 3

LA COQUILLE

During her many years in Africa, Anne publicly dropped her guard once—in 1967, when she gave an interview to journalist and TV executive Barry Wynne. Wynne, a warm, engaging, and tenacious interviewer, was writing a book about the first decade of the Flying Doctors Service. Published in 1968 under the title *Angels on Runway Zero 7,* the book had a tiny press run and died an untimely death. Today, most copies available on the Internet are library rejects.

When she gave her interview, Anne had been with the Flying Doctors for only three years. While she selectively parsed critical details, she divulged far more than she ever did with other journalists or in her memoirs, published three decades later. Perhaps a few beers or a bottle of wine made her drop her guard. Maybe she was struck by an overpowering desire to impress Wynne with her derring-do. One year later, when he read how much Anne had disclosed in *Angels on Runway Zero 7*, her brother, François, expressed his displeasure. Reprimanded for her loose tongue, Anne kept the existence of the book to herself for the rest of her life and on one occasion dismissed Wynne's account as "a pack of lies."

Wynne's skill as an interviewer and Anne's ill-advised candor were biographical windfalls, bringing to light Anne's early, often dangerous months leading up to war.

—◄o►—

In the spring of 1918, in the last days of World War I, Henry Spoerry had decided that his wife, Jeanne, then in the final trimester of her pregnancy, would be safer in the South of France rather than deal with anti-French uncertainties in German-controlled Mulhouse in disputed Alsace. She arrived in Cannes on May 12 and a day later gave birth to her first daughter, Anne Marie. The Spoerrys already had a son, François, born six years earlier. By some accounts, Henry had wanted another son. One member of the family claimed that the father never disguised his disappointment at having a girl. As she matured, Anne would do all to please him, even cutting her hair short and wearing trousers rather than dresses.

Anne was born into a family rooted in commerce. Her parents, both from Swiss Calvinist stock, were heirs to separate textile fortunes. Her father ran Voucher (later SIEC), a company founded by his grandfather in Switzerland and Alsace. Her mother was born Jeanne Cécile Schlumberger. Neither Anne, her younger sisters, Martine and Thérèse, nor her brother, François, spoke much of their mother. Because he considered financial matters far too weighty for a woman, Henry managed all her assets, accumulated by hardworking forebears from Fischenthal in the canton of Zurich. In thrall to his formidable intellect, she accepted her role as household manager. For Anne and her siblings, their pious and comforting mother was a much-appreciated but near-invisible family fixture.

When Anne sought a role model, she looked to her father, Henry. She was proud of his wartime record, having survived Verdun, the most devastating battle of World War I. She boasted that as it raged around him and shells whistled overhead, he set his cool, analytic mind to perfecting a circular mapping system—a methodology that later proved useful to the French army. Scholarly, theoretical, and focused, even in battle, he was Anne's first ideal.

Anne was so awed by her father that although he was her height once she was fully grown, she always remembered him as a towering figure. His sharp eyes, angular nose, and distinguished suits and hats evoked a gentleman scholar, more British than French. Most weekdays, regardless of weather, he walked a mile to his office. Officially, he was there to manage family finances, especially large holdings in Voucher. Unofficially, according to his grandson Bernard, he spent his office time indulging scholarly interests, such as teaching himself classical Japanese. Anne never dwelled on these inconsistencies, preferring instead to fixate on his intellect. Yet, because Henry's scholarship, special interests, and hobbies absorbed so much of his time, little remained for portfolio management. At the time of his death, a large family fortune had been substantially squandered.

Anne grew up in one of Mulhouse's stately homes, the Spoerry family seat at 1 Rue du Sundgau, built in the English style by Anne's great-grandfather in the late nineteenth century. Set on a hillside in a quiet shady neighborhood, it still breathes discreet prosperity with its high walls encircling a secret garden of ancient oak, cedar, and beech. Even today, far from the hurry and bluster of commercial Mulhouse, the estate evokes a hush. Anne saw Rue du Sundgau as a safe house against interlopers, an impenetrable vault, welcoming close family members and trustworthy friends. Tutors and governesses came and went, strengthening family bonds and enforcing

Spoerry codes of rectitude, service, and sport. Discipline began in the nursery. At the dinner table, children were permitted to talk to their father only after being addressed by him. While all learned German in school, at home that language was outlawed, as a reflection of Henry's aversion to Germany's former annexation of Alsace. There were other rules guiding table talk in the Spoerry household. Whenever one of the children wished to talk, he or she was compelled to construct sentences grammatically, logically, and in full command of the facts. Opinions were of lesser value, to be reached as the summation of facts. With such strict rules of conversation, Anne kept her own counsel. She never took issue that at 1 Rue du Sundgau men reigned.

—◄o►—

Outside in the estate's large garden, rules varied. Here Spoerry children were free to be themselves. Behind its ivied walls, in the shade of its great specimen trees, Anne, her three siblings, and their friends played war games and tested each other's nerves, climbing high, jumping far, and, in Anne's case, mimicking the antics of boys. At Rue du Sundgau, Anne advanced from commanding a regiment of wooden soldiers to forming garrisons. In doing so, she impressed into service her compliant sisters and willing friends.

Over the course of the year, Henry arranged the calendar to accommodate a circuit of Spoerry estates. Once school had adjourned, the family decamped to its villa in the South of France, three hundred meters from the Baie de Cavalaire, halfway between St.-Tropez and Toulon. Next, during the months of August and September, the Spoerrys moved en masse to their family seat on Switzerland's Lake of Zurich. Their sixteenth-century manor house lay outside the village of Männedorf on 1.3 kilometers of private lakefront, fronted by a massive boathouse, which Spoerry children came to designate their private sporting club.

Anne's generation of Spoerrys possessed two passports—French and Swiss. In Switzerland the Spoerrys carried the title "Freemen," in recognition of the good deeds of their great-grandfather Henry (or Heinrich) Spoerry, the scion of the family who, in the 1840s, began amassing a fortune that would provide four generations of family with more than adequate means. Anne always boasted that through descent she, too, was a "freeman"—the closest the Swiss ever went to awarding titles. She was never as vocal about the other benefit Switzerland accorded her, dual citizenship, though later in life she hinted that dual citizenship provided her with the comfort of knowing that if France refused her, she would find refuge next door.

As she grew into adolescence, Anne came to be seen as *un garçon manqué,* a tomboy, so drawn was she to prove herself against men. While competitive, her generosity to others, especially her sisters, was never questioned. Once when Thérèse's favorite goldfish died, she brought it back to life—albeit with different markings. Seventy years later, Thérèse still remembered this charming expression of devotion. It stood out in a relationship that was often fraught, for Anne was always reserved with her sisters. While thoughtful and impulsively generous, she remained aloof—a quality Thérèse found troubling. She could never fathom why Anne preferred sailing alone on the Lake of Zurich, in her dinghy, *La Coquille,* without the company of her little sisters. This detachment, Thérèse claimed, remained a constant, well into old age.

With her brother, François, Anne was altogether different. In childhood, he held absolute—some claimed oppressive—power over her. While she campaigned ferociously for his attention, he appeared indifferent. Undeterred, Anne water-skied, downhill skied, and sailed far from shore—all to catch his eye. François was unmoved. In time, Anne would dress as a boy to win him over. One friend contended that François interfered with Anne's adolescent identity by allowing—even encouraging—her to wear trousers while other girls her age were discovering their femininity in dresses and skirts.

At the age of fourteen, Anne joined the Girl Guides. On Thursdays, with school adjourning early in Mulhouse, she and fellow scouts set up mock camps in the Rue du Sundgau garden. There they perfected rope skills and made plans for the three-week summer outing beneath the shade of giant conifers at Camp du Ventron. Discipline, physical challenges, and the company of fellow adventurers gave Anne the confidence denied her by her brother. Wearing a long pleated skirt and a billowing kerchief, Anne developed independence, purpose, and leadership. In time, she rose through the ranks to *cheftaine* and began calling three Girl Guides her best friends. Scouting inspired dreams of adventure—climbing mountains, portaging around waterfalls, penetrating jungles, and surviving storm-tossed seas. It also would help her, in unforeseen circumstances, to overcome soul-shattering privations.

In contrast, at home in the men's world of Mulhouse, Anne was powerless. At the dinner table, while François spoke freely, she could only watch and listen. Henry Spoerry, unabashed Anglophile, encouraged conversation in English. Thanks to her bilingual nanny, Cinette, by the age of twelve Anne spoke English well enough for her father to consider an English boarding school.

The motto of the Francis Holland School, just off London's Sloane Square, was "That our daughters may be as the polished corners of the Temple." Anne took the words to heart, for the student body's Englishness. She was one of the school's few boarders; most of the girls lived at home in nearby Knightsbridge and Kensington. Years later, she claimed that at Francis Holland she never once suffered from homesickness. In this prosperous corner of London she developed an ear for upper-class contextual subtleties, and in no time Anne's friends looked upon her as "one of us." Many of the girls she befriended at Francis Holland remained close for life.

Thérèse recalled that Anne had only two boyfriends, one a Boy Scout. A Parisian friend of Anne's remembered another boyfriend—an architect—but the relationship was short-lived. Anne offered scant encouragement. In conversation with girlfriends, she expressed little interest in heterosexual relationships or, for that matter, marriage. According to Thérèse, when their mother suggested she accept the hand of an especially ardent suitor, she snapped, "It takes two to be married."

After Francis Holland, the Institut Polytechnique in Strasbourg was dreary, uninspiring, and friendless. Forced to memorize dull principles of philosophy and rules of science, Anne hurried to complete her final two years of schooling before university. In her last year, she developed an interest in biology. Soon she began to consider a career in medicine. The prospect of taking up a traditionally male profession was, for Anne, a draw. Liberated by scouting and the Francis Holland School, she thrilled to the prospect of breaking with convention and upsetting bourgeois assumptions of family.

When François told his father about Anne's career choice, Henry was horrified. For years he had hoped his bright daughter would take up a womanly pursuit—perhaps reading art history at Oxford and then going on to become curator at the National Gallery. When he learned she preferred medicine, he did all he could to change her mind. Now, away from the dinner table, Anne freely spoke her mind.

She began her premed studies in 1937 at the Faculté des Sciences in Paris. During this time, she lodged in a boardinghouse on Rue Denfert-Rochereau. She remembered its stern landlady and the "appalling" food—discomforts she never raised with her father, for if she complained, she knew he would use her words to entice her into another career.

Over the Easter holidays of 1938, Anne and other medical students cruised the eastern Mediterranean. For Anne, the trip's highlight was traveling inland from Beirut to the oasis of Palmyra with all its impressive antiquities. There she encountered her first Bedouins. In one account, she noted that the memory of that desert meeting kept her alive and hopeful during the dark years of war.

Shortly after Anne passed her premed exams, Henry Spoerry bought his two eldest children a Paris apartment. This fifth-floor pied-à-terre, at 1 Quai Voltaire, was convenient to the Beaux-Arts for François's architectural studies and the Faculté des Sciences for Anne. Halfway between the staid *rive droite* and the bohemian *rive gauche,* it lay in a respectable but artistic quartier. The apartment was a sensible purchase by a wealthy, solicitous, and shrewd father. It was, in fact, Henry's final attempt to lure Anne back into the arts. Anne never picked up on the hint. Instead, she saw 1 Quai Voltaire as a means of having François all to herself. It was where she hoped to prove herself at last.

During a break from school, on September 1, 1939, Anne and François joined their parents at Pardigon, overlooking the Baie de Cavalaire in the South of France. That evening, an English guest rushed into their drawing room to announce he had just heard on the wireless that at dawn Adolf Hitler's Wehrmacht had attacked Poland. The siblings struggled to process the news, then they gathered around Henry, veteran of Verdun, for his thoughts. He too was at a loss for words. Two days later, on September 3, when Great Britain and France declared war on Germany, their father shook his head, still nonplussed.

Anne returned to Paris, determined to continue her studies and maintain a safe house on Quai Voltaire for her brother. But like any other educated French girl who had heard her parents' accounts of World War I, she suspected that with Europe again in turmoil her life would never be the same.

CHAPTER 4

WE ARE FINISHED

During my four days in the desert with Dr. Spoerry in 1980, I knew I had still not breached her walls of silence. With only a half-baked view of her, my article was incomplete. About two months later, I called her for another interview. So it was she asked me to join her for the weekend at Sabukia, her farm.

Sabukia, lying halfway between Nyahururu (formerly Thomson's Falls) and Nakuru, on the eastern edge of the Great Rift Valley, was then about a three-hour drive from Nairobi. In those days, game was plentiful, often standing in full view by the side of the road. Were it not for the flicking of their tails, Thomson's gazelles might have been cast in bronze. Candelabra euphorbia lent shade to guinea fowl, and by Lake Naivasha zebras, all torsos, no legs, appeared to float dreamily in the heat haze. I stopped in Gilgil to buy samosas from a street vendor. Before I drove off, an earnest kid, flashing a notepad, approached, begging me to bankroll the purchase of his school uniform. As I dug through my pockets, three more boys, pencils in hand, descended on me, all with identical pads. This was 1980 urban Kenya—needy and street-smart.

As I drove north, the game thinned, driven off by smallholdings and fenced tin-roofed farmsteads. I circled about for a while before finding Anne's unmarked gate. I opened it and drove through. After closing it behind me, I faced a gauntlet of full-throated Flemish geese. Inching my way through them, I parked on a verge of grass beside a bungalow of unknown ancestry. Anne emerged from the front door at full throttle, greeting me with a quick Gallic kiss. I told her how taken I was by her farm; with all its luxuriance it was a far cry from the desert. She nodded, having heard it all before.

Outside, Anne's house was gift wrapped in bougainvillea; inside, it was all elegant tattiness. Anne made no excuse for the disarray. What mattered to her lay beyond the hedges—tussocky rows of coffee, mounded hillocks of melons, and smiling staff, the men tipping balaclavas, the women all curtsies, as we passed. With a dismissive wave of the hand, she noted that the Agricultural Society of Kenya had just awarded her first and second for her Nantes carrots and Carentan leeks. All this was said at lightning speed as she climbed a fence to show me her Friesian cattle, minded by a herdsman, dressed in a cast-off dinner jacket and a pair of Colonel Blimp shorts, ventilated in irreverent places from years of use. As we toured the land she had tamed, meeting the people she employed was a mandatory ritual of welcome. I began to see her twenty-five acres as an independent nation-state within Kenya, because even seventeen years after independence Anne still could not shake the demeanor of colonial chatelaine, ruling over others' lives.

In the evening after a dinner of fresh courgettes from the garden and fish from the coast, we moved outside with two stem glasses and a bottle of Sancerre. There we listened to the pinging of bats and the warble of tree frogs. At the time, I was unaware I was occupying a historic place of confidences. Tonight I was simply a guest, certainly not an insider. Revelations would only be a string of affable African stories. While talking up a storm, Dr. Spoerry skirted over all matters of the heart. I took in the bougainvillea and the perfumed fecundity of her Africa. She had created an oasis. Buoyed by the wine and warmed by a burgeoning friendship, I breathed deep and asked, "What did you learn in the war that helped you in Africa?"

Dr. Spoerry exploded: "This conversation is over. I told you to stay off that subject. Bloody hell." She slammed the front door as she vanished into her bedroom.

In the morning, I apologized, stuttering that I understood why war was off-limits. I knew many veterans from my parents' generation who kept the subject to themselves. Dr. Spoerry nodded, barely listening. She seemed to have forgotten the whole matter. Tea or coffee? she asked. Coffee please, I said, ever mindful of the rules.

By the end of breakfast, rain clouds had massed above the Aberdares and a lone fish eagle circled the pond. The ionized air seemed to make Anne even more energetic. As she introduced me to her geese, I asked about the little girl we had encountered on our desert trip. "Aaah, Kabala," she said, smiling. It was then she told me of the happy ending when she returned to seek out the mother and then arranged for the girl's surgery in Sololo, home of the feared Gabbra. The operation was "a grand success. End of story."

"But," I retorted, "it was more than that. You saved a life."

Anne rejected my compliment. "For every Kabala," she said, "there are a thousand more."

As thunder built, a friendship was born. It would last over twenty years.

◄○►

In the spring of 1940, François departed 1 Quai Voltaire. As an out-flanked France fought the Wehrmacht, he abandoned his studies in Paris, obtained a commission in the Pioneers, and joined a regi-ment of the *infanterie coloniale* on the Somme, knowing it would have been folly to pursue an education in architecture when all France, its monuments, and its institutions faced imminent devas-tation. Anne continued her studies at the Faculté des Sciences while apprenticing as an extern at the hospital of the Pitié-Salpêtrière for the destitute. Without François, 1 Quai Voltaire was a desultory col-lection of rooms.

Paris was now on high alert; at every street corner and in cafés friends brooded over the German advance. They gazed north, where the Wehrmacht's armored and motorized Panzer divisions and the Luftwaffe's Junkers and Messerschmitts were seeing little resistance as they overran Norway, Denmark, Holland, and Belgium. The British Expeditionary Force was incapable of halting the advance and, sardined onto the French coast around Dunkirk, was rescued by a madcap flotilla of sailboats, fishing craft, and skiffs. Altogether some 340,000 infantrymen were welcomed home to Britain at the end of May, in a torrent of patriotic fervor. In stark contrast, in France, the mood was all gloom, with many resigned to defeat. Already over 100,000 French soldiers had been killed and 225,000 wounded. With nowhere to go, La République's demoralized fight-ing force was no match for Germany's spit-polished Wehrmacht.

Northern France fell, region by region, and whole cities were evacuated, with families abandoning homes and taking to the roads. From his vantage point in the South of France, Henry Spoerry, vet-eran of Verdun, was stupefied by the absence of French officers. Seeing images of ten million of his fellow countrymen fleeing the German advance, toting family portraits, grandfather clocks, and Virgin Marys, the old hero was sickened by his government. By the end of May 1940, François was still deployed near the Loire, some thirty miles from Paris, his retreating regiment in tatters. Ominously, he wrote to Anne, "We are finished. There is no hope. We cannot find any officers above the rank of major and even they are few and far between. Be careful and look after yourself. Our country is lost."

From her balcony in early June, Anne's nighttime view was of a bloodred sky from burning fuel storage tanks, hit by Luftwaffe bombs. For the next fourteen days Paris choked on smoke. Now not even the seventh arrondissement was safe. Neighbors locked their windows to save their lungs and preserve their sanity. Holding to Girl Guide principles, Anne determined not to abandon her post at Pitié-Salpêtrière, where she cared for the terminally ill. On June 14, 1940, when the Germans entered Paris, she was at a patient's bedside. As she squeezed the old man's hand, he was alert enough to understand all was not right in Paris. She told him not to worry. Then he stopped breathing. Lucky man, she thought.

With her shift done, Anne left the hospital, crossed the Seine, and, once on the Champs-Élysées, stopped to watch in horror as German soldiers goose-stepped to the Place de la Concorde. She was stricken. A few days later Adolf Hitler, architect Albert Speer, and Hitler's favorite sculptor, Arno Breker, posed for victorious portraits in front of the Eiffel Tower. "For a week, the Germans poured into Paris in waves," recalled Anne. The sight of French tricolors replaced by swastikas incensed her. For headquarters, the Germans commandeered buildings by the Arc de Triomphe and on the Rue de Rivoli. On June 17, from his bastion in Vichy, puppet prime minister Marshal Henri Pétain, the grand old hero of the Battle of Verdun, spoke to all France, disregarding the stern advice of his generals in the field and his British allies across the channel: "We have asked the enemy his conditions for an armistice . . . between soldiers, with honor."

No member of the Spoerry family saw honor in France's capitulation. The nation that had once championed *liberté* and the rights of man had surrendered with hardly a fight. Anne heard Pétain on the radio, urging all Frenchmen to lay down their arms and "control their anguish in order to be led only by their faith in the destiny of the fatherland." Believing she was being fed a pack of lies, Anne expressed her contempt for the occupiers through small acts of sedition—cold-shouldering anyone speaking German, misdirecting officers, and, in cafés, spiking the sugar bowls with salt.

Watching officers desert their troops left François despondent. Knowing his future did not lie in the military, he abandoned his uniform, traveled to Marseille, and set out to continue his studies at the École des Beaux-Arts. The armistice Pétain signed allowed the Reich to occupy over two-thirds of France, described by an arbitrary line drawn from Compiègne on the Oise in the east to the Spanish border in the southwest. South of this line, where François and her parents resided, there was a semblance of normalcy. Anne, listed as a resident medical student in Paris in the occupied zone, was cut off from her family through the arbitrary line dividing France.

Anne's *Ausweis* (permit) granted her, as a medical student, only the right to move freely within Paris city limits. She wanted more. Soon she formulated a plan—to cross the frontier into the unoccupied zone: for her, arrest and imprisonment were worth the risk.

Anne's dramatic crossing began on a cold morning in February 1941 when she hoisted her bike onto a southbound train. Reaching Burgundy, she disembarked at a siding and biked to a hotel in Chalon-sur-Saône, the designated rendezvous point where she was to meet her *passeur,* who would spirit her past German guards into the unoccupied zone. After a long wait, the concierge frantically whispered that her *passeur* had been arrested and that she was to vacate the premises immediately before arousing German suspicions and placing the concierge at risk.

Determined to find another crossing, Anne set off on her bicycle.

By the end of the day, she had reached Montceau-les-Mines, with its central canal, serving as frontier between the two Frances. Sitting in a café, Anne overheard a party negotiating fees with their *passeur,* a hard-drinking Polish coal miner. She waited until they had left before approaching him. Anne began with small talk. He stopped her. For a hundred francs, he would escort her into unoccupied France. A deal was struck.

Anne and the Pole bicycled to a heavily guarded canal lock. She was alarmed at the prospect of crossing here, because German guards, patrolling the canal, would have a clear view of her. The Pole put his finger to his lips. With wind whistling through the bare branches of chestnut trees and ice forming on the lock, the two set off, balancing bicycles on their shoulders. Halfway across, Anne spotted another column of Germans and was certain she was caught. To her astonishment, they looked away. Clearly, her *passeur* had a special arrangement. Once safe in the free zone, Anne gratefully slipped him a hundred francs. As she did so, he gave her his final advice: on her return she must fool the guards by changing the time on her watch to South of France time to indicate her residency and then wiping her shoes clean of mud to demonstrate she had traveled openly on paved roads.

Once arrived at Pardigon in the South of France, Anne was fed copious amounts of seafood—at the time an exotic treat for Parisians. Her two younger sisters listened wide-eyed to her account of the adventure, while François sat off to one side, studying his sister with bemusement.

At the end of 1941, Anne chanced another frontier crossing to visit her family at Christmas. Again she headed for Montceau-les-Mines. On arrival, she learned that her Polish *passeur* was in jail. Anne now had to go it alone.

This time she was arrested straightaway and taken to a farmhouse for questioning. Steadying her nerves, she cast about for a place to hide her forged unoccupied zone identity card. The stove was not an option, because the fire was cold. Beneath the kitchen table she opened a trapdoor, dropped in the shredded document, and snapped it shut seconds before her German interrogator entered. Suspecting that she had been hiding evidence, he went straight to the stove. Not finding anything, he spent the next hour leaving and returning, attempting to catch her in the act. While Anne won this game of nerves, she was arrested and jailed in the medieval prison of Chalon-sur-Saône because her captors had evidence she had crossed into the unoccupied zone illegally. Finally, after fifteen days, and payment of five hundred francs, she was let go. This time, when she arrived in the South of France, François could not conceal his admiration.

―◄○►―

In November 1942, during her fourth year of medical studies, Anne received a coded message from François hinting that it might be useful for her to spend yet another Christmas with the family. Avoiding Montceau-les-Mines, Anne crossed the frontier far to the west, near the historic Château de Montaigne. Avoiding detection, she scurried across a bridge spanning the Dordogne. Within a day she was on the Mediterranean. At Christmas lunch *en famille*, François said little, appearing impatient to have time with her alone.

On December 26, the two set off north to Aix-en-Provence, the seat of François's nascent architectural practice. At Cours Mirabeau in Aix, he toured her around the Hôtel d'Espagnet, which their father had bought for his offices. Its purchase had been bundled together with the historic Château de Cabanes, to the north. Still secretive, François gave her a bicycle and indicated for her to accompany him along back roads. At dusk they arrived at the eighteenth-century château, beside the Durance River. There they settled into the grand hall, on chairs still in their two-hundred-year-old upholstery. In dancing candlelight, François opened up: his architectural office in Aix was a front, he explained, with weapons cached in fake rafters. Now working full-time for the Resistance, he was the head of an underground *réseau,* a network known as Spindle.

Anne was thrilled by her brother's secret. As sparks from the fireplace fell on the stone floor, she learned that one of François's co-conspirators, a regular visitor to his offices, was the celebrated medical researcher Jean Bernard. Would Anne, François now asked, join him to work in a Paris satellite network connected to Spindle?

On that cold December night in the castle, Anne vowed to join the Resistance, promising François her allegiance. By her own admission, she did so less for her love of country than for her devotion to François. Over the course of four and a half months from the end of December 1942 until April 1943, she would work for Carte, attached to "le réseau SPINDLE" supporting Britain's SOE (Special Operations Executive), F (French section), headed by Colonel Maurice Buckmaster.

Between 1940 and 1945, there were an estimated 300,000 to 500,000 active resisters in France. Not until a decade or more following the war was the role of Resistance women, like Anne, fully recognized. Their motivations varied. Agnès Humbert, for instance, was shaken into action by a scene of everyday injustice, when, next to her on the Métro, she observed a French soldier, seated next to a "big, beefy and pink" German soldier smoking a cigarette and looking contemptuously on the French. Humbert watched as the German condescendingly offered the Frenchman a cigarette. This soldier returned the gaze, studied the cigarette, and, much as he craved it, icily refused. "He will never know how much pleasure he gave me," recalled Humbert. "That little unknown soldier, defeated and betrayed, but still so proud and dignified." That innocuous incident was a turning point. A month later Agnès Humbert began distributing underground anti-German pamphlets and, by the end of the year, she was serving on the editorial committee of an illegal newspaper named *Résistance*.

Countless other women fought gallantly, like Anne, in the cause of French freedom: Claire Chevrillon, Charlotte Delbo, Lucie Aubrac, and Americans like Drue Tartière, Virginia Hall, and Devereaux Rochester. Countesses and peasant girls—the Resistance had many heroines, willing to fight and die for France. The Romanian-born Englishwoman Vera Atkins, who headed Anne's F section of the SOE, recruited many of these women. (After the war, Atkins, familiar with Anne's work and life in detention, would reappear at a brief but distressing moment.)

Returning to Paris, Anne was instructed to secure safe houses for British operatives working behind the lines. Forgery of identity cards and ration coupons would be a central feature of her work. A fellow medical student, demobilized from the French army, had the cunning to pocket a République Française copper stamp. With artistic retooling, Anne made it a vital weapon in a growing arsenal of duplicity. Forged identity cards, disguises, and a listening device: soon Anne's apartment resembled a war room. François had schooled her to trust no one. In occupied Paris, appearances were undependable, and anyone too eager to join would instantly set off alarm bells in Anne's mind.

A few weeks after her induction, François sent Anne instructions to travel to Annecy, near the Swiss frontier, to deliver a parcel to a "gentleman of importance." For purposes of identification, she would need a Michelin map and a special edition of *Radio Journal*. The paper was to protrude from her elbow so the mystery man, known only to François, could recognize her. Anne found the map, but all editions of *Radio Journal* had been sold out. Undeterred, Anne marched around Annecy's esplanade, proffering the Michelin map. When no one approached, she made for a hotel, which seemed appropriate for a "gentleman of importance."

Anne's hunch proved correct. At first the operative held back, suspicious of Anne's Teutonic features. Eventually, he noted a resemblance to François. The two spies nodded, then slipped into a hallway to complete the exchange. Having followed all her brother's instructions, Anne felt delicious comfort on her return to Paris. The two were now linked together in an enterprise vital to the future of their beloved country.

In later years, Anne described her role as a "liaison officer." In February she received a *pneumatique* (compressed air pipe message) from André Marsac, assistant to André Girard, head of Carte. It directed her to rendezvous early the following morning at an improvised airfield on the outskirts of Paris. There she was to meet her first "customer," a passenger on a Westland Lysander, the lightweight aircraft that Britain had designed to deliver agents in and out of enemy-controlled Europe.

"Roger" was a music hall parody of an Englishman—all trilby, brilliantine mustache, silver whiskey flask, and Terry-Thomas Franglais accent. He hauled two suitcases, one filled with millions of French francs and the other a heavy radio transmitter. While Roger had been introduced as a seasoned operative, Anne found him, at first, a perfect buffoon. What amateur had dreamed up his comic-opera disguise?

Anne rushed Roger back to her flat, sat him down in the guest room, and treated him to the first of several tongue-lashings. It was a bloody miracle, she told him, that his costume had not blown her own cover. "Now look here," she said. "I've got to go to the hospital today . . . People can see into the rooms . . . For goodness' sake, do not open the windows in the front room." And "whatever happens do not go into the street."

On her return to the apartment that evening, there was no sign of Roger. Anne suspected the worst. She bolted out, ran down the staircase four steps at a time, landing loudly before the concierge, a lady of uncertain loyalties. Anne asked whether she had seen her "tall cousin" as she swiveled one finger against her temple—the universal sign of lunacy. "You see he is not too good in the top story."

The concierge knew about him and appeared to share in the joke. "He is a little strange, *n'est-ce pas*? I found him trying some doors. He seemed to have forgotten your flat! Strange for a cousin," she said, toying with Anne. Then she pointed toward the Seine.

On a bench, facing the river, sat Roger. Anne stormed up to him and, after a tongue-lashing, marched him back to 1 Quai Voltaire, where, guiding him like a nanny, she deadpanned loudly for the concierge, "These are the stairs, that is the way to my flat. How many times must I explain, silly boy . . . Perhaps next time you'll remember."

<o>

A few days later, while Roger was tuning his shortwave radio, came a knock at the door. He immediately slipped into a closet while Anne set the chain and peered through the opening. Even after the visitor introduced himself as a fellow member of Carte, Anne barred the door. The stranger had calamitous news: that morning, on the Champs-Élysées, Marsac had been arrested, carrying a list of two hundred members of Carte as well as a *pneumatique* addressed directly to Anne. The Germans would soon know all; in effect, their network was "*brûlé*," finished.

The arrest of Anne's boss was a bonanza for the Germans. André Marsac's captor was *Unterfeldwebel* Hugo Bleicher, a sergeant in Germany's labyrinthine military intelligence apparatus, the Abwehr. On his instructions, Marsac was dispatched to Fresnes Prison, where Bleicher interrogated him. When Marsac refused to speak, Bleicher leaned in, squeezed his forearm conspiratorially, and confessed that he had lost faith in Germany and was horrified by Nazi excesses. He agreed with Marsac's Resistance sentiments and was now planning to defect. So, taken by Bleicher's sincerity, Marsac opened up. Over the course of the day, he revealed Carte's members, its plans, and details regarding the imminent arrival in France of SOE group leader Peter Churchill and his radio operator, Odette Sansom, code name "Lise."

Partially as a result of Bleicher's manipulation of Marsac, Churchill and Sansom were intercepted, questioned, and imprisoned. In Fresnes, a German officer tried to make Sansom talk by pulling out her toenails and pressing hot irons to her spine. Divulging nothing, Odette was transported to Ravensbrück, Germany's only concentration camp purpose-built for women, for execution. Miraculously, she survived.

Marsac's arrest was the beginning of the end for Anne. In possession of her name and the identity of others, the Abwehr sought out all members of Carte, taken from his list. Immediately, Anne told all other operatives to burn evidence of their association with the network. Knowing François was in the greatest danger of all, she telephoned a Girl Guide friend and in code told her to bicycle at high speed and catch a train to Aix, where she was to tell François to flee.

Before Anne could save herself, she had to deal with Roger. She raced across Paris to a ministry, where she found a secretary willing to sign a movement order, allowing Roger, under a French alias, to escort two members of Pétain's youth movement out of Paris. The clerk signed it and Anne solemnized it with her trusty République Française stamp.

Once outside, Anne checked her surroundings, knowing that German officers often waited by the entrance to catch agents. With studied theatricality, she affected the manner of a window-shopper. Soon she observed a van following her. Now survival depended on her fervor for shoes, sausages, and hats. The van stayed close as she studied a window filled with women's accessories. The moment she found a one-way street she broke into a run. At its end, she whirled into a shopping arcade, slowed to ponder a collection of stickpins, and looked left, right, and behind: no van.

Booking a railway passage in Paris to destinations outside the occupied zone presented another hurdle. Anne knew she would have to wait forty-eight hours for a German security permit. Again, she found a well-placed friend who was willing to circumvent channels. In record time, she presented the special document to Roger. Moments later, she watched him, sans radio, trilby, and silver flask, escort two "Pétain youth movement" brothers onto the train, bound for the south and freedom.

Immediately, Anne returned to her apartment to "sanitize" it. She looked around, saying her good-byes, taking pride in the knowledge that it was from here that Roger had successfully transmitted vital intelligence to London. Anne's satisfaction was short-lived. Forged papers, stored under floorboards, were burned, the République Française stamp hidden in a water pipe, and everything related to Roger destroyed. At last the apartment was "clean." Simultaneously, two hundred miles away in an "architectural" office in Aix, François and fellow *réseau* members were destroying all evidence of their Resistance work.

The moment Anne heard the knock on her door she went on high alert. The visitor was an ingratiating woman, speaking good Parisian French, claiming an old and warm friendship. The woman then began asking questions. She knew much about Anne's activities in the *réseau*. Realizing this was a trap, Anne played the innocent: Of course she had nothing to do with Marsac, and what was all this talk of a *réseau*? "Marsac, Marsac: sounds Basque, no? A name I don't recognize." Anne warmed to this persona of the dim ingenue. "I am just a medical student, going about my studies," she whimpered.

Now the stranger came in for the kill: "So where are you working?" The moment Anne responded "Hérold Hospital," she knew she had blundered. The woman left, but Anne knew it was only a matter of time before her colleagues would be questioned and the truth about her double life revealed.

In the early months of 1943, the Abwehr had relaxed travel restrictions between the occupied and the unoccupied zones. Henry Spoerry took advantage of the new rules to catch a train to Paris to visit his daughter for the purpose of urging her to flee to neutral Switzerland. Within a day of his arrival, Anne received a postcard from her mother. She showed it to her father. In code, it delivered the news they most feared: "I am sorry to tell you that your brother has had a very serious operation and has had to be moved to a clinic in Marseille."

"There I told you," said Anne's father, knowing instantly that François had been captured. "You must leave immediately. I have your papers. Come with me to Switzerland." Anne promptly agreed, but before boarding the train, she would have to destroy incriminating papers stored in her desk at Hérold Hospital. Setting off at a run, she shouted to her father, "Give me an hour and I'll be with you."

Anne's decision proved catastrophic. For the rest of her life, she would recall the missteps she made on April 21, 1943—how she ran back to her desk at Hérold, heard muffled German commands, slamming of doors, tramp of boots. The receptionist did all to protect Anne by claiming she was somewhere else. It was no use. Minutes later, a hatchet-faced officer stared down at Anne: "Fräulein Spoerry?"

Breathing deep, Anne said she would cooperate. First she needed to change her clothes. Once out of his sight, Anne found a friendly nurse and told her to destroy all papers and take her Swiss railway tickets across Paris to Café St.-Germain, where she would find Henry Spoerry. "Tell him . . . I've been arrested." With that, Anne returned upstairs and followed the German officer into a waiting Citroën. Their destination: 11 Rue des Saussaies in the eighth arrondissement. No Paris address was more dreaded. Anne knew the stories—the torture, tears, screams heard up and down the street. On the walls of the cell into which she was thrown, she would read her predecessors' last written words: "Don't talk"; "Never confess"; "Honored to be condemned by the Boche . . . Good-bye forever to France and my loved one"; "I am afraid."

Eleven Rue des Saussaies was a holding pen, with cells the size of closets, arranged around interrogation rooms. Virtually all jailed suspects were found guilty, transported to Fresnes Prison, for transfer to Germany. Anne was forced to stand before a seated interrogator. Under the lights, she ran many risks. If her answers displeased her interrogator, she would be beaten and members of her family put on "a list." Through the walls, Anne heard a fellow Resistance fighter saying his final prayers.

In the first round of questioning Anne stuck to her claim that she was an innocent bystander with no interest in the Resistance. At first, her interrogator appeared to believe her. Wanting details, he directed guards to escort her to her apartment on Quai Voltaire. When the car stopped at her favorite corner, Anne weighed the odds of bolting through the entrance gate, dashing down a back alley, and escaping. Instead, she turned the key in the lock, shoved open the heavy door that always stuck, and ushered the Gestapo inside. They began a sweep, surgically examining each room, under carpets, in drawers, through closets, under floorboards. It was perfect. They found nothing and would never know that this fifth-floor apartment at 1 Quai Voltaire had once been a safe house.

In the end, Anne was foiled by the discovery of Marsac's list and his subsequent confession. Her interrogators, having found her guilty of espionage, shipped her to Fresnes Prison, seven miles south, on the outskirts of Paris, on April 26.

A few weeks into her incarceration, Anne experienced a brief moment of joy when a guard presented her with a sweater, a present from her brother. He, too, she learned, was in Fresnes, in fact, on the same floor. While she would never see him and while he could offer no other help, Anne was overjoyed at this brief display of solidarity.

Happiness was short-lived. From whispered conversations with others, Anne learned that few Fresnes prisoners were ever acquitted. Here, political prisoners were as worthless as Jews and Gypsies.

In Fresnes, Anne spent much of her time battling an uncontrollable fear of arbitrary assassination. While many others learned to escape into private worlds, Anne spent her days imagining the worst. Her most painful fear was that faceless strangers would select her for a firing line or a hangman's noose. This self-described thrill seeker was not ready for death. In spite of great physical bravery, a deep dread of dying would cause Anne decades of tribulation.

    A PUKKA PLACE

*In loving memorie of the Keffirs working in
vein to please me.*

—Inscription drawn in concrete, on failed dam
effort in Laikipia, circa 1930s, by a settler who
subsequently left Kenya in ruin

Anne spent more than half her life in Africa, and in time the continent defined her. There she was not just Dr. Spoerry. She was Mama Daktari. When Anne got around to writing her memoirs—*They Call Me Mama Daktari*—more than 80 percent of her book was set in Africa. In measuring her life experience, she made Africa out to be her rudder and sail.

Anne joined a long roll call of expatriates defined, enriched, and elevated by Africa. Victorian and Edwardian Britain made press heroes of the intrepids who plumbed its interior—Dr. David Livingstone, Henry Morton Stanley, Sir Samuel and Lady Baker, Sir Richard Burton, Frederick Selous, Colonel J. H. Patterson. More recently, Wilfred Thesiger, Peter Beard, Quentin Keynes, Kuki Gallmann, Angela Fisher, Carol Beckwith, and others joined their ranks—men and women who would rather live in an untidy land than in a suburb with streetlights. In the bush, they found liberation and reinvention, cheating death, confronting dark fears, staring down the barrel at magnificent truths. In Africa they were Peter Pans, preserved forever in the amber of youth.

So it was with Anne. She gave herself up to adventure and chance, responding to unimaginable needs, saving lives on an industrial scale. To fellow romantics, this indomitable woman was their Olympian, their noble monument to compassion, aviation's unrivaled risk taker and one more romantic hostage to Africa—or so it seemed.

—◦—

In 1949, no one in the British Crown Colony of Aden except Anto Besse had any inkling they were dealing with anyone more complicated than a strong-willed young woman from a wealthy French family. Anne Spoerry did her job efficiently and knowledgeably. The hospital was lucky to have such a novice doctor with seasoned diagnostic skills and a nose for spotting communicable diseases, like tuberculosis. Dr. Cochrane was thrilled he had in his employ a junior doctor willing to work for a pittance and stay on forever.

Publicly, Anne kept her intentions to herself. Privately, with her contract to expire in August 1949, she was in a muddle whether or not to renew. With a modest allowance from home, it was hard to make do in a colony where it was de rigueur to have a cook, gardener, night watchman, and waiter. A large household staff would require her to beg her father for more money, not a request she was prepared to make at the time.

Anne shared her concerns with Heron Bruce, Antonin Besse's best friend. Bruce had been a commander in the Royal Navy and was now assistant superintendent of the Aden police force. Privy to a wide range of local intelligence, he was a most useful ally of

Antonin Besse. The friendship went beyond business. Sharing confidences over drinks, the two often fell into ruminations about country life, to which both were devoted. They delighted in driving tractors, improving the pedigrees of livestock, and awaiting bumper crops. Every summer, Antonin Besse recharged himself at a farm called Le Paradou in Provence; for Bruce, it was Kenya. Both retreats were relief from Aden's blistering August heat.

The Bruces' Kenya refuge was a small farm, in the up-country outpost of Thomson's Falls. A week before Anne's contract expired, she joined Mary and Heron for dinner at Aden's Polo Club. Over several gin and tonics, the strikingly tall couple enchanted her with tales of their East African colony. Kenya boasted a glacier-capped mountain, untouched forests, broad rivers, a great desert, and a very sporting farming community—mostly composed of British soldiers/settlers. And serving them was a most willing and cooperative workforce. By morning Anne had made up her mind.

A week later, she stepped onto the tarmac of Nairobi's Eastleigh Airport. By the apron, she passed a sign proclaiming Nairobi the crossroads of the world. On it, wooden arrows radiated in all directions—one pointed to Juba, another to Kampala, still another to Dar es Salaam, and finally one to London, 5,030 miles away.

Anne spent her first night in Torr's Hotel, and in the morning she explored Nairobi. At the junction of a great avenue, policemen, mounted on pedestals, directed traffic with military precision. Their skin was nearly dark blue, their shorts as white as clouds. Unlike Ethiopia, which had had only a passing flirtation with colonialism, Kenya had lived under British rule for over fifty years. Now all was Anglicized, the city library called "McMillan," a shopping street "Sergeant Ellis," the widest avenue "Lord Delamere," and the principal hotels "the Norfolk" and "the Stanley." Hardly anyone, at the time, was concerned that some forty thousand whites were guiding the destiny of more than six million blacks.

When Anne strode out onto Government Road, everything was exotic—vivid bolts of cloth called *merikanis* snapping in the breeze, Asians pedaling sewing machines, spear-brandishing, *shuka*-draped Masai, fresh off the plains of Tanganyika. Anne relished the colony's tone and approved that the British owned the banks, shopkeepers were Indian, and African women balanced titanic loads on their heads. In 1949, Nairobi was, if anything, orderly. Hotel menus were even typed in Franglais: "Pate de Foie Maison, French sardines a l'Huile, roast duckling Villageoise, Mignotte of beef Garni, Coupe Flamingo." Wine lists featured French wines, most prewar. Even a dry 1942 Pommery & Greno champagne could be had. To a European smarting from the pain of war, Kenya appeared to offer style, peace, and oblivion.

On day two, the Bruces' driver collected Anne for the four-hour drive up-country to their farm near Thomson's Falls. Within an hour, she saw her first herd of zebras and Thomson's gazelles. The road ran beside a steep escarpment; it skirted volcano-framed lakes streaked pink by flamingos. Once arrived at the Bruces' farm, Anne leaped from the car. The air was cool, reminiscent of long-ago summers in Switzerland.

From the start Anne found Heron and Mary's lifestyle to her liking. They were a social couple, loved entertaining and being entertained. When at home before the fire, they talked of the land and the game. Neighbors ran mixed farms of beef and dairy cattle, tea, wheat, maize, pyrethrum, even coffee, along with a rich array of vegetables. On the loamy slopes of the Aberdares and Mount Kenya, eight thousand feet above sea level, a farmer could plant almost any crop and soon thrill to the sight of its tendrils bursting through clods of earth. An eager staff tended their cutting garden of tuberoses, lilies, and orchids. In the evenings, the flowers' perfume drifted through open windows into the drawing room, mixing with an animal fat used to wax hardwood floors. At sunset, a liveried houseman set fires in both drawing and dining rooms, and soon Anne inhaled the perfume of burning acacia, reminding her of Ethiopia and that hallowed night lulled to sleep by Amharic laughter.

For Anne, Kenya's highlands outdid Ethiopia's. The days were brisk, the heat dry and never sultry like in Aden. Twelve months a year, on the equator, the moan of emerald-spotted wood doves announced the dawn. Twelve hours later, to the minute, chill darkness descended with a chorus of tree frogs. Evening drove Anne and the Bruces indoors in search of jumpers, a crackling fire, and restorative sundowners.

On two different afternoons, Heron and Mary drove Anne to meet neighbors. Their homes were not the sprawling mansions of wealthy nobility, the Happy Valley set, famous for its licentious ways, exchanging drugs and wives ("Are you married or do you live in Kenya?"). In this corner of the highlands Anne met hardworking gentry, living from harvest to harvest. The principal entertainment of the Bruces' neighbors was sport—polo, tennis, and golf. The floor plans of their homes were laid out on notepads at the club— higgledy-piggledy affairs that would soon be wreathed in flowering vines, with doors scratched by pawing dogs. The interior furnishings, verging on the scruffy, satisfied Anne's practical nature. One Nairobi factory appeared to hold a monopoly on a line of boxy, easily sprung armchairs and sofas. To keep up appearances, settlers covered worn spots with leopard skins. On the walls, beside faded English prints, hung trophies of the chase—Cape buffalo, Grant's gazelles, and bongo—all mounted regimental style, at precisely the same height. Dining room tables were large and heavy and served as parade grounds for battalions of condiments—House of Parliament, Bovril, and Major Grey's chutney. Following along rode a cavalry of mismatched silver sauceboats and tureens.

Anne scrutinized a variety of bookshelves. She found a consistent theme—textbooks on farming, worn copies of Alan Quatermain and other Rider Haggard novels, Everyman's editions of Richard Burton's, David Livingstone's, and Samuel Baker's explorations. Masai shields and Makonde carvings, purchased from Mombasa street vendors, served as bookends. On a sideboard, the "wireless" assumed pride of place, almost a religious icon, with its dial frozen on the BBC World Service. In these settler homes, family treasures rarely survived intact. Porcelain was chipped, books foxed, chair legs rigged with wire. Africa was hard on heirlooms.

"You did not have to be rich in the Kenya of the time," wrote Anne years later, "to lead what would have been a princely lifestyle in Europe." Even in straitened circumstances, a settler family could afford staff. And there never was a shortage of candidates, waiting patiently in the shade. With limited culinary skills of her own, Anne lingered a while to study a cluster of hopeful chefs. Somewhere in this hodgepodge of faces she might find her man. She knew from the Bruces that while most up-country cooks were illiterate, all had committed to memory their previous memsahib's array of European recipes and could put together crêpes suzette in no time flat.

No matter the family's status, it was almost a religious duty for waiters to serve dinner in uniform—typically white *kanzu* and red fez. A loyal staff member was usually identified by one name, perhaps Babu, Josphat, or Merciful. When a headman was out of earshot, the man at the head of the table might get a chuckle by calling him "our wrinkled retainer" or "Number One Boy."

At the time, few whites found anything untoward about Kenya's colonial conventions. Very few in up-country settlements hinted of premonitions that one day there may be a price to pay for such patronizing racial insensibilities. At Francis Holland School in London, Anne had embraced the peculiarities of the British class system. Many of the up-country farmers she met appeared fair and evenhanded, going to great lengths to treat "the labor" with respect, learn the customs, and accept their ways. It was not unusual for European children to grow up blood brothers to the children of their African servants. In many instances, cooks, kitchen *totos* (young boys serving as sous-chefs), and *ayahs* (nannies) became inseparable members of European families.

Anne approved the tone of Kenya, often dubbed "the officers' mess," in contrast to Southern Rhodesia (later Zimbabwe), which tended to attract working-class English. Anne was comforted that white Kenyans were usually "gentlemen"—people she considered cut from the same cloth as her father or brother. Kenya Colony's policy favored public school graduates, with many possessing Oxford and Cambridge degrees; a good number were sons of peers. So what if some Old Etonians landed in Kenya because of "a spot of bother" back home. Anne knew that she would be recognized for her background and would rise to the top of the pecking order.

In 1948, Kenya's farming community, comprising twenty-two hundred white-owned farms, was compact and more or less homogeneous. Up-country farmers had a nodding acquaintance with nearly all their peers, having crossed paths at sporting meets, gymkhanas, holiday fetes, weddings, funerals, or spontaneous "bun fights" in country hotels or sporting clubs. While few in number, Kenya Colony settlers possessed a robust gossip mill, powered by a workable postal system and party telephone lines, that allowed for the free exchange of intelligence, whether intentional or uninvited.

Even in remote hinterlands, white society was vibrant. After farmers spent their weekdays outsmarting predators, pests, and the labor force, they rewarded themselves with weekend "socials" at the club. Few Kenyan settlements lacked one. On their playing fields, settlers performed feats of athleticism; at their bars, they complained about "the labor," vented rage against the central government, and exchanged confidences about budding romances, some licit, others not so. In up-country Kenya, there was much to share, especially regarding the capriciousness of nature and the unreliability of marriage. Far from the tedium and mediocrity of Europe, these men and women had lucked onto a place where rules were invented to suit the moment, and the magnanimity of geography had afforded them near-feudal privileges. Here you could set yourself any goal, unburdened by British obsession with service, scholarship, and sainthood. In Kenya at the time, eccentricity was applauded, and an unexceptional man might even become the club champion.

Anne found the Bruces' neighbors direct, self-deprecating, and manly—qualities she admired. Some swaggered but, as far as she could tell, with some justification. No one was getting rich, and overdrafts were a running joke. Not every settler was British, for after both world wars Kenya had attracted an assortment of Europe's dispossessed—German Aryan, Jew, Czech, Dane, and Italian. Thus Anne would not be the first "foreigner."

Because the absentee landlords Mary and Heron Bruce were not exactly representative of the community, Anne spent some of her holiday driving out to meet others outside her host's circle. While no one precisely matched her circumstances, in Kenya Colony of the time an unmarried woman seemed not to ring any alarm bells. The settlers she met were too polite to pester her with questions. Men seemed bemused and women little threatened.

Anne saw opportunity in the Kenyan highlands because many communities did not have a doctor. If white settlers needed emergency care, they set off at breakneck speed over rutted roads to hospitals in Nakuru or Nanyuki or, if the situation was dire, Nairobi. Locals depended on traditional witch doctors, or *mgangas,* or stood in long queues at government dispensaries. For African women pregnancies were often fatal. Burns, spear wounds, disfigurements, were left untreated, often with calamitous results. Every day, the local population faced early, violent deaths. For Anne,

Kenya seemed a better prospect than Aden, for it offered independence, scant bureaucratic oversight, and the prospect of helping
tribal people, without interference. Waving farewell to the Bruces
was hardly painful, for she knew she would be back.

—◦—

Once back in Aden, Anne kept her Kenya dream a secret from
Monsieur Besse, who was doing everything in his power for her to
remain nearby. Already he had helped her immeasurably, banishing
the gloom, introducing her to a future far from Europe, drawing
the curtain on a new beginning. For him, leaving Aden for Kenya
would be a betrayal.

With unfinished academic work in Europe, Anne returned for
what she hoped would be a short visit. She began in Mulhouse,
where she enchanted her two young sisters with tales of "Arabie,"
Ethiopia, and Kenya. The new, positive Anne also impressed her
father. When her brother, François, heard of her Kenya plans, he
gave her his immediate blessing. The security and anonymity provided by a British colony were precisely what she needed.

For the next nine months Anne set about completing several
outstanding medical requirements. At the Université de Paris, she
finished a thesis on amebiasis, a tropical gastrointestinal infection.
At the same time, across the border at the Swiss Tropical Institute in
Basel, she met her final diploma requirements. When not at school,
she holed up in the Spoerry manor in Männedorf.

When Anne was in Paris, she stayed at her apartment on Quai
Voltaire and kept to herself whenever possible. One person she
could not avoid was a Parisian childhood friend, Odette Bonnat
Allaire, to whom Anne had lent the apartment during her time
away in Aden. More than fifty years later, Odette recalled what happened the evening she raised the subject of her behavior during the
latter days of her wartime imprisonment: "I . . . whispered to her,

'Are you continuing this same behavior? You are making a mess of things wherever you go . . . operating with an atrocious insolence.' Anne didn't care. I asked her to sit down with an analyst and bring order to her past and her memories. She barked back at me, 'I'm not crazy.' So Anne never wanted to confront all this . . . She was a mystery to me . . . She had no fear of anything." Odette, who would live with her imprisonment's emotional wounds the rest of her life, could not comprehend how Anne could recover so quickly, without apparent regret. For Odette, that long-ago conversation on Quai Voltaire had proven to be a disaster. Anne simply would not listen.

In June 1950, the Université de Paris accepted Anne's thesis. Under normal circumstances, a diploma would have followed, allowing the honoree to carry the title "doctor of medicine." But on July 4, Anne was informed the dean was withholding it—a setback she admitted to no one but her brother and father. Anne would have to wait two years—until October 20, 1952—to be accredited. Yet there is no evidence the delay bothered Anne. She had her mind set on being a country doctor in Kenya, where bureaucratic irritants, like withheld diplomas, were immaterial. Without one, she knew no one would have the nerve to question her right to practice medicine.

In the autumn of 1950, Anne disembarked in Aden, packed up her belongings, and flew to Nairobi, slipping away quietly to escape facing her mentor, Anto Besse. Once in Kenya, she began a job hunt. The director of medical services at the Kenyan Ministry of Health offered her three positions. The first two she rejected out of hand because she did not wish to work in cities—Nairobi and Mombasa—where she would be on public view. The third appointment was in Marsabit District, virtually an oasis in a desert. It would have been perfect, but her candidacy met opposition from the local district commissioner, who exploded: "What? A woman doctor, and unmarried? Unthinkable. She would be a most unsettling influence on all my young officers!" Anne faced a sequence of other rejections, driven by the prevailing sexist bias within the British civil service.

Learning of her obstacles, Heron Bruce called to tell her that the community of Ol Kalou was in need of a doctor. The township lay along the same railroad line as Thomson's Falls and consisted of a police station, a few Indian stores, and a polo club that doubled as a church while the official Anglican church was under construction. Ol Kalou seemed the perfect fit for Anne. From this township radiated large mixed farms, embracing valleys, hills, copses, and stands of hardwoods. Every inch of the country, at an altitude of eight thousand feet, was radiantly green. To the east stood a great forest, blanketing the Aberdares, inhabited by an elusive antelope called a bongo and giant forest hogs. It seemed a place of mystery and romance.

At the time of Anne's arrival, there were sixty settler families in Ol Kalou. In need of a resident doctor, they had raised money and advertised. After two months without a single application, they were about to concede defeat when they received a response from a single Frenchwoman, with no previous African experience. Without even an interview, the Ol Kalou board hired this one candidate on the spot. No one thought to request a background check. No one suspected that at the time Anne Spoerry did not possess a medical diploma.

As soon as she arrived, Anne found a house three miles out of town. It was a bungalow set on a parcel of 150 acres, part of a large farm belonging to Mary Patten. Anne also leased commercial space in the village behind an Indian *duka,* store, for her surgery. There, five mornings a week, she would minister to her patients. Anne also maintained a clinic in her guest cottage for out-of-hours emergencies.

The white community was immediately taken by Anne's deep pockets, replenished by an allowance from her wealthy French father. Before her first paycheck, she had assembled a sizable household staff, purchased a spanking-new Peugeot 203 station wagon, and acquired a string of pricey polo ponies. She reasoned that if the Peugeot got stuck, she could always do her house calls on horseback.

During her first year, Anne's neighbors found her eccentric in other ways—especially for her obsessive indulgence in a pack of dogs. Soon after arriving, she acquired six mixed terriers. Guests at her dinner parties had to shoo Bridie, a spoiled brindled bull terrier, prone to heavy drooling, off the couch.

Anne's preference for utilitarian clothes also attracted attention. "We never thought she wore a bra," recalled Biddy Davis, a neighbor. Another neighbor added, "The one time we saw her in a dress, whilst attending a wedding, it was so out of place that it caused a stir." When Anne joined the Ol Kalou Polo Club, she provoked even more wonder by her insistence on joining the polo team, as its sole woman player. Many came out to see her first outings and were struck by her brio—riding fast, shouting jubilantly. One lady thought her "very jolly."

Anne's loud equestrian technique was not for everyone. John Platter, a young member of the team, found her inept as a teammate: "She was atrocious, a complete nuisance, being always in the wrong place on the wrong side. What a joke . . . nobody cared to say to her, 'Really, Anne, you must find something else to do.' People just put up with her."

The polo club was the social vortex of Ol Kalou. While there might be smarter gathering places—Thomson's Falls or the Gilgil Country Clubs with their golf courses—the Ol Kalou Polo Club, framed by tennis courts and a polo field, met all the community's needs. With its gleaming bar, attentive staff, hushed dining room, and manicured lawns, Anne happily described it with her latest Anglo-Indian colloquialism: "pukka."

Every Saturday, club managers Alec and Margaret Scade, a Scottish husband-and-wife team, hosted gymkhanas, horse shows, and themed dinners and dances, with New Year's Eve the year's ne plus ultra ceremonial occasion. Once a month Mr. Preston drove two tin canisters up from Nairobi for a film show. Favorites were *Mrs. Miniver* with Greer Garson, *Kind Hearts and Coronets* starring Alec Guinness, *The Third Man* with Orson Welles and Joseph Cotten, and *The Small Back Room* about Nazi land mines during World War II. No one could recall whether Anne attended the latter.

All children remembered Anne's brusque manner in the examination room and her terrifying injections. One recalled "the syringe being a foot long . . . the size they used on horses." In her dispensary, there was little small talk. "Bend over" was Anne's imperious command. So help a white boy or girl if he or she screamed or cried out. Once making a house call, she passed the bedroom of a ten-year-old, paused to look in, and asked, "When are you going to tidy up your room?" On the spot, the girl concluded Dr. Spoerry was "monstrously bossy."

In the early 1950s, whenever Anne was in Nairobi, she stayed in a spare room at the house of her friend Enid Grant. From the start Mrs. Grant noted that Anne did not conform to the colonial code: "She preferred a casual appearance where dress was concerned." Once, when invited to a garden party at Government House, the most desirable address in town, Anne "proposed going in her denim skirt and blouse. We all were horrified and insisted on dressing Anne up." After the makeover, Enid called Anne "very glamorous."

Enid also noted even greater peculiarities: "When first I met her, two things struck me . . . She couldn't bear to be in a room crowded with women. She hated crowds in any form . . . it gave her claustrophobia. The other thing was that when Anne was served with a plate of food, she set to and ate it very quickly, as though she might not get any more."

Yet for all Anne's eccentricities, few disputed that she was generous. Unlike most struggling Ol Kalou farmers, precariously balanced between harvest and overdraft, Anne, with her princely allowance, seemed forever flush with extra cash and always prepared to enjoy spending it impulsively on humanitarian projects. This side of Anne was known to at least one friend as her "secret charity." Once, on hearing that a sixteen-year-old girl had her heart set on becoming a veterinarian, Anne presented her with a large equine health encyclopedia. When Anne then learned that the girl's mother, Madge Onslow, was enduring hard times, she sent her a round-trip ticket to Hong Kong to visit her son. Another neighbor, Heather Griffin, also aged sixteen, returned from an overnight stay in Nairobi to discover that the suitcase enclosing her entire wardrobe had flown off the roof of the car. The next day Anne arrived at the Griffin house with "the most beautiful emerald green kimono."

Weekends in Ol Kalou were a whirl of parties. During the war Heather Rooken-Smith's mother had taken to throwing Saturday soirees "to raise morale." The custom prevailed into the early 1950s, with Anne a regular guest. The lively Mrs. Griffin loved to play the piano and watch guests cut up across the dance floor. Her favorites were the Lambeth Walk, the Military Two-Step, and a variety of Strauss waltzes. Much to Mrs. Griffin's dismay Anne wore no makeup and refused all invitations to dance. Instead, according to Heather, she hung out, talking "men talk," with "a whiskey in one hand."

For Anne, now aged thirty-two, Ol Kalou was a godsend. On this continent of second chances, she was able to live hopefully, cosseted by a cadre of farmers who did not pry. All marveled at her determination to fit in, to master the ways of Kenya and its peculiar metaphors. More than anything, Anne wanted to belong. In December 1950 she advertised for an assistant and hired the first applicant to show up at her clinic. His name was Francis Karua Thuku, and soon she would call him her "trainer"—an odd description because her settler friends were more comfortable designating him her "assistant." This sixteen-year-old goatherd, educated by Christian missionaries, became Anne's interpreter, informant, and alter ego. He taught her rudimentary Swahili, the lingua franca of East Africa, and helped her understand the ways of his tribe, the Kikuyu, by far the largest of Kenya's forty-one. In no time, Anne relied on him without hesitation: "Francis, what is this man talking about? Francis, hold his arm . . . Francis, quiet this child. Francis, you bloody well learn how to change a tire."

A few well-meaning neighbors cautioned Anne against placing too much trust in the goatherd. "Spoil the African and you'll pay for it" was a regular white rejoinder. Others, less measured, said he was just another "shifty Kikuyu." Anne was stubborn. She knew what she needed, and no one could tell her how to manage her affairs. Francis Karua Thuku was here to stay.

The great majority of Anne's patients at her Ol Kalou clinic were Africans. They appreciated Anne's no-nonsense medical style because it yielded material results: aspirin dispelled headaches; chloroquine usually helped abate the symptoms of malaria. Most Africans welcomed Dr. Spoerry's no-frills medicine, her approach suggesting to them she favored them over whites. According to Sarah Higgins, Anne regarded whites "as a pampered race compared to the people she was dealing with regularly." When a white settler boy was struck by lightning while driving a tractor, Anne treated him in her clinic in quick order. The bolt had gone straight through his left side, welding together a collection of keys in his pocket and pile driving him into the ground. According to his half brother, Richard Morgan-Grenville, Anne "sorted him out, dusted him off," and "duffed" him out of her clinic the moment he opened his eyes. A few months later, when the same young man was shot in the forearm by a friend while playing with a .22 pistol, "Anne put a plaster on it and said, 'Bugger off. I don't want to see you anymore.'"

Those who knew Anne during her Ol Kalou days could not recall any love interests. She famously pooh-poohed the prospect of marriage, claiming she was far too busy to settle down with a man. Fifty years after her days in Ol Kalou, questions remained unanswered. Prue, the young aspiring veterinarian, wondered whether her brother, Richard Onslow, might have been more than just a friend of Anne's. "The two were confidants and I never asked him, since he was an honorable man." Another neighbor remembered there had been some chemistry between Anne and Heron Bruce but in the same breath found the suggestion of romance preposterous because Anne was equally devoted to Mary Bruce. Some wondered if Anne "might have preferred the ladies," but no one could provide hard evidence for such a notion. The general consensus was that Anne was asexual, with little or no interest in men, or women.

Almost all held an opinion about Anne's explosive temper. Her friend Sarah Higgins recalled two incidents while at Champagne Ridge, Sarah's favorite campsite, to the north in Samburu National Park. The first episode was prompted by a container of avocado soup that Anne had had her chef carefully prepare at home. "She roared up to our cook, handed him the thermos, and ordered him to serve it to us in bowls, chilled. Somehow the poor old man always thought that whatever came in a thermos had to be hot. Scared to ask the ferocious memsahib anything, he heated up the avocado soup and served it to us. The result was totally disgusting. Anne had one sip, then laid into him verbally . . . She got very hot, very cross, very quickly. Poor man. He didn't know what hit him. Her explosion dumbfounded all the kids. A few minutes later it ended. We got back to our drinks and telling naughty stories. After explosions like these, Anne always calmed down and carried on as if nothing had happened.

"The other occasion was over a breakfast of eggs, bacon, sausage, and baked tomatoes," recalled Sarah Higgins. Anne looked out across the plains and, through shimmering heat haze, said she had spotted an elephant. "'No,' corrected my stepson, age twelve. 'That's a zebra.' Anne went apoplectic and lambasted my husband: 'What are you doing, bringing your son into a park and he not knowing the difference between a zebra and an elephant?' So my husband challenged her to a bet of a hundred pounds. Knives and forks were thrown down, and across the plain we drove to settle the bet. What did we find? A Grevy's zebra. Anne said not one word. We returned in silence to our now-congealed breakfast . . . You just move on after these explosions. For anyone else, the incident would have been embarrassing. Not with Anne."

Because Anne refused to open up about her wartime past, she invited speculation. While her Ol Kalou friends were too discreet to probe, many privately wondered whether her temper was her way of preserving privacy and evading awkward questions. How, they pondered, could a woman, disciplined in so many ways, regularly lose it? Were her tantrums an artifact of childhood, war, or just her way of keeping the world at arm's length? Some wondered whether her ban on matters dealing with war might be a sign of good breeding; she was simply reluctant to boast about her own bravery. Others pondered whether she had been mutilated in some unspeakable way. One friend asserted that her fierce temper resulted from "a bad case of shell shock."

Through temper, silence, and bold independence, Anne set her own agenda in Ol Kalou. A few months after her arrival, she formed a Girl Guide troop, much like the one she had adored as an adolescent during summer days at Camp du Ventron. Her company was composed almost exclusively of African and Asian children.

Onlookers, passing by her parade grounds, marveled at the sight of teenagers precision marching while a uniformed middle-aged white woman bellowed commands.

For all her idiosyncrasies by 1952, Anne had become a much-admired member of the Ol Kalou community. Neighbors were singularly impressed by her readiness to attend to emergencies, even at midnight. All marveled at a Frenchwoman, just arrived in Kenya, playing helter-skelter polo, leading Girl Guide troops, setting high community medical standards, and curing people of every color. One settler called Anne "plucky . . . and brave." But within a few years, some members of the Ol Kalou community would have second thoughts.

TOP: Anne, age six, marshaling her troops.

MIDDLE: Anne, age eight, with "Peggo," Mulhouse.

LEFT: Anne in the South of France the year before Germany declared war.

24. — La morgue ?... Non, l'hôpital...

TOP: "The morgue? No, the hospital." Violette LeCoq's memory of Ravensbrück.

MIDDLE: Violette LeCoq remembers the gas-chamber selections in 1945, when her fellow prisoners were no more than "twigs."

BELOW: Ravensbrück entrance recalled by Anne a year before her death.

30. — Sélection pour les gaz. Rameaux 1945...

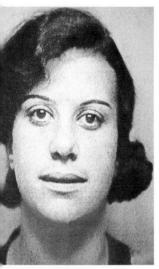

LEFT, TOP: Carmen Mory in her late teens, soon after abandoning Adelboden.

LEFT, MIDDLE AND BOTTOM: Carmen Mory in prison.

BELOW: Carmen Mory hearing her death sentence, February 4 1947.

RIGHT: Carmen Mory dead in prison.

ABOVE, LEFT: Anne and her "trainer," Francis Karua Thuku, outside her Ol' Kalou dispensary during Mau Mau. Note revolver belt.

ABOVE, RIGHT: Miss Mary's last passport photograph.

RIGHT: Miss Mary O'Shaughnessy and Anne near Hell's Gate, circa 1967.

LEFT: Anne and a Turkana girl.

BELOW: Anne and an aged patient in his final days, 1981.

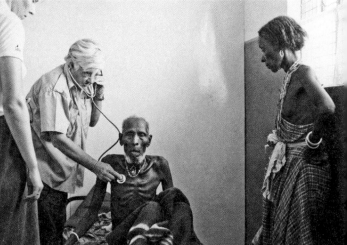

ow, TOP: Anne pulling oth without anesthesia.

ow, BOTTOM: Success!

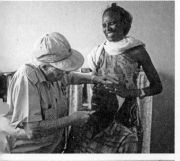

ABOVE: A coastal clinic not far from the Somali frontier.

TOP: Anne catching up on local news.

BOTTOM: Anne fast asleep at the controls of Zulu Tango.

TOP: Dispensing medications just before takeoff.

MIDDLE: Anne at the controls of Zulu Tango over the Northern Frontier District, Kenya.

LEFT: Passport portrait.

TOP: Anne's Sabukia farmhouse today.

MIDDLE, LEFT: Anne's grave in a sand dune, Shella, Kenya.

MIDDLE, RIGHT: AMREF shrine to Anne after her death.

LEFT: Ten years after Anne's death, Mary Ndegwa proudly shows the author a photograph of Anne, Mary, and fellow primary school teachers.

CHAPTER 6

❖ *THE EMERGENCY*

> *I found myself haunted by an impression*
> *which I myself could not understand: I kept*
> *thinking that the land smelled queer. It was*
> *the smell of blood, as though the soil were*
> *soaked with blood.*

—Carl Jung, upon arriving in Africa

After breakfast on her farm during my 1980 visit, clouds built, and we readied for a donnybrook of a storm. As we gathered up to go indoors, I mentioned Mau Mau, the Kenya insurrection of the 1950s. Anne smiled as she tumbled the words around in her mouth, like bonbons. When we settled into the drawing room and listened to rolling thunder, she asked whether she had told me any of her stories. I shook my head as she smiled with the memories. "All jolly good fun."

With limited understanding of Mau Mau at the time and because I had not yet grasped Anne's genius for burnishing history, I never called her out for her joyous smile or asked her why a time of mass killings could have been such a lark for her. Mau Mau, I would learn, was an especially horrific time for the Kikuyu. For them it was anything but "jolly good fun."

Measured against her past, Mau Mau was Anne's tipping point. Some would see it as coda to her actions during World War II.

—◦—

When Anne Spoerry settled in Kenya in 1950, she believed she had found the perfect bolt-hole, far from Europe. She swiftly made friends among the whites; as for the Africans she encountered, she found a docile, willing, happy folk, with infectious smiles. Every day she thrilled to their merry lullaby of laughter, ringing out from her staff quarters.

Like many other whites in Kenya, Anne did not see the storm bearing down portentously upon Kenya Colony. Ever since 1903, when the protectorate government first invited Englishmen to settle Kenya Protectorate, newcomers had viewed the land as theirs for the taking. Neither the government nor arriving settlers considered the possibility that indigenous peoples, especially the largest tribe of all, the Kikuyu, held prior claim to the land. Englishmen had the temerity to call the colony's most fertile land the White Highlands. Later, following both world wars, the British government added to a list of injustices with the "Soldier/Settler Scheme," giving away seemingly "vacant" land to British war veterans in search of a new life. Black Africans had also served in the wars, fighting alongside the British, sharing privations, even leaving their bones on foreign soil. For those Africans who survived and returned home, there was no hero's welcome. Instead, they faced the spectacle of pale-faced people making merry on land that had once been theirs.

Africans, especially the Kikuyu, endured other insults. In the early twentieth century, the colonial government engineered several population shifts, expelling over 100,000 Kikuyu from "the White Highlands," along the Great Rift, and settling them on less fertile land, called the Kikuyu Reserve. The Kikuyu was not the only tribe subject to relocation. In 1904, the British government divided the Masai into two groups, the northern branch relocated in the Laikipia region, the balance along the southern border with German East Africa, but the colonial government reserved special attention for the Kikuyu. Between 1919 and 1947, the government compelled workers to carry the *kipande*—an identification pass that prevented them from circulating at will. In addition, Kikuyu farmers were saddled with confiscatory and, to them, perplexing land taxes.

The rural Kenyans Anne met were mostly illiterate. Labor was cheap, and a settler saw nothing extravagant in hiring two to do the work of one. An extensive staff relieved a settler's wife of disagreeable tasks, like serving at table, washing dishes, raking gravel, weeding gardens, and scrubbing toilets. In Kenya, even settlers of modest means could afford a sizable staff. Now comfortably settled in Ol Kalou, Anne had no qualms asking her father to cover her domestic needs. In France and Switzerland, the Spoerrys had always employed servants. In Kenya, Anne could hire on the grand scale, beginning with a headman, Njugana, a chef, Ndetto, a scullery maid, a night watchman, and three others, charged with garden, horse, and the care of six dogs.

Anne would have noted that her white neighbors were, for the most part, politically conservative; they opposed multiracialism, integration, and wage increases for anyone but whites. In most upcountry homes employees were virtually invisible. Both in front of them and behind their backs, whites could patronize, even ridicule them, without consequences. Who could stop one's friend at the club from joking about poor Juma, who thought he could polish silver by scouring it with sand, or howling over Mwangi, who mistakenly poured ice cream over the fish, believing it to be "white sauce"? Not all but some Ol Kalou settlers were flagrant racists, notably Anne's neighbor Major Harold White, known to correct staff infractions with lashes from his rhino hide whip, or *kiboko*. Today, fifty years after he departed Kenya, his crumbling home, inhabited by descendants of the men he once whipped, still carries the name Kiboko.

◄○►

During Anne's early years, some neighbors objected to her "modern" approach with staff, especially the young man she called her "trainer," Francis Karua Thuku. John Platter, who rode to hounds with her and played polo alongside her, believed the community saw her unquestioning relationship as unsettling: "She shielded Francis and entrusted him when all Kikuyu . . . were treated with great suspicion."

Even with a degree in tropical medicine, Anne had never encountered such a collection of disorders. Most common were coughs, resulting from lives lived inside smoke-filled huts. Children were brought into her clinic suffering from horrific burns from having slept too close to open fires. Most prevalent were tuberculosis, dysentery, and eye infections, as well as wounds caused by skirmishes with wildlife. Initially, without a diploma, Anne set bones, sutured wounds, and delivered children. Serious emergencies, resulting from road accidents, cattle-rustling wars, household disputes, and breech births, she transported to specialists and surgeons in Nakuru or Nairobi. On these journeys, Francis sat in the passenger seat, ready at all times to do his boss's bidding, whether repairing a puncture or silencing an obstreperous patient in the back.

The accommodating young Francis, faithfully trotting behind, was uniquely positioned to influence Anne's understanding of Africa. His singular worldview revolved around the Kikuyu universe, with its complex potion of superstition, prejudice, and spirituality. His influence was shrewd, pointing out whom to trust, whom not to hire, and when to watch her back. Like many other

Kikuyu, he smoldered over ancient grievances against other tribes, including the Kalenjin around Lake Baringo, the Kamba to the southeast, and the Luo and Luhya by Lake Victoria. Generally, he favored Europeans, lavishing groveling praise on them whenever possible. His fawning ways should have alarmed Anne, but, new to the land and its people, she was slow to apprehend Francis's gift for manipulation.

In Anne, Francis clearly saw an opportunity for self-advancement, by using her to gain the trust of other whites. When alone with her he could drop hints, withhold information, share his enemies' list, ignite fears of nocturnal vengeance, all the while advancing himself as her indispensable factotum. Within a year of his hire, he had won her over completely, making his ideas hers and embedding himself in her life with unchallenged male influence not unlike her brother's. This lone white woman, lacking fluency in Swahili, was no match against a tactically placed word by a political insider.

Anne's troubles began on October 7, 1952, when her wireless sprang to life with news that the Kikuyu senior chief Waruhiu, an outspoken opponent of Kikuyu rights, had been murdered in broad daylight near Nairobi. Within a few days, Britain announced it was sending troops to quell the uprising, still undefined. On October 20, after a string of killings, Anne was at the club when she heard the BBC announce that the British government had declared "a state of emergency."

When the uprising's alleged ringleader, Jomo Kenyatta, was sentenced to house arrest and sent to a remote corner of Kenya, his Kikuyu followers declared open warfare on the British. The colonial government, headed by Governor Sir Evelyn Baring, retaliated by interning over two thousand Kikuyu suspects and threatening execution of any Kikuyu found to have administered an oath. By November, the international press had conferred a code name on the insurrection—Mau Mau.

◄◦►

By the end of 1952, Ol Kalou was prepared for war. Knowing her foreign citizenship afforded no immunity, Anne locked exterior and even interior doors at night. At dinner, Anne's neighbors had already taken to placing loaded guns beside the dinner service, and at night pistols were positioned an arm's length away on bedside tables. By the end of the month, Kenya gunsmiths' inventory had been exhausted. Anne wrote to her father to send her a pistol. She knew what she wanted: a Walther UP Model 1. Upon its arrival at Eastleigh, an alert customs inspector, unfamiliar with Dr. Spoerry and possibly a bit suspicious of continentals and guns manufactured in Germany, impounded it and sent Anne a "Notice of Seizure." Instead of collecting it, Anne purchased a Smith & Wesson .38 Service Special. It would remain in her possession the rest of her life.

In 1952, carrying arms in the White Highlands was an act of patriotism, with the commissioner of police advising settler households to keep weapons "loaded and ready . . . for immediate use." In addition, all "Kikuyu staff" were to be out of the house and "in their quarters before dusk." He urged settlers to ensure they "had a gun ready at hand if a servant were allowed to enter the house after dark."

Whispered talk of Mau Mau's secret oaths, foisted upon gang members, fueled panic. According to one of Anne's new friends, these "beastly" Kikuyu practices were deemed far too indecent for tender female ears. Anne was the exception. Invoking medical privilege, she demanded to be told. Francis, eager for political advantage, accommodated her. The novitiate's first step was to remove all European clothes and to drink a mixture of blood and meat. The next step might involve sexual intercourse with a dog, placing a piece of meat in the anus of an old woman, tasting a needle after pinpricking a dead man's eyes, eating the brains of the dead, drinking the menstrual discharge of a prostitute, inserting a dead goat's penis into a vagina, then dipping it into blood for the woman to lick. The final oath, dubbed the Kiberichia Cocktail, combined beans, sugarcane, and sweet potatoes as well as the initiate's semen, a chopped-up sheep's vagina—all mixed in a bowl of blood. The recruit was forced to drink this concoction while repeating, "Or this oath will kill me and all my seed will die."

Under Anne's grilling, Francis explained that an oath made the initiate feel so debased he or she was driven to engage in increasingly bloody and horrific acts. Oath taking was the force that transformed a devoted and loving house servant into a serial killer.

In her memoirs, Anne never wrote about her association with Francis Karua Thuku. He appears only once, in a photograph caption, described as her "trainer" (in the French edition, he is not identified by name). Clad in white linen surgical gowns, standing in midday sun outside the clinic, the two assume a grave pose, shoulder to shoulder, with Anne making no effort to disguise her gun belt, weighed down by the Smith & Wesson .38 Service Special beneath her scrubs. In Ol Kalou, during and after the emergency, Anne was armed even as she examined patients in her clinic.

Eventually, Mau Mau's tentacles reached out to Ol Kalou. At the end of the year, Erik Bowker, living alone, was killed in his bed. This gentleman had been fast asleep when his farm laborers burst into his bedroom and slashed him beyond recognition. Anne was among the first Europeans to come upon the carnage.

A few days later, in nearby Thomson's Falls, Mau Mau broke in to the home of a retired naval officer, Ian Meiklejohn, and his wife, and attacked them with *pangas* as they read by the fire in the sitting room. Only Mrs. Meiklejohn survived.

On the night of January 1, 1953, violence struck close to Anne's home. The victims were another elderly settler, Charles Ferguson, and his young farm assistant, Dick Bingley. Both were known for their pro-African views and egalitarian ways with staff. Convinced that their modern outlook inoculated them from harm, they refused all neighborly advice to lock their doors and carry sidearms. On New Year's evening, as they dined in dressing gowns, a gang of fifteen, wielding *pangas,* set upon them and hacked them to death. The first neighbor to come upon the scene found they had been cut "practically into mincemeat." The sight was so unnerving he withheld details from all women, including his wife, believing she would "have fainted straight away." He made an exception of Anne Spoerry. When he showed her the bloodbath, he found her immune to shock.

Like all settlers, Anne (whose call sign was "Alpha Two") was required to radio twice daily into the Laikipia Emergency Wireless Network. Even children were taught to operate the single-sideband wireless. One was eight-year-old Caroline Blore, a neighbor of Anne's, who had been coached, in the event of an attack, to rush to her parents' bedroom armed with a hockey stick. Nearly sixty years later, she recalled the terror: "So when we heard our house broken in to, we were under the bed. Our call sign was Alpha Seven, but we couldn't get to the radio in time. As we listened to the sounds of Mau Mau ransacking our house below, I lay under the bed shaking all over. I'm amazed we weren't taken out. I was as scared as I have ever been in all my life."

With entire dairy herds of cattle hamstrung and housefuls of loyal servants butchered in their quarters, Anne never moved without her Smith & Wesson on her belt. One old former Mau Mau terrorist recalled her as "a one-woman army." According to him, she was friendlier with her animals than with fellow humans. Once he saw her reward her horse, after a ride, with a bottle of Guinness.

◄०►

Six decades after the emergency, three Kikuyu men who had observed Anne during her Mau Mau years came forward, each claiming that beginning in 1953 her assistant, Francis, did much more than serve her as bodyguard. They alleged that in his fanaticism as a British loyalist he used Anne's Ol Kalou clinic, at night, as a torture chamber, maiming and murdering suspects held by him and his followers. In the clinic, Francis and his men dealt with anyone who would not confess by poisoning or castrating them, with most left to bleed to death. In 2011, one castrati was said to be alive, although suffering from dementia. When asked how many Francis tortured and killed, one informant waved his hands and claimed "well over a hundred."

If Francis did torture, maim, and murder, where was Anne? Did she know? Was she complicit? Or simply willfully blind? If she was not aware of Francis's activities, another settler, Bill Delap, a neighbor of Anne's, certainly was. According to his widow, Bubbles Delap, he had, at first, been a staunch member of the loyalists in their efforts to suppress the uprising, but when he learned of Francis's nocturnal castrations, he walked out and said he would have nothing more to do with the loyalists. If Bill Delap knew about Francis, wouldn't Anne know as well? How could she not notice evidence of Francis's nocturnal activities when she arrived at her dispensary in the morning? While the testimony of three old Kikuyu men may not provide conclusive evidence of Anne's complicity, it does suggest that Francis was overly brutal and that Anne was blind to his excesses.

Anne did admit these were times of pure terror. The tipping point was when she heard Dot Raynes-Simson and Kitty Hesselberger's story. One evening, early in the New Year 1953, while listening to the BBC, these two women had become increasingly alarmed by their Kikuyu waiter's behavior. Kitty, an expert marksman, cocked her pistol. Suddenly five men, with *pangas,* burst through the door. One grabbed Dot by the throat and was strangling her when the women's boxer set upon him. Kitty opened fire, killing the assailant and, by mistake, her boxer. She then wounded another attacker. Both women, their pistols blazing, then took off after the gang and, in a dark passageway, inadvertently killed their cook. When they heard a rustling from the bathroom, they shot through the door. This time they killed two men and wounded their elderly "houseboy."

Anne feared their story could easily be hers. She promptly decided that she would not docilely follow the other women of Ol Kalou, sleeping every night on pews in the vicarage, while their husbands patrolled the forest. Instead, she would volunteer with the Kenya Police Reserve (KPR). Already several military units had been deployed along the Eastern Rift to fight the insurgency—C Company of the Kenya Regiment, regular police, members of the General Service Unit, the Kenya African Rifles, and the Tribal Police. Anne signed up with the Kenya Police Reserve. Her uniform included military drill, with epaulets on her shoulders, and her .38 Service Special swinging from her belt. As a part-timer she was one of the few women officers in a company composed of Kenya-born men, all conversant with the sounds and smells of Africa. With them, she would fight an enemy she barely knew, hike terrain altogether alien, and share risks other women never imagined. She later described her role as an "inspector," her assignment to work with other mounted scouts, "mostly mopping up" after raids in the Aberdare Forest, as well as locating, identifying, and fingerprinting corpses. On one occasion, as she removed a bullet from the leg of a Mau Mau leader manacled to a hospital bed, he confessed, providing her team with precious intelligence—or so she claimed.

Not all saw merit in her work. Helen Hallowes, a neighbor in Ol Kalou, claimed Anne was an absolute liability: "Unlike the men, she didn't know the local sounds and signs, i.e., scraping of utensils or the call of the nightjar—all part of Mau Mau 'telephone' language." Helen's Kenya-born husband, Rupert Hallowes, was conversant with the language of the forest from childhood and could call back to Mau Mau enemies, even making them laugh. Anne, deaf to the subtleties, was "an embarrassment to all."

Kenya Police Reserve veteran Colin Davis recalled a telling incident on patrol, when the men waited to ambush a Mau Mau cell in the forest. For hours during the night the team waited, shivering against the cold, listening out for every sound. At five in the morning, "Anne decided to have a pee. She quietly dropped her blue dungarees and squatted. A blade of grass tickled her in the wrong place. She thought it was a snake, jumped up, and gave it both barrels, thus giving away the patrol's location. The commander of the platoon stood up and said, 'Okay, chaps, I think we can go home now.'"

During these days, Anne lived by the gun. She knew her right to use her pistol in self-defense and more in the execution of her duties was uncontested. Her well-thumbed Kenya Police Reserve handbook suggests she consulted it frequently to verify this right: "Any person . . . who fails to stop after being challenged by an authorized officer, may be arrested by force which force may, if necessary . . . extend to voluntarily causing death."

It was said that Davo Davidson, a colorful character, recently arrived, like her, in Kenya, had encouraged Anne's predilection for gun toting. Davidson was a Scot who had knocked around Australia before finding his way to America, where he had allegedly been one of Al Capone's gunmen during Chicago's Prohibition wars. Anne was said to have been drawn to Davidson's colorful ways. Historian Ian Parker wrote, "Davo certainly did carve a rather unique slot for himself—turning up more as self-appointed sheriff than a feature of the establishment. He definitely was K.P.R., did turn up in forest operations festooned with grenades and all manner of Superman gear—attaching himself to units whenever he thought there would be action." Davidson's prowess with pistols left a deep impression on Anne.

Unfortunately, even under his tutelage, Anne did not always

follow basic safety rules. Admittedly, she was not Ol Kalou's only trigger-happy resident. One member of the Police Reserve made the mistake of carrying a pistol into the bath. When he slipped, it fell, hitting the rim, tripping the trigger, and killing him instantly. On another occasion, two young brothers found a gun in a wardrobe. One pointed it at his brother and shot him dead.

Anne's misstep would leave a blot on her reputation in the Kenya Police Reserve and color her Mau Mau days, at least among her contemporaries. In later life, Anne deftly evaded the subject, only dropping a few enigmatic hints—that she once suffered from "traumatology" and that "quite a few bullets found the wrong target."

The incident that ended Anne's Police Reserve career occurred in February 1953, on patrol. At dusk, her small band had set out to locate Mau Mau operatives in the forest abutting Mary Patten's farm. Along with Anne came Erik Hovmand, newly arrived in Ol Kalou from Denmark, with his wife, Rudi. Assigned radio call "Alpha Five," he enlisted in the reserve at the urging of his neighbor and fellow continental Anne Spoerry. That evening, the moon rose late and the Mau Mau gang appeared to be on the alert. The KPR patrol only heard tree frogs and owls. At midnight, the forest hushed completely, coming to life near dawn, when the reservists heard a lone turaco call out. The men knew these were real forest birds sounding dawn's reveille. Suddenly Anne heard a footfall. She called out, "Who goes there?"

Or so she claimed. One neighbor believed Anne did not follow procedure and never shouted the universal command. Another conjectured that the Dane, Erik Hovmand, not fluent in English, was confused by the words. What is certain is that Anne opened fire and, at point-blank range, shot Erik Hovmand in the leg.

"It was absolutely dreadful," recalled Heather Rooken-Smith. "Everyone in Ol Kalou was stunned . . . Anne simply took him to hospital . . . She just got on with it." Erik Hovmand's recovery was long and painful. Heather believed Anne paid all his medical costs as well as a lump sum, "to keep the incident under wraps." According to Rooken-Smith, Erik's leg was amputated from the knee down, and he spent the rest of his life in pain. The Hovmands were not fully appeased by Anne's financial gesture. They sold their farm at a loss and stormed off to Australia, never again to speak to Anne or return to Kenya.

After an inquiry, Anne was dismissed from the Kenya Police Reserve. John Platter remembered that the shooting "raised questions about her demeanor under duress." Heather Rooken-Smith speculated that "the Hovmand incident must have been on her conscience forever." If so, Anne never let on. For the next fifty years, she never spoke the name Erik Hovmand or revealed that she had been dishonorably discharged from the Kenya Police Reserve.

—◦—

Drawing a curtain over her past had now become an old habit. Because she had discontinued the habit of journaling, there is no certainty whether she suffered from inner turmoil. Chances are, if she did, she would not have admitted doubts to her journal or to anyone but closest family. What is certain is that she would not let Hovmand distract her from her master plan for Africa. One scrap of paper shines a light on her resolve to stay and begin again.

On a sparkling October morning, Anne answered a knock on her Ol Kalou door. Facing her was an employee she had not seen since the early days of the emergency. She recognized the old man, and in an instant she intuited that he had taken the Mau Mau oath and had been living as a terrorist in the Aberdares. No doubt he too had once plotted to kill her. Now, after nearly three years, he wanted his job back.

"Jambo, Mama." The old man handed Anne a one-page document, printed on cheap paper and bearing the franked signature of

Governor Sir Evelyn Baring. It read, "The bearer of this pass wishes to surrender. He is to be given fair treatment, food, and medical attention if required. He . . . is not to be prosecuted for any offence connected with the Emergency." (Anne kept this paper the rest of her life to consecrate a critical moment of her life.)

In 1955, a wary peace had settled over Ol Kalou. While doors remained locked at night, chairs and bureaus were no longer jimmied against them to thwart attacks. Anne looked into the man's rheumy eyes and liked what she saw. She stayed on the doorstep talking with him longer than she planned, studying his feet, encased in rotting shoes. Perhaps she noted the cicatrices hatching his face while inhaling the aroma of his campfire smoke. Dressed in a dusty double-breasted suit jacket, discarded by a former employer, he appeared more stooped than before. It was astonishing that such a fragile and gentle specimen was once her sworn enemy. There was a time when he would have hacked her into mincemeat.

In the old man, Anne saw the Africa she wanted for herself—innocence, forgetfulness, and impartiality. She had come here in search of absolution. Could she not extend the same courtesy to this old boy, in dusty clothes and a smile?

"*Ndyo.* Yes," she said. He now would have his old job back, no questions asked. With toothless glee, he pumped Anne's hand, oblivious of the gift he had just bestowed upon her.

CHAPTER 7

THE PIPER

*Home is where you go when you run out
of home.*

—John Le Carré, *The Honourable Schoolboy*

By the end of the emergency, Francis Karua Thuku's company, previously essential, was proving toxic. Knowing his fellow Kikuyu loathed him, Anne discharged him. Further association would have weighed on her reputation. In his place, she hired a succession of other assistants. While all were equally industrious, none proved to have the command and cunning of Francis Karua Thuku.

In firing Francis, Anne was free. Now she would set out for a very different Africa, where, in time, she would enjoy a friendship with someone her polar opposite, as well as a new direction for her life. As far as journeys go, this would be a short one—only thirty-six miles, but in respect to her heart, the longest journey of her life.

In 1955, Ol Kalou was all tranquillity, with front doors open to admit the morning breeze, lorries hauling bumper harvests to the Gilgil market, and laborers ingratiating themselves like never before. It was easy to believe that Mau Mau was a moment of passing lunacy and the good old ways were here once more. Many Ol Kalou settlers believed they were poised for at least another decade of colonialism.

Yet within a few years, the 1960 Lancaster House Conference in London shattered that confidence, with the British government making clear its intention to grant Kenya independence, or *uhuru*. Events moved fast as settlers faced the first signs of "the winds of change," with Africans winning seats in the legislature and, even under house arrest, Jomo Kenyatta being elected president of the Kenya African National Union.

On August 1961, at settler clubs around the country, the gloom was compounded when regulars listened to wireless reports of Kenyatta's release from prison and his jubilant arrival in Nairobi, cheered on by unexpectedly large crowds. At the bar of the Ol Kalou Polo Club, members were in a "what the hell" buying mood. Assured that Kenyatta had been the mastermind behind Mau Mau, they saw the future as not only uncertain but dangerous, with a purported murderer soon to become Kenya's first president.

Each passing month saw portents of change. At the end of 1961, independence had become a certainty, and by 1962 many settlers began making plans to emigrate, in advance of what they imagined would be the "inevitable bloodbath." In 1963 a new constitution, providing for a bicameral legislature, was written. It was immediately filled by members of the Kenya African National Union, who readily elected Jomo Kenyatta the nation's first prime minister. On December 12, 1963, the Duke of Edinburgh officiated at the transfer of power. *The New York Times* reported, "With Britain's Union Jack replaced by the black, red and green flag of the new states, political power in Britain's last East African colonial holding slipped from the grasp of its 55,759 whites and was taken up by its 8,365,942 Africans."

Few attended the New Year's celebration at the Ol Kalou Polo Club. Only three couples danced. Anne was alone at the bar, whiskey in hand. When diehards sang "Auld Lang Syne," she stood with them at attention for a "last post." Promptly at midnight, the band packed up, wives corralled their tipsy husbands, and Anne slipped across the lawn to her Peugeot to drive home to be with her dogs. If she were to stay in Kenya, she would have to adapt to a new order, which would reduce her to serving Africans who once served her. Was she capable of such reinvention? On the other hand, what were her options? France was out. What about another African outpost? No doubt, the Rhodesias, in turn, would fall as well. So too all the others. She had spent a dozen years making a home in Kenya, only to find it was never hers.

Weighed by uncertainty, Anne kept to herself. She now knew she had miscalculated when, in 1959, she purchased the adjoining farm, Lokolwa, a thousand acres of beautiful rolling pasture, rich cropland, and swaths of Aberdare Forest. "Farming," she asserted, "was in my blood." Behind the purchase lay a more complex motive—to thwart its purchase by a certain Heinrich Platter (in her memoirs she misspelled his name "Plater"), an elderly German. "Apparently he had been a very good soldier in the Wehrmacht during the First World War," she wrote, but "I must confess we did not get on very well together." His role in World War II was a mystery, even to his son. Was Anne's ill will a response to historic Alsatian grudges, or was she venting her own wartime prejudices? In her memoirs, she failed to explain the dispute. She had vowed Platter would never become her Ol Kalou landlord, no matter how uncertain the future of landownership in Kenya. With ten thousand pounds, transferred by her father, she outbid Platter and became the chatelaine of Lokolwa. The moment she acquired title to the land, she bought a tractor, plow, and harrow and, with a large team of Africans, began planting barley, corn, and pyrethrum on 150 acres, with the remaining land fenced for polo ponies, dairy cows, beef cattle, and sheep. Now, as full-time farmer, Anne put her medical profession on temporary hold. Hers might have been a sensible decision, for the many Africans who once queued each morning at her clinic now stayed away. According to an African neighbor recalling those times, locals feared the clinic's history of torture and death. They even believed it was haunted, claiming they heard screams in the night, from ghosts of the dead.

Five years later, at independence, Anne's Lokolwa idyll came to an end when she learned her land was slated for nationalization through the "One Million Acre Settlement Scheme"—a pact signed by Britain and the new Kenyan government to acquire large tracts for division into fifty-acre lots to satisfy land-hungry Kenyan farmers. Fertile Ol Kalou, the historic heartlands of the Kikuyu, was at the top of the land board's list for buyout. In her memoirs, Anne claimed that she received "adequate compensation" for the loss of Lokolwa, but others disagree, saying she took in less than half the acquisition cost and nothing for any of the improvements she made. In 1992, Anne broke down to the writer Annie Kouchner, admitting that losing Lokolwa was *"un crève-coeur,"* a heartbreak.

In 1963, the sight of friends packing up their life's gatherings deepened Anne's sense of failure. Every day another Ol Kalou family piled its farm lorry high with faux-Chippendale breakfronts, tarnished polo trophies, and chipped Wedgwood dinnerware and kicked up dust, bound for new lands. Some returned to England, others made for the Rhodesias, South Africa, Angola, New Zealand, and Australia.

As late as mid-1964, Anne stayed on in the same modest cottage she had first occupied in 1951. Fierce dogs, trotting behind her by day, barking by night, were comforting. While Jomo Kenyatta had promised whites, "We are going to forgive the past," Anne worried about less measured Kikuyu, still drifting out of the Aberdare Forest. She had seen images of them in the *Daily Nation* and *East African Standard*. Smelling of wood fires, coated in animal fat, draped in leopard skins, with hair in dreadlocks, they were menacing in their looks. Would they be as quick to forgive?

Much to Anne's distaste, in 1964 her former employee Francis Karua Thuku ran for a parliamentary seat. While he suffered a crushing defeat, he managed to bedevil Anne by successfully acquiring four of her best fifty-acre Lokolwa plots. Anne saw his greed as betrayal. As always, when she traveled, she brought along her dogs and the Smith & Wesson.

Rather than take in African members or close altogether, the board of the Ol Kalou Polo Club handed the property over to the local African Council. In despair, a former board member wrote to Anne, "There are already accusations of racial reasons for closing and I am hoping this generosity will put a stop to them." There would never be another Saturday film show, weekend polo match, or Sunday curry lunch. And Anne would never set foot there again.

The only familiar faces left in Ol Kalou were members of her own staff—Ndetto, her cook, two guards, and the scullery maid. The nearest opportunity for a good gossip was Thomson's Falls (soon renamed Nyahururu) or, after a long drive, Nairobi. Weeds in the cemetery beside the Ol Kalou church covered the graves of her landlord, Mary Patten, as well as, ironically, her enemy Heinrich Platter. In November 1963, Anne received a letter from her friend Joan Isaac, now living in South Africa: "I wonder what you are going to do. If it is a case of *sorti tout de suite*, you know I have a room." Anne did not accept the offer, even though she was now a squatter on land she once owned. In fact, she held the dubious distinction of being the last remaining white settler in Ol Kalou. The African patients she once treated had fled from her practice in favor of local witch doctors. Anne's cottage, filled with books and one voluminous safe, housing guns and sensitive wartime papers, became her last refuge. At night she listened to voices drifting down the hill from the staff quarters. Where once she enjoyed their laughter, now all she heard were harangues. In *The Flame Trees of Thika*, Elspeth Huxley captured the contemporary settler state of mind: Kenya "is a cruel country that will take the heart out of your breast and grind it into powder, powdered stone. And no one will mind."

Soon after losing Lokolwa, Anne took a job as a medical officer for the new district of Nyandarua. It encompassed a large swath of villages and townships, requiring extensive time away from home. Anne's solution was to kit out two Land Rovers as roving dispensaries, each with its own medical staff. But working for government, on a paltry salary, was, at best, a stopgap measure. Anne needed more.

On weekends, Ndetto, who had cooked for Anne since her arrival in Kenya, served her luncheon in the garden. Sunbirds came to the feeder, and on the ground there was usually a wagtail bobbing for scraps. Above, vultures circled. Anne held bateleur eagles, with stub tails and streaked red heads, in high esteem. She also reserved a special place for harrier hawks, African gymnogenes, on account of their death-defying aerobatics. One day, above the raptors, she spotted a new bird—an antique Tiger Moth biplane. She watched it circle, bank sharply, then fly above the surrounding camphor, cedar, and Hagenia trees. From Anne's perch in the garden, it was as beautiful as any eagle.

◄○►

Anne scheduled her first flying lesson for June 23, 1963, on an airstrip near Sabukia, thirty miles northwest of Ol Kalou. Her teacher was Bill Bunford, a fellow veteran of the Kenya Police Reserve. Determined not to fail, Anne came to view his old Piper Colt warhorse, so beat up that winds whistled through cracks in the fuselage, as her way out of the all-absorbing confusion of her life.

At age forty-five, Anne was no natural pilot and the Sabukia valley, notorious for its turbulent winds and erratic midday thermals, hardly the ideal training grounds. Anne lived in dread of the shrill stall warning, alerting the pilot that the plane was about to fall from the sky. Seasoned pilots claim there is no better way to learn the intricacies of flight than with rudimentary instrumentation in a tail dragger, but flying just above stall speed at low altitude is an invitation to disaster, especially in a Piper Colt. Anne had taken on a colossal challenge and progress was barely detectable.

The greatest hurdle was landing. Not aligned with the prevailing winds, Sabukia's short, narrow, high-altitude airstrip was pitiless. Anne consistently failed to gauge her height above the ground as she came in to land. One observer, Biddy Davis, called her kangaroo hops, verging on ground loops, "hysterical." Finally, six weeks into her lessons, Anne latched upon a trick and, in time, turned the corner. She discovered she could estimate height above the ground by comparison with grass stems bordering the runway. After she adopted this strategy, Bill Bunford remarked that she was making progress.

Success immediately went to Anne's head. Confident she had mastered the intricacies of aviation, she proposed a long trip with her friend Dermott Bailey, Biddy Davis's brother, to revisit her old stomping grounds in Yemen. The two took off from Nairobi, crossed the Red Sea, and began their descent into Aden's international airport. All went smoothly until the final moments before touchdown. With the surrounding terrain all but desiccated, Anne could not find one blade of grass for reference. Her landing proved catastrophic, with the plane hitting the runway, bouncing, stalling, and then plunging into the ground. The force of the crash sheared off six inches of propeller. As pilot and passenger walked away from the wreckage without injury, Anne offered no apology for having smashed Dermott's plane. She expressed her remorse not in words but in the form of a gift, treating Dermott to a six-week tour of Yemen—an act of generosity he never forgot.

—◦—

"Flying over the Highlands and the Rift Valley," Anne wrote of her early adventures in Kenya, "was a continual enchantment and a wonderful reward for my long months of effort, doubt and, sometimes, fear." Set loose to roam the clouds, she found a world of new possibilities. Above Lake Nakuru, with three million flamingos turning its glassy surface pink, her heart quickened. Over calderas, teeming with buffalo and giraffe, she imagined childhood kingdoms. On the edge of deserts, she saw human life as she liked, not messy, but one orderly thatched-roofed hut after another. Here, set loose in a big sky, over a miraculous continent, Anne fell in love with her adopted home all over again.

By July, Anne had soloed, and a month later she qualified to fly cross-country. By the following year, she was a private pilot, and at the beginning of 1964 she bought her first plane—a Piper Cherokee 235—for $10,655, paid by her father in a wire transfer to Wilken Air in Nairobi. There would be only one other plane in her life— another Piper, slightly larger, more powerful, and considerably more expensive. Why Anne was devoted to this particular brand puzzled fellow pilots; for them, high-winged Cessnas, while marginally slower, were better suited to Kenya's rough high-altitude terrain. For Anne, speed trumped common sense, because Pipers always arrived a few minutes ahead of Cessnas. Her plane, speed queen Anne insisted, was "the perfect machine to fly in Kenya."

One day, while practicing "touch and goes" at Sabukia, Anne spotted a small farm not far from the airstrip. In the afternoon, she drove out for a look. Its previous owner, an elderly colonel, had fatally crashed his plane while landing at Sabukia. Now his grieving widow wanted to flee the scene of the tragedy and return to England. Anne made, by her own admission, an "absurdly low" offer. The traumatized widow accepted it, and Anne closed on the farm in record time. According to journalist Annie Kouchner, Anne bought the Sabukia farm to prove to the world she had not failed in Africa. The one individual she most needed to reassure was her father, Henry Spoerry, still uncertain of his daughter's dependability.

Without pausing to reflect, Anne returned to Ol Kalou. There she loaded up her Peugeot, trailer, and lorries with dogs, horses, firearms, a voluminous safe, and a library of books. In the rear seat sat Ndetto, her cook, as well as a *fundi* (carpenter). Anne never said farewell to Francis.

–◆–

The Sabukia farm, on the road between Nyeri and Nakuru, was an impulse buy: twenty-five well-wooded equatorial acres, eight thousand feet above sea level, bounded by two streams as a secure perimeter fence. Because land around Sabukia had escaped the compulsory purchase orders of independence, it still boasted a robust expatriate community. Here Anne would never feel alone. While commercial farming in Sabukia could not measure up to Ol Kalou's, its mild climate, high altitude, yellow-barked acacia, and views conspired to make it a favored refuge for settlers willing to take a chance in postindependence Kenya.

Ol Kalou's lurking memories, with former Mau Maus ghosting out of the forest, had tormented Anne. Sabukia, by comparison, appeared to be a sanctuary. While its higgledy-piggledy architecture, smoky fireplace, and threadbare couches imperfectly mirrored her gathering wealth, the farm became the source of Anne's solace, a place devoid of lurking fears. At Sabukia, Anne could start over, with a new, eager staff.

Within the year, Anne had begun to set aside a corner of her sitting room for the many gifts bestowed on her by penniless patients. In time, this African reliquary of goat bells, Masai spears, and beaded calabashes, pungent with wood smoke, became a source of some pride—evidence of Africa's gratitude.

Anne's farmhouse was a simple bungalow, only slightly grander than her previous cottage in Ol Kalou. It boasted four bedrooms and one toilet. Anne did not mind that her dwelling lacked electrification. She was content reading by the glow of a hand-pumped Tilley lamp, after dinner in the drawing room, and later waiting for sleep in her narrow, monastic bed. Anne claimed the cottage's decoration bill was greater than the purchase price of the entire farm. If so, the investment seems of questionable merit: the walls were cement block, the tin roof, rusted and peeling, the windows, small and barred. Typically, Anne deplored ostentation, and the bungalow is a monument to thriftiness, never reflecting the architectural grandeur of her French and Swiss childhood. She settled for quintessential Kenyan luxuries—large staff, well-stocked library, plentiful food, spirits under lock and key, fierce dogs, and heart-stirring sunsets.

Within months, Anne's bookshelves, bordering the fireplace, bowed from the weight of her library, originally assembled in Europe, enlarged upon in Aden, pored over in Ol Kalou, and now devoured all over again. The lower shelves were dedicated to French medical references. Above them she arranged her favorite African and Arabian travelers' tales. One can visualize Anne's delight, by the fire, as she reread Alan Villiers's *Sons of Sinbad,* with dogs at her feet and .38 Service Special, out of its holster, perched on a side table.

Anne had to dip into a family trust to purchase the Sabukia farm. As her cash reserves multiplied following the death of her father in 1966, she expanded her staff to over twenty full-time resident employees. Anne looked to Sabukia as her larder, a showplace to delight her European visitors, and a refuge from dangers real and imagined. The three hundred coffee trees flourished in Sabukia's warm days and cool nights. Friesians—later Jerseys—met Anne's and everyone else's dairy needs. Dogs and a flock of "alarm" geese provided security. In Sabukia, with its full staff, Anne ruled as if Kenya were still a colony and she a feudal sovereign. Over her nearly forty years in independent Kenya, no one ever chided her for her colonial memsahib ways.

In her first year at her new farm, Anne continued her work as a medical officer for Nyandarua County. Once her two-year contract came up for renewal, she quit "without regret," having grown frustrated battling bureaucracy. Now without steady employment, Anne set her mind to farming and practicing pro-bono medicine— setting workers' broken fingers, stitching wounds, and delivering babies. Her white neighbors, previously lacking a resident doctor, saw Anne as a godsend.

It was not long before Anne showed signs of restlessness. She was in need of a rousing adventure. To that end, in 1964 she began planning to fly her single-engine plane seven thousand miles from Kenya to France and back. Admitting she had limited experience, she enlisted her friend Dermott Bailey, formerly a navigator in the Royal Canadian Air Force, as co-pilot. He, in turn, recruited his cousin Tim Llewelyn-Smith as "baggage master," in charge of refueling and weight distribution. Recognizing she was still "very green" as a pilot, Anne looked to her crew to fill in the gaps in her aviation education. Years later, Dermott speculated that Anne had conceived the trip because she was "bored." He also felt that "deep down" she aspired to "recognition in Kenya," that she needed a bold transcontinental journey to bring her out of seclusion. Perhaps she would attract someone's attention.

The outbound leg north from Kenya went without hitch in spite of Anne's tantrums. According to Dermott, whenever she lost her temper, he responded, "'Okay. Calm down.' Then it would all

blow over." The team successfully negotiated thunderheads pil-
ing up over the Sudd, the massive swamp where the Nile wanders
through a maze of aimless channels in the heart of southern Sudan.
Approaching Khartoum, they flew blind on instruments into a
haboob, a dust storm. In Egypt, when Anne's manly trousers and
bush jacket met with the disapproval of Muslim customs officials,
she changed into a dress. Safely arrived in Greece, Anne, Dermott,
and Tim lashed down the Piper and went off to sail the Pelopon-
nesus with François, Anne's brother. At the end of the junket, the
three aviators flew to France, where Anne introduced Dermott and
Tim to the rest of her family. Thérèse and Martine seemed in awe of
their older sister. After a week, Anne had grown impatient with the
calm of Provence. She clapped her hands to announce to Dermott
and Tim she was ready to return home to Africa.

Just out of Malta on the Mediterranean leg to Benghazi, Dermott
spotted fuel seeping from a wing tank. This proved to be the trio's
first emergency. According to Dermott, Anne stayed cool, turning
the plane back to Malta, issuing an SOS on the RAF frequency, low-
ering the undercarriage, and executing a perfect landing, just as the
engine failed. During the perilous minutes when Anne, Dermott,
and Tim considered ditching the plane in rough seas, Anne never
flinched.

When finally Anne landed the Piper at Wilson Airport in Nairobi, news of her feat traveled fast among members of Nairobi's
Aero Club. The flight was Anne's longest cross-country—a noteworthy international exploit even for aviation-hardened Kenya.
Most critically, Anne's feat caught the eye of Dr. Michael Wood,
one of three founders of the Flying Doctors Service of East Africa.
For a few years, Michael Wood, who had come to Africa for his own
health and then become one of its leading health providers, had
been hearing about the no-nonsense French doctor with her own
plane. Now with impressive cross-country credentials to her name,

she appeared the right fit for the Flying Doctors. Still, Wood had no illusions his colleagues, opposed to hiring a woman for "men's work," would share his enthusiasm.

Long before she learned to fly, Anne had hoped to meet the Flying Doctors, especially its founder Sir Archibald "Archie" McIndoe, famed for his pioneering work during the Battle of Britain reconstructing the disfigured faces of Spitfire and Hurricane pilots who had been shot down. McIndoe's revolutionary skin graft technology, based in a hospital in East Grinstead, Sussex, gave these acutely scarred men new faces and the prospect of reasonably normal lives. By the end of the war, Dr. McIndoe had successfully grafted noses and ears onto over thirty-five hundred men. To honor their rescuer, they formed "the Guinea Pig Club." In turn, the king acknowledged Britain's debt by knighting McIndoe. In time, his field of medicine would come to be known as cosmetic surgery.

After the war, New Zealand–born McIndoe took time off to go on safari in East Africa. Immediately, he fell under its spell and, back in England, began making plans for a return. This time he brought along two of his most promising medical students— Michael Wood, who already knew Africa, and Tom Rees, born to Mormon parents in Utah. In time, Michael Wood would move his family to East Africa and purchase a succession of farms, the first on the slopes of Mount Kilimanjaro. Tom Rees's infatuation took another path. For much of his career, he would leave his highly successful New York practice, bobbing noses, augmenting bosoms, tucking tummies, to volunteer a month a year to work pro bono in Africa, rebuilding the lives of the impoverished. In Kenya and Tanzania, one of Rees's proudest achievements was reconstructing the faces of severely scarred kids who lacked eyelids—a disfigurement that kept them from sleep and rendered many blind. Rees's surgical intervention gave them their lives back.

McIndoe, Wood, and Rees, soon to be known as "the white

knights of medicine," had formed a remarkable partnership, all because of an obsession with Africa. Their enterprise began with one flying surgeon and a nurse, intending to service rural mission hospitals in Kenya and Tanzania via regularly scheduled flights. Their overarching plan was to bring plastic surgery to the bush.

Delivering medicine to places of greatest need was, at the time, innovative. Prior to the establishment of the Flying Doctors in 1957, if a pastoralist sought Western medicine, he or she had to walk vast distances, at considerable peril, to a township, possibly occupied by a hostile tribe. Michael Wood was among the first to right this wrong. What began with a truck, outfitted as both dispensary and operating theater, soon took to the air. Flying his small Piper Tri-Pacer, he learned to meet patients on their home turf; almost immediately the experiment proved a wild success. His only problem was the size of the plane, limited to carrying only one patient and a stretcher. Knowing their project needed critical mass to be effective, he, McIndoe, and Rees charged off to Britain and the United States to raise funds for a bigger, bolder idea—larger planes, specialist pilots, ground crews, doctors, nurses, and the installation of a Nairobi-based communication network. The American talk show host Arthur Godfrey was one of the charity's earliest benefactors, with the donation of a Piper Aztec and then a Piper Cherokee.

The organization's simple premise struck a chord with Anne. She knew firsthand the challenge faced by nomads, whether Masai, Samburu, Turkana, Rendille, or Pokot, and how women were at the gravest risk of all. In her up-country practice she had seen traditional female circumcisions go devastatingly wrong and unattended pregnancies turn deadly for both mother and child. As early as 1965, she recognized that women's health especially was neglected across Africa. If she could talk her way into the worlds of McIndoe, Wood, and Rees, she might be able to bring a woman's sensibility to health issues and achieve an enduring dream of bush medicine and derring-do.

Anne had little trouble convincing Michael Wood of her worth. Now she needed the buy-in of his colleagues, especially Tom Rees.

In 2004, the New York plastic surgeon recalled the moment of his conversion. Under pressure from Wood, he agreed to meet Anne on Nairobi's Norfolk hotel terrace, a popular expatriate rendezvous. He also saw it as a neutral venue. He had already made up his mind: he would buy her a beer and politely tell her she was not up to it. "I was worried," he explained, "about a woman doing this very dangerous job."

When Rees cast his eyes across the crowded terrace, Anne was already waiting for him. Introducing himself, he noted her firm handshake and winning smile. Once they found a corner table away from the hubbub, he ordered a round of beers. They soon dispensed with small talk; Anne was intent on pitching him about her medical skills. She ordered a second round and presented him with three reasons why he should hire her on the spot: she was a skilled pilot, she loved challenges, and she knew battlefield medicine. Rees tried to mount a counteroffensive: "But you'll be alone in a land of men." Anne stared him down like a raptor. He could not escape her eyes. There was something about her, he thought. Maybe Michael was right. Anne Spoerry was no everyday lady: "From her first words, I knew she was up to it. I could see she was fearless, and there was something better: she had a smell for disease—the acumen for sniffing out bad situations."

Michael Wood and Tom Rees hired Anne Spoerry on a handshake. Old-world courtesy excused her from further scrutiny. Neither doctor asked about her past. No one requested references. The two doctors simply offered her the job. As long as gentlemen ran the Flying Doctors Service, Anne would be safe. According to Rees, "In those days, no one questioned."

Henry Spoerry did not share Anne's enthusiasm for this new scheme. On his office stationery, dated May 19, 1964, he wrote, "I am not in favor of contributing your airplane to this cause, but if you accept—and I believe you already have—you must ask them for substantial compensation." Anne disregarded her father's advice, so committed was she to the Flying Doctors dream. She was firm in her resolve to be a flying doctor, even willing to work for next to nothing. Years later, with gathering wealth, she even dispensed with a salary altogether and dug into her own pocket to pay for aviation fuel.

Two days after cautioning Anne about compensation, Henry Spoerry wrote again. Assuming she had overruled his advice, he asked whether she was looking for a property next to Wilson Airport. Henry Spoerry knew he was powerless against his strong-willed daughter.

◄o►

When Anne signed on to the Flying Doctors and began wearing the uniform—a khaki shirt with blue and gold flying wings—she became the first woman flying doctor in the world. In addition, she and Michael Wood were, for a time, East Africa's sole full-time members of the exclusive profession.

In her early Flying Doctors days, Anne flew cautiously, always seeking out the advice of more seasoned pilots whenever she prepared to land at an unfamiliar airstrip. Never complaining of privations or discomfort, sleeping alone beneath the wing of her plane, Anne immediately won the respect of her colleagues. Especially impressive for Wood was her skill improvising splints from tree branches, recycling old tourniquets, and splitting doses of antibiotics when supplies ran short.

In her early Flying Doctors years, Anne held dominion over some 680,000 square miles of Kenya's outback, annually flying her

Piper over 39,000 miles. It was not unusual for her then to fly several hours for a single patient. Once she flew 600 miles for a nomad woman speared by bandits. In those early days, when she stepped out of her plane into Africa's pulsing heat, the sight of her terrified many. In 1967, she told her friend Ann Steel, "Some . . . have never seen a white woman in their lives before . . . They giggle among themselves and can't believe their eyes. But once they realize I am a doctor everything is usually all right." At the time, Anne estimated that in these wild lands there were thirty thousand patients who needed her help every year. She now was reasonably fluent in Swahili, and while not all her rural patients spoke it, it greased the wheels in most situations. "They are stoic people," she said. "They appreciate you and don't say much. The amount of pain they can bear is amazing." When Ann Steel asked Anne Spoerry why she worked so hard, her response was evasive: "Because it is interesting and rewarding."

"She was a fabulous diagnostician and I feel honored to have known her," recalled Dr. David Hartwright, an orthopedic surgeon who briefly served her as apprentice. "As a Western doctor we have all sorts of scans to rely on. She had no access to them. Her skills were highly honed to pick up visible signs from her patients. The smallest change she noted . . . She recognized all problems instantly, just from observation."

Anne's bush clinics were rudimentary—a card table, two chairs, and several large plastic containers of tablets, mostly aspirin. In her notebook, she kept track of as many as 150 patients a session. Dr. Hartwright exclaimed, "The speed of her conclusions was dazzling."

In 1969, the Flying Doctors changed its name to AMREF, African Medical Research Foundation. In that year Anne, aged fifty-one, appeared in an obscure documentary, *The Flying Doctors of East Africa*, directed and produced by famed German director Werner Herzog. In the voice-over, he introduced Anne simply as the "Swiss doctor." Her hair was now uniformly silver, her manner assured, even brusque. Her bush skills were solidly on display as she girdled the tires of her plane with thornbushes to repel hyenas. "Why hyenas prefer Firestone tires, no one knows," said Herzog's narrator. The sequence then cut to show Dr. Spoerry on the radiotelephone informing AMREF headquarters that she would be flying an injured twelve-year-old Masai boy to Nairobi. During her eight-minute appearance, the enduring impression is of a seasoned and efficient bush doctor, with a trace of sulkiness when responding to Herzog.

The gruff persona Anne affected on camera was not the one known to friends. One of Anne's greatest was Maddie DeMott. Shortly after joining the Flying Doctors, Anne had met this well-heeled California widow in Nairobi. Having just completed a monthlong East African safari, Maddie told her she had fallen irreversibly in love with the continent. Learning that she had once been a Red Cross nurse, Anne insisted she come to work for her in Nairobi.

Maddie began as Anne's assistant. Soon she was appointed California fund-raiser for the Flying Doctors. Anne and Maddie's friendship, spanning thirty-four years, comes to life in a touching correspondence, preserved by Anne. "Dearest Maddie," all Anne's letters begin. "Lots of love," they end. Theirs was a cozy, prosaic exchange in which they shared family news, lamented their many losses, and commiserated with each other about the chaotic fortunes of their beloved Flying Doctors. In one letter, Maddie told of her joy with the birth of a new grandchild. By return, Anne described her bliss upon learning her nephew Bernard had finally married his girlfriend, Anita, with whom he had already sired two children. Fund-raising was a constant. Whenever Maddie returned to the United States, her assignment was to beat the bushes for money to keep AMREF's airplanes in the air.

In 2003, in failing health, Maddie was admitted to a California

nursing home. Even then, this gentle ninety-year-old, still passion-
ate about Africa, had no trouble recalling her adventurous days
with Anne. To Maddie, Anne was her "exotic" African friend: "She
really didn't need me [to work for her]. She just wanted someone to
take intelligent messages [on the phone] and to do her errands. She
was bossy. She liked to run the show. Still, she was one of the most
remarkable people I ever knew." One 1969 note illustrated exactly
how Anne ran the show. In it, Anne commanded Maddie to run
into Nairobi to get her "12 doses of Leftovax [Anne probably meant
LeptoVax, a dog vaccine], 5 lbs. of apples, Kodachrome film, a car-
ton of Embassy cigarettes and a bottle of Haig whiskey." Maddie
complied.

In a more personal note from 1969, Anne lamented that her
future as a flying doctor was now uncertain: "We are again short
of funds and flying hours have been reduced to 120." Everyone, she
noted, no matter how senior, had gone off, hat in hand, to beg for
money—Michael Wood to Europe, and Tom Rees to New York.
Anne did her bit, writing to friends in Basel, Switzerland, but her
success was modest compared with her colleagues'.

Three weeks later, a large check from New York arrived at Nairobi headquarters. Instantly, the Flying Doctors Service was flush,
its physicians again airborne. Anne jubilantly renewed her pilot's
license and wrote to Maddie, "I got my medical passed on my return
here and got a flight test and went off with glee, into the blue."

During their many years of friendship, Maddie regularly stayed
with Anne at the farm in Sabukia. She recalled frequent evenings
talking late, with sausage beetles crashing against Tilley lamps.
Much of their conversation was about joys, losses, and regrets. Maddie was too much a lady ever to press Anne about World War II—
what she described as Anne's "no fly zone"—but on a few notable
occasions Anne raised the topic of her own volition, one of the few
instances when she broke her famous vow of silence.

-◄o►-

From her California nursing home in 2003, Maddie recounted one chain of events. That night, there were three of them, she recalled—Anne, Maddie, and another, unnamed woman. The exchange took place around a bottle of wine, beneath the bougainvillea smothering the house (the site where, in 1980, Anne gave me a dressing-down for inquiring about the war). The wine, Maddie believed, made Anne chatty. Maddie whispered to me the word that began the memorable exchange: "Ravensbrück."

"There," recalled Maddie, "Anne told me her life changed, because she allowed herself to be protected by the Germans. It all happened because she agreed to kill people. She did not want to but she had to." After the admission, Anne looked away, "heavy with it all." Because she helped the Germans, Anne told Maddie, her life was spared. Maddie tried to respond, but she never found the words. I asked her what happened next. "Nothing much," Maddie said. "Anne excused herself and went to bed."

Baffled by this account, I asked Maddie to elaborate. After a silence, she switched stories. This one was about Anne and her brother in Lamu over the Christmas holidays, several years later. On Boxing Day, after Anne popped a bottle of champagne, she again dropped her guard. When Anne raised the subject of war with François, Maddie was "all ears." Anne's volubility apparently aggravated her brother. With theatrical exaggeration, he tiptoed across the terrace. With his face inches from Anne's, he put his finger to his lips. Anne instantly hushed. Maddie saw in these coded gestures a deep and wonderful expression of love: "they were sworn to secrecy, you see," and no one but François had the nerve to discipline Anne. Anne's obedience implied a special brother-sister bond. Perhaps because Maddie had no idea what François was concealing, she described the moment as "so cute."

When Anne made her admission to Maddie, she had already

disclosed her Ravensbrück story to someone else altogether—the unnamed woman sitting beside Maddie and Anne at Sabukia. While Maddie remembered the silent woman knitting, she could not recall her name. Whoever she was, she was certain "she knew a lot." The unknown woman was, in fact, the only person in Africa who had breached Anne's wall of silence.

I t is a puzzle that for much of her life in Kenya Anne kept the name Mary O'Shaughnessy to herself, for Mary was a heroine and their friendship inspirational. One might expect Anne would have extolled this brave lady with words similar to the ones she reserved for her adored and celebrated brother. Instead, she embargoed all talk of Mary, treating the name, as she did Ravensbrück, as private property.

I might never have known of Mary had it not been for a call, a few years after Anne's death, from my friend MaryAnne Fitzgerald, living in Nairobi. Aware of my interest in the famed flying doctor, MaryAnne thought I should know she had stumbled upon a parcel containing the passport of a woman who was said to be a friend of Anne Spoerry's.

For upwards of an hour I studied the passport photograph. It was of a prim lady, her hair done up in a bun, her face tempted by a smile. I was drawn to what had been written in the document in green ink beside the heading, "special peculiarities." No further information accompanied the passport. When I asked around Kenya, few could recall Mary O'Shaughnessy.

Knowing only that Mary was British-born, I began a search of all O'Shaughnessy telephone numbers, beginning in the north of England. Later, through sheer good luck, I narrowed the hunt to Lancashire, calling number after number for over a week. At last, an elderly man heard me out and, with tremulous voice, said he knew Mary O'Shaughnessy. He was, in fact, Denis, her nephew and sole survivor. This was the breakthrough I needed. Thanks to him, I was able to stitch together an era pivotal to Anne's secretive Africa.

—◦—

Mary O'Shaughnessy entered Anne's Sabukia life in 1966. There she would remain, invisible to most, a puzzle to others. This fastidiously dressed woman spoke with precision, husbanding words, economizing emotions, easy with silence. So determined was Mary O'Shaughnessy not to draw attention to herself that some presumed she worked for Anne as a kind of amanuensis or perhaps a lady's maid. Others imagined a liaison of the heart.

"Miss Mary"—the appellation used by those who knew her during her Kenya years—was twenty years Anne's senior. Unlike Anne, she tended to feminine apparel and, according to most, was rarely attired in anything but a dress, often festooned with a brooch, even when performing farm chores. Her eyes were a haunting blue gray, her silver hair meticulously arranged in a bun. By all accounts, Miss Mary was not chatty, but when she talked, her voice was so delicate listeners leaned forward to revel in her lilting Lancashire diction.

At Sabukia, Miss Mary always preferred to stay apart from the social whirl. While Anne invariably commanded a central speaking role at gatherings, Miss Mary contented herself with the periphery, often busy knitting. When Anne was flying across Kenya during the week, Miss Mary supervised the farm, attending to duties assigned by Anne. Because the elderly lady did not drive, she rarely went out in public. For five days of every week, Mary O'Shaughnessy was invisible to the outside world.

When one first met Miss Mary, what caught the attention of all, white and black, was not only her graceful manners but the absence of a left hand—the distinctive feature she noted in green ink in her passport under "special peculiarities." To avoid embarrassment, she concealed her prosthetic in a long tasteful glove that somehow defied Africa by remaining perfectly white. Ariane Besse, Anne's sister-in-law, noted how, even with an artificial hand, Mary sewed, knitted, and washed effortlessly. Whenever Ariane offered to help, Miss Mary brushed her away, saying she could manage "just fine."

In Kenya it was no secret that Miss Mary had suffered a reversal of fortune and that bighearted Anne had come forward with help. Some wondered whether the two first met during the war. No one could be certain, and because most of Anne's neighbors had been raised not to probe, few ever knew. All accepted the two women as rare birds, set down on African shores, their pasts dwarfed by their new lives.

Whenever the two laid on a Sunday curry lunch, Anne held court, while Miss Mary contented herself listening. One acquaintance called the two "a matched pair." Nicky Blundell Brown, a friend of many years, claimed Anne was at her "most comfortable" in the company of Miss Mary.

◄o►

One of four children of working-class Irish immigrants, Miss Mary was born in 1898 in Leigh, twelve miles north of Manchester.

Mary's impoverished childhood was compounded by a congenital deformity—her missing hand. With her parents unable to afford a prosthetic, Mary learned to cope, devising many stratagems to disguise her handicap. She hid it under a jacket, in a school bag, behind her back. Rarely were schoolmates fooled, and Mary suffered years of school-yard heckling and bullying.

A week after she turned twenty-three, Mary was raped. Too shamed to report the incident to anyone, including her parents, she withdrew in silence, only to discover that she was pregnant. In Leigh of the time, abortion was not an option and illegitimacy, no matter the circumstance, a lifelong stain on both mother and child. "There was great shame having a child out of wedlock," Denis explained. "This town had its share of bigots." Soon after the birth of her son, Mary, unwilling to endure a lifetime of scorn, packed up, handed the boy over to the care of her parents, and fled Leigh and England.

Within six months, both Mary's parents fell ill and died. Far from Leigh, Mary learned the news. Much as she wanted to return for their funerals, she dreaded further ridicule and humiliation. She knew her son was in better hands than her own, having now been adopted by her uncle and aunt, Denis's parents.

Denis never met the estranged Mary. He believed that for much of her life she never spoke of her son, the circumstances of his abandonment, or the guilt that she felt for having hastened her parents' death. He also assumed that her self-imposed prohibition lapsed when she came to stay with Anne. In the company of a woman equally tormented, he speculated, Miss Mary "found her resolution."

After abandoning her son, Miss Mary O'Shaughnessy boarded a ferry in Poole and disembarked at Cherbourg. Prior to job hunting in Paris, she invested in an expensive prosthetic hand and two sets of white gloves. The profession Mary chose for herself in France was, paradoxically, the care of children. Her first position, serving as governess for a titled Angers family, three hundred kilometers southwest of Paris, lasted twelve years. A photograph shows three girls and one boy posing for the camera before their family château, with Miss Mary standing deferentially to one side. Even in grainy, informal shots, one senses the children's devotion to Mary. Also apparent is her effort to hide her gloved left hand behind her back.

When Mary turned forty-two, after years of careful saving, she bought a small apartment in Paris. Her timing could not have been more inopportune. The year was 1940, and Miss Mary, like other Parisians, soon watched in horror as Germany's Wehrmacht invaded France and overran Paris. Almost from the first days of the occupation, Miss Mary worked for the Resistance, providing safe houses for downed British airmen and facilitating their escape from occupied France through the port of Marseille. For two months, she cared for one wounded pilot near Angers, until he was fit enough to return to England. During this time and beyond, she sent the MI5 network sketches of suitable bombing targets for transmission to the RAF.

In 1943, the Gestapo, increasingly suspicious that Mary O'Shaughnessy was a British spy, broke into her Paris apartment. When Mary came upon her treasures in disarray, she realized the web was closing and there was now only one course of action. Throwing a few belongings into a suitcase, she slipped out of her door for the last time and headed for the south. Her intention was to escape France and cross into Spain, which, at the time, offered sanctuary. At a border town, she accepted a friend's invitation for tea at a hotel. It was a fateful error. A few minutes after she and others settled into seats around a table on the terrace, Nazi officers arrived, seizing them all, including Miss Mary. Only one woman was allowed to go free: the supposed "friend." Miss Mary watched as the informer scuttled away from the scene of her betrayal.

Mary was first imprisoned in Montluc, a fortress near Lyon.

Under intense questioning by the Germans, she was ordered to disclose all names of fellow Resistance operatives. Miss Mary refused. Guards thereupon subjected her to rounds of scalding baths, followed by immersion in ice water. Even after thirteen sets (she counted them with great precision) over a span of nine days, Mary held to her resolve of silence. Frustrated, the Germans threw her into a cattle car with hundreds of other prisoners. Five days later, the train arrived at the women's concentration camp, Ravensbrück. Miss Mary, one of its few English prisoners, was again tortured. Again, she refused to name any of her colleagues. In frustration, guards threw her into a dreaded block housing some 1,150 women. For five months, Mary witnessed every sort of "German bestiality," including the sight of one unhinged guard kicking prisoners one by one until they died. Not long after her arrival, a woman guard was so enraged by Mary's lack of fluency in German she lashed out at her, breaking eight of her teeth. When Mary continued to resist, the guard landed a roundhouse punch to her face, breaking her nose.

Mary escaped death on at least three occasions. Once, a friend assured a suspicious guard that the woman lying at his feet was a corpse. To check whether rigor mortis had set in, he kicked the inert Mary, who somehow kept still. Satisfied she was dead, he left. When he was out of earshot, Mary opened her eyes and fled.

More than once, Mary saved others, using her prosthetic hand for passing secret messages between blocks. In the end, the disability became a liability. During the final month of war in 1945, Mary was handed a pink card, transferring her to the adjacent Uckermark Camp for girls, now repurposed as a staging post for "women who were sick, no longer efficient, and over 52 years old." Realizing that in the eyes of her German captors she met most of these thresholds, Mary had no doubt she was being readied for execution. For the first week, she was locked in an overcrowded block, with no water, food, or sanitation. Beside her, women lay dying in their own excrement. Those who showed signs of life were led out into the snow, forced with rifle butts into the bed of a truck, and then delivered to the gas chamber. Wondrously, a female guard who, over the week, had shared personal confidences with Mary took pity on her and showed her how to hide from the daily "death transports." For her final week in Uckermark Camp, no one, but one friendly guard, knew Mary existed.

In April 1945, the Swedish Red Cross liberated six hundred Ravensbrück prisoners. One of the lucky few to join the first westbound convoy was Mary O'Shaughnessy. After transiting Denmark, Sweden, and Scotland, she reached England, where an RAF airman she had saved in France took pity on her and brought her into his home until she had recuperated sufficiently to travel on her own. In October 1945, a Birmingham newspaper, *The Journal,* reported Mary was still "a mere shell of her former self." In the interview, she reported she had no money, only one set of clothes, a few honors, and a weekly pension of eight shillings—barely enough for sustenance. Through *The Journal,* she "appealed to the men she saved, most from the R.A.F., to come forward as proof of the good work she did, as her troubles may then be solved."

In 1946 and 1947, Mary returned to Germany to provide testimony for the prosecution in the Nuremberg and Hamburg war crimes tribunals, the latter consisting of seven trials for war crimes committed by Ravensbrück camp officials and prisoners. Once back in England, she set out to write a book about her years in Ravensbrück and Uckermark death camps. The project came to nothing, for, before she had even completed her first chapter, a Fleet Street friend told her the book was doomed since the British public was "fed up" with war stories and now needed uplifting tales. Mary glumly took his advice and resumed her life as a nanny. In 1948, Tuppy and Anne Manton of Tunbridge Wells, Kent, hired Mary as a governess to look after their two sons, Roger and Johnny, the latter handicapped and in need of special schooling. In 1956, when Tuppy was transferred to Kenya, Miss Mary followed with the boys, arriving in Nairobi on November 26, in the final days of Mau Mau. She remained in Kenya in the employ of the Mantons until 1966, when, at the age of sixty-eight, Miss Mary informed them of her wish to retire.

—◦—

How Anne Spoerry and Mary O'Shaughnessy connected is not entirely clear. The coincidence of two Ravensbrück survivors, living alone in Africa, might have been incentive for mutual friends to make an introduction. Two single women, even at a geographic remove from each other, were almost certain to encounter each other in Kenya's postindependence white community. One of Anne's friends was quite sure they met at the Nakuru Hospital, where Miss Mary had volunteered after leaving the Manton household.

It is more than likely that during that first encounter Anne was not forthcoming, being compulsively wary of anyone too friendly or connected to Ravensbrück. Still, Miss Mary would have impressed Anne with her reserve, impeccable manners, discreet mien, and perceptiveness.

Within two weeks, Miss Mary moved onto the farm. The decision made good sense for both women. Sabukia's crisp climate was exactly what Mary, with a heart condition and at loose ends, needed. Quiet, polite, and with proven managerial skills, she offered to exchange board for housekeeping. There was no question that Anne, absent five days a week, needed help with the farm.

Arriving at Sabukia, Miss Mary opened her one bruised suitcase, unpacked her few belongings, and settled into a guest room. Each Friday when Anne buzzed the house after distant tours of Kenya, Miss Mary had vases filled with cut flowers. Under her gentle guidance, the household staff was turned out in white *kanzus,* and the Tilley lamps shone like Georgian silver. Within weeks of Miss Mary's arrival, Sabukia went from encampment to home. Soon Anne could not do without Mary.

For Anne, the foremost attraction of a permanent guest was conversation. In the privacy of Sabukia, the two women had all the time in the world to exchange confidences. The older woman was a fine judge of people and was no stranger to weakness, failure, and unintended consequences. Having lived through Ravensbrück and having sat in the witness box for the prosecution at two war crimes trials, she was painfully familiar with frailty and compromise. Should Anne clear her throat or cry, Miss Mary knew to look away, pick up fallen petals, iron a jumper, mend a sock, or brush wine drops from a tablecloth. Mindful of her own history, she steadfastly held to the belief that one woman has no right to judge another, no matter the circumstances.

Five years into her stay, Miss Mary began to decline. A neighbor's 1970 letter to Anne hinted of a serious condition: "I do hope Miss Mary is feeling a bit better now. It is so sad to lose old friends even if they are better in more peaceful harbors." Over three years, Miss Mary rallied and by mid-1973 appeared sufficiently recovered to travel to England to join a gathering of Ravensbrück survivors. While quick to pay Miss Mary's airfare, Anne had no intention of joining her. A holiday with François in the South of France was far preferable.

Early in September, Miss Mary flew to London and caught a train to Brighton. There she checked into a hotel along with other Ravensbrück survivors. The reunion began on a high note for Miss Mary. But after one day, it proved too much. Miss Mary's frail heart gave out at dinner on September 11, 1973, when she suffered a massive heart attack. By the time the doctor arrived at the hotel, she was dead. Vera Atkins, the Special Operations Executive's famed intelligence officer and assistant to Maurice Buckmaster, held Miss Mary's hand at the end.

When Miss Mary's body was removed for burial, Vera Atkins found an address book in her purse. In it she came upon the name of one other O'Shaughnessy. Denis answered the call and promptly caught the first train out of Manchester. In Brighton, at the funeral, he said little, awed by tales of the aunt he never knew. The eulogies all spoke of a woman of exemplary bravery, generosity, and modesty. "I felt extremely humbled by their accounts of her life." In time, he would write an article for the BBC, calling Mary O'Shaughnessy "an unsung heroine of World War II."

Riffling through the address book on that September evening in Brighton, Vera Atkins found another name. This one she recognized. During the Hamburg war crimes trial of 1946 and 1947, Atkins, sitting in the balcony, kept hearing about a certain "Dr. Claude," or Anne Spoerry. While never a defendant at the trial, Spoerry, Atkins learned, had refused to serve even as a witness to help save a supposed friend of hers, one of the defendants, facing death. Was it cowardice or survival? Atkins never forgot the consistently damning testimony against Spoerry. After the war, Anne had heard that Atkins had publicly spoken out against her, despite their never having met. Now, during his day with Vera Atkins, Denis watched the illustrious intelligence operative pick up the phone.

The day was September 11, 1973. From the brief conversation, Denis detected no trace of condemnation in Atkins's voice. All he could assume was that the former spymaster recognized Anne as a friend and patron of Mary's. Atkins simply wished to inform her of the latter's death. Even though Denis listened to only one side of the conversation, he had the distinct impression Anne burst into tears.

A few weeks later, back at home, Denis O'Shaughnessy received a letter from Anne. In it, she described Miss Mary's death as a "bombshell" and "a terrible shock" and begged him to call her so he could hear for himself details of the life of Miss Mary, "who was a wonderful woman." For reasons lost to time, Denis never made the call—a failure he said he has "regretted the rest of my days."

—◦—

It is difficult to calculate Miss Mary's impact on Anne, who regularly kept private matters shrouded in mystery. Still, records show that from the time of Mary's arrival in Sabukia Anne applied herself with ever-increasing energy to the Flying Doctors. It was as if she had no other thought than to turn away from the past and to better the lives of entire tribes, across vast swaths of Kenya. Whether or not this colossal resolve—bringing community health care to whole populations—was driven by Miss Mary is a matter of conjecture, but the coincidence of a woman's arrival and a renewed lease on life is hard to dismiss.

It is also noteworthy that in later life Anne never divulged she once had a friend who came to stay for seven years. The only artifact from their time together was Miss Mary's battered suitcase, containing photographs of a noble French family, as well as her neatly cased brush and comb.

Following Miss Mary's death, Anne kept that suitcase in a place of honor—perched on top of her bedroom wardrobe, visible as a final touchstone each night as she slipped off to sleep.

CHAPTER 9

L'ENFER DES FEMMES

> *The reality of the camps appears to burst*
> *the bounds of imagination, the precincts of*
> *conceivability. It still triggers diverse forms*
> *of defense meant to exculpate conscience, to*
> *extinguish memory.*
>
> —Wolfgang Sofsky, *The Order of Terror:*
> *The Concentration Camp*

Two decades after Miss Mary's death, Anne, in collaboration with French writer Claude Chebel, wrote her memoirs. Éditions Jean-Claude Lattès published *On m'appelle Mama Daktari* in 1994 in Paris, over the protests of Anne's brother, who, according to his son Bernard, felt that "Jews would be outraged by the way she was conducting her life." Anne overruled her brother, arguing that her enemies, after fifty years, were either dead or in their dotage.

In these reminiscences, Anne restricted her life to defined periods—early years in Europe and five decades of adventuring in Africa. *They Call Me Mama Daktari,* as the English-language edition was called, is an exciting read, and while partitioned into eras, it comports with its author's exacting rules of silence. The book astonishes less for what it says than how it censors—not a word about Mary O'Shaughnessy, and, most startling of all, the distillation of nine months in Fresnes and thirteen months in Ravensbrück into one ambiguous paragraph:

> I was arrested a few days after François while I was at work in Hérold Hospital. I was incarcerated in Ravensbrück, from which I was freed on the twenty-fifth of April, when the camp was emptied by the Swedish Red Cross, thanks to the intervention of Count Bernadotte. Five days later Hitler committed suicide. The horrors of Ravensbrück are described in detail in Germaine Tillion's *Ravensbrück*. It is, I believe, the definitive work on the subject.

Nowhere else in this book's 200 pages does Anne draw lessons from her life as a concentration camp survivor. While *They Call Me Mama Daktari* provides an inspiring account of an energetic career, one craves a few words of self-reflection. How satisfying would it have been to encounter the intimate Anne as she picked herself up from "broken Europe" and started again in Africa? Why did she not credit "If—," her favorite poem, as a guiding principle? In the spirit of Kipling, if she had treated Disaster with the same wisdom as she treated Triumph—and then wrote about it—would that not have made for a richer story? Instead, her autobiography evolves as a series of hard-fought victories. One understands her need for privacy, but, if so, why be so selective in her public reminiscences? Personal memoirs are a tricky genre, rendered more so if the author parses the truth and conceals his or her identity.

Right up to the end of her life, Anne continued to say little, even when pressed. One year before her death, a Flying Doctors colleague, Ellen Sabin, interviewed her on videotape for a summing-up of her magnificent career. In the final minutes of the interview,

Ellen mustered the courage to ask Anne about Ravensbrück. For the camera, Anne maintained her composure and answered calmly. With a wave of her hand, she dismissed the place altogether. "It was inconsequential. I did not suffer," she claimed. Sabin never challenged her.

—◦—

Ravensbrück proper is a suburb of Fürstenberg, and from the end of the war until 1989 both lay behind the Iron Curtain. While Ravensbrück's past is as somber as Auschwitz's or Dachau's, from a distance the setting seems almost quaint, nestled in a conifer forest, on the edge of a lake. Here, in spring, couples circle the lake in small boats, and swans imperiously paddle in and out of the reflection of a church spire.

The first fairy-tale discontinuities are towering brick walls, some sixteen feet high, with chimneys even higher. When a visitor walks through the gate, nothing can prepare him or her for the sight of the central enclosure, nearly the size of a football field. This is the *Appellplatz,* the prisoner marshaling ground, and here one can stand on occasional tiles polished white by inmates shuffling off to the gas chamber. Nearby is an alley where thousands were shot by a firing squad. Except for a wilted bouquet of roses lying on cobblestones, who would know that the narrow defile separating two dull stucco walls was a killing zone of industrial proportions?

At first, Ravensbrück seems as dull as a bobbin factory. Its horror lies in its very ordinariness, the unsettling banality of its architecture, its low-slung buildings still, after all these years, exuding menace.

On the foundation of what had once been the camp infirmary, twenty meters from Anne's block, a marker reads, "SS doctors carried out medical experiments on prisoners here, including 74 experiments on Polish women." Nearby is a place designated "Bed of Roses"—a mass grave of three hundred prisoners executed just before the camp's liberation. The inscription reads, "Two memorial stones are dedicated to the Jewish victims and . . . the Sinti and the Roma." Another stone indicates the site of the gas chamber, which once led to the death of thousands.

Today, Ravensbrück is a public museum, modestly popular, or so it appeared on May Day, a public holiday. Most of the visitors were old ladies—of an age and demeanor that suggested they had been survivors of the camp.

Ravensbrück's perimeter walls outside the central enclosure merge into the brickwork of the SS administration offices. Before Russian Allied troops liberated Ravensbrück beginning in April 1945, the Germans razed the gas chamber in a cockamamie effort to destroy all traces of its existence. After Ravensbrück was liberated, Russian soldiers were billeted in the wooden prisoner blocks, but within a year they burned them to the ground. Today, only the outlines of their foundations remain.

Leaning on canes and walkers, trailed by children and grandchildren, the elderly women limped from site to site, most unmarked. Saying little, these survivors of one of the earth's most unspeakable crimes paid wordless respect to lost lives—their friends' as well as their own. Pausing at their stations of the cross, they communicated mostly through gestures—a cane thrust there, a shaking of the head here, hand reaching for support from a wall, pocked by bullet holes. One small child helped her grandmother to lay a rose on the floor of the crematorium.

◄○►

As soon as she arrived in Fresnes Prison, south of Paris, in May 1943, Anne Spoerry knew her chances of survival were bleak. By all odds, she would meet one of two ends—death in France or death in Germany. During the nine months she was incarcerated in the aging prison, Anne was, by her own admission, terrified for herself and her brother, locked away, she understood, nearby.

In Fresnes, Anne relied, as best she could, on her Girl Guide training to handle discomforts. During that summer of 1943, she became adept at hopping from side to side to avoid slugs slithering across the floor of her cell. By November, the cold had penetrated her clothes and was leaving hoarfrost on the walls of the cell. She refused to complain, each day trying to gulp down two entrées of slop, thrust through a hatch, one at dawn, the other dusk. Anne could manage discomforts but was undone by uncertainty.

On her eighth day in Fresnes, guards marched Anne into a small office for questioning. For two hours, she was interrogated by Commandant Verbeck, seated in front of a giant swastika. He confined his questions to her activities at the beginning of the year. At first, Anne gamely played along as the innocent. The meeting's dynamics changed when Verbeck produced a sheaf of papers, many in her own handwriting. She was trapped. Verbeck stared her down in silence. Finally, Anne owned up to having served as a "mailbox" for her brother. Verbeck wanted more—the names of her friends in the Resistance. Anne refused to rat on anyone, or so she claimed after the war.

In September, another female prisoner moved into Anne's cell. The encounter came to my attention in a four-page letter that Anne had hidden away in Kenya. It was written in 1967, twenty-four years after the two met, and signed with an indecipherable signature. The letter recalled a friendship that, from its tone, appeared to have been important to both. The woman, by 1967 settled in Beauvais, France, had been, like Anne, a casualty of *Nacht und Nebel*—Night and Fog—Hitler's decree silencing political opponents and Resistance fighters by removing them from judicial oversight and strictures of the Geneva Convention. Initiated late in 1942, *Nacht und Nebel* made political prisoners vanish into "night and fog." Through it, the German High Command assumed the right to execute all political prisoners, like Anne and her friend, without cause.

From the letter, it is evident the two women, living uncertainly, grew deeply attached. The Beauvais lady was intelligent, well read, and from a privileged background, much like Anne. The letter began with an explanation of how she was able to track Anne down from a newspaper account of her stellar African flying doctor career. "I would love to see you again," she wrote. Referring to the time since her arrival in Anne's cell, she continued, "It is certain life has weighed on both of us with enormous heaviness and that you are looking to rediscover, in vain, the girl with shaved head who arrived in your cell and who you found attractive. I am now a grandmother . . . And you are no longer the 'young boy' in short hair who appeared like a soothing bath after the horrific hours of captivity . . . I felt it was a dream."

The extent of the relationship between Anne and the stranger will remain a mystery. From the letter, it appears that their few days together brought them both passing warmth, comfort, even love. But the attachment was short-lived; soon guards transferred the Beauvais lady to another cell. Alone again, Anne returned to her brooding about imminent death. Release seemed implausible and deportation, followed by execution, increasingly likely.

In October 1943, Anne was trucked to Avenue Foch in Paris for further questioning by the Gestapo. This time, from Anne's account to her attorney after the war, her interrogator was ill-informed and easy to manipulate. On the return drive, Anne peered through the small barred window in the rear of the van and saw her beloved city, now gray, wind soaked, leaves stripped from chestnut trees, swastikas snapping against slate skies.

In December, guards caught Anne circulating news of Allied successes at Montecatini on the Italian front. For this indiscretion, she was sentenced to fifteen days in a dark cell with no toilet, soap, or soup. She claimed she survived these privations honorably, according to the account she provided to her attorney after the war.

One morning in late January 1944, now returned to her former cell, Anne heard the clatter of mismatched shoes passing her cell. With a clank of keys, her cell door was flung open, and a guard indicated she was to gather up her belongings and join the procession of prisoners. She and the rest were trucked to Compiègne, a transit point in northeast France. After eight days in limbo, Anne and a hundred prisoners were marched to a railroad siding where they were jammed into a *chemin de fer* cattle wagon.

For three days the train lumbered east. By night Anne huddled alone in a corner. At dawn through slats she saw terraced hills, neglected farms, and teetering church spires. Slush gave way to snow. Anne wore a long coat and François's sweater, and in a pocket she rubbed a rosary, not for its spiritual powers, but because it was a favored family heirloom. She bundled the fringes of her coat under her head for a pillow, closed her eyes, and covered her ears to muffle out the whimpers and sobs of other women. In written testimony, she said that she and a friend attempted to cut a hole in the wooden slats with a penknife. When others threatened to expose her, the two abandoned the scheme and settled in for a long imprisonment. In Cologne, the German Red Cross provided the prisoners with porridge, black coffee, and bread. The journey now was disorienting—muddy railroad sidings, barked orders, food chucked onto the floor, and a vicious scrum of women, fighting over scraps. Where were they headed—Bergen-Belsen or Auschwitz? One woman, seeming to know more than all the others, spat out the word "Ravensbrück." On the third night, facing a wind off the Baltic, guards used bars to break the ice, levering the heavy door along its rails. As it slid back, Anne steadied herself and, blinking from the security lights, saw the sign FÜRSTENBERG.

SS troopers, male and female, with guard dogs, marched the

prisoners in columns of five along cobbled streets. In windows, children rubbed sleep from their eyes, while their parents jeered. Anne's disjointed company of women marched across a snow-covered field, then between two gates, ten meters apart. After they passed, guards slammed the gates shut as a woman whispered in Anne's ear, "L'enfer des femmes [women's hell]."

—◦—

No woman ever forgot her first sight of Ravensbrück. Before block-houses in the *Appellplatz,* in light refracted by dust rising from bare ground, thousands of women stood to attention, heads shaved, faces streaked, emaciated bodies draped in thin, striped, numbered tunics. This was *Appell:* one of two daily roll calls, dreaded by all.

The brick wall to Anne's left was topped by barbed wire. Crowning each corner were pillboxes manned by guards with machine guns. Beyond the wall lay the SS canteen and military hospital. Before Anne stood thirty-two blockhouses, whose doors were framed by flower boxes where, in summer, guards would plant pansies (Louise Le Porz, a fellow Ravensbrück survivor, remembering the flower boxes, said that after the war whenever she saw a pansy, she threw up). To Anne's right, beside the gate, stood the administration building, kitchen, and toilets, with floors puddled up in excreta. Here, around the clock, women queued for relief. Beyond the toilets lay a long brick building of grated windows—the special punishment block, with seventy-eight cells, each measuring two meters by two and a half—where women, singled out by guards as miscreants, endured solitary confinement.

In operation between May 1939 and May 1945, Ravensbrück was purpose-built as a concentration camp for women. According to one Hamburg wartime tribunal prosecutor, its aim was to make the lives of women intolerable: "an organized attack on the life of womanhood." Not only did Ravensbrück destroy women's minds and lives, but through its menacing reputation it silenced husbands, parents, and children, too scared to identify their loved ones' whereabouts, in fear of reprisals.

In March 1944, when Anne arrived, Ravensbrück's prisoner population reflected a cross section of Germany's perceived enemies: Poles, Czechs, Russians, Dutch, Belgians, French, English, Americans, Spanish, Swiss, Italians, Germans, Jews, Jehovah's Witnesses, Gypsies, Communists, any Caucasian who intermarried a black or a Jew, dubbed a "race defiler," and, as in Anne's case, Resistance fighters or political prisoners.

When built in 1937, Ravensbrück was intended to accommodate no more than 6,000 women prisoners, with the central *Appellplatz* designed for thirty-two blockhouses, each to house 150 prisoners. A few months after the camp opened, numbers increased at an alarming pace, and before Anne was liberated in 1945, there would be more than 40,000 women in a space intended for one-sixth of that. Over Ravensbrück's lifetime, between 115,000 and 123,000 prisoners passed through its gate.

Estimates of mortality vary. The most acceptable claim is that five out of six prisoners, or ninety thousand, died in Ravensbrück. The healthiest arrivals were assigned outside jobs, as farmhands, quarry workers, or factory labor. Starvation, epidemics, and guard brutality accounted for much of the mortality. In Ravensbrück's final four months before liberation, hundreds were eliminated each day in the gas chambers. Even today, there remains a broad variance in numbers of women estimated to have been assassinated, for as prison administrators and guards fled, they set fire to many files. Even had they been preserved, the deaths of untold numbers of women, dying at night, were never recorded. Each morning, unlucky survivors were assigned to go from block to block, bunk to bunk, looking for corpses, these to be dumped, unnamed, into wheelbarrows, for incineration in the crematorium.

"Within a few hours" of arrival, wrote Germaine Tillion, Anne's fellow prisoner (and the author of the book Anne endorsed in her memoirs), "we became brutally aware of reality: the forced labor, the experimental operations on young girls (we soon saw for ourselves their miserable, martyred limbs), the *transports noirs* [death transports], individual and mass executions, the ill being 'put out of their misery,' the dogs, the beatings, the gas chambers."

The faces of Anne's fellow Ravensbrück prisoners were unreadable. Were they suffering from dullness, fatigue, or suspicion? Whom could she trust? Ravensbrück was a petri dish of Europe's near-tribal societal divisions, ranging from the destitute to the prominent, women such as Geneviève de Gaulle, General de Gaulle's niece (largely for their heroism in Ravensbrück, in 2015, de Gaulle and Germaine Tillion were both formally reburied in the Panthéon), and photographer Marie-Claude Vaillant-Couturier. Countesses, writers, scientists, artists, shared the torment of the camp with SOE operatives, including Denise Bloch, Cecily Lefort, Lilian Rolfe, and Violette Szabo (executed at Ravensbrück).

Side by side with them were the "asocials"—common criminals, lesbians, prostitutes, and Gypsies. Who was to be trusted? Germaine Tillion wrote, "Here ordinary conventions and hypocrisies were swept away and true natures revealed—the *'grande dame'* who turned out to be a thief, the Communist who showed herself as a cheat and hoarder, the Gaullist 'patriot,' zealously working for the German war effort in order to get her dish of soup."

Anne had arrived in a slave labor camp with all healthy inmates forced to work crushing hours to support the German war industry. Like other concentration camps, Ravensbrück fell under the control of *Reichsführer* Heinrich Himmler, Hitler's chief of police, minister of the interior, and head of the SS. Ravensbrück was special to him because, holding personal title to its real estate, Himmler leased it back to the German High Command. So attached was he to this cash cow he regularly traveled the sixty miles from Berlin for surprise visits. His business model was pitiless and simple: charge war industries as much as possible for labor, invest as little as you can in a worker's well-being, and when you have worked her to the edge of death, starve, shoot, or gas her and then find a readily available replacement.

Anne soon learned that to survive, she must, at all costs, avoid the attention of guards. While guards were trained for brutality, some were more—sadists, alcoholics, and, according to Germaine Tillion, insane. All were permitted to torture and murder at will. For Anne, death was literally in the air, with the crematorium belching smoke and sprinkling human dust over the blocks. Late in 1944, a second and a third crematorium were constructed to keep pace. In the first days of 1945, a gas chamber was also added. Along with the crematoriums, it remained in operation, around the clock, up to the liberation of the camp.

On February 8, 1944, Anne was assigned Block 26 along with a thousand other Frenchwomen. For five days she awaited unspecified "formalities." With women sleeping seven to a bed, Anne found herself a corner on the floor. During this time, she set up an infirmary in the ablution area and did her best to help others, even though she had at her disposal few medications.

—◄○►—

Two weeks into her internment, Anne and hundreds of others were herded into a holding room and forced to strip out of their clothes. Having heard rumors of gas vents, a few women became fixated on anomalous apertures in the ceiling. Naked, and huddled together, they stared up in dread. Hours passed before they heard the hiss. To the relief of all, water trickled from the showerheads, coating them for a minute. Now, wet, cold, and still in fear for their lives, they waited another hour before two uniformed men, identifying themselves as a doctor and a dentist, entered. Without explanation these two examined each naked woman, some with prurient scrutiny. When the "doctors" reached the end of the queue, the women were bundled into a second room for what appeared to be a head shearing. It was at this moment Anne sensed another prisoner gazing at her. She turned and saw a woman, attired unlike all others. The stranger wore a shift and a scarf, modishly draped around her dark brown curly hair. She was, as far as Anne could tell, the only prisoner excused from the head-shearing procedure. The woman attracted the attention of one of the guards by snapping her fingers, indicating Anne. With few words, she directed the barber not to cut her hair.

Approaching Anne, the woman explained that she recognized her as a fellow Swiss. Anne was taken back. "Adelboden," the older woman said, naming the town where she was born. To Anne, Adelboden conjured images of snowdrifts, balconied chalets, cobbled streets, and horse-drawn sledges. After uttering the charmed word, the mysterious fellow Swiss whispered that she could help Anne by concealing her sweater, soap, and rosary. She explained that it was essential to get these items out of the reach of thieving guards. She then introduced herself: "Carmen Mory."

Why the normally wary Anne put her confidence in a perfect stranger is a puzzle. Perhaps she felt unassailable trust in a fellow Swiss national. Possibly she was attracted to the woman's authority. Anne did not hesitate. She handed over her sweater, soap, and rosary. Two other women were equally gulled, thrusting books and jewelry into the hands of Carmen Mory.

A few days later, Anne learned that enemies in the prison administration exposed Carmen Mory, charging her with trafficking in black market goods in exchange for preferential treatment with SS prison guards. Mory was sentenced to two and a half months of solitary in the *Strafblock,* and Anne would never see her family possessions again.

For the next six months, the two women—Anne, quarantined in Block 13 for infectious diseases, and Mory in her punishment cell—lived apart. These were especially trying times for the medical student, the sole medical provider for eight hundred in a space with little sanitation. Nearly half her patients, she later wrote in an affidavit, suffered from diphtheria, scarlet fever, erysipelas, and "purulent ear infections." With a meager ten to twenty aspirin a week and "some paper plasters," Anne did all she could. On any given day, she was treating as many as forty infected prisoners, while surviving on a diet of ersatz coffee and the occasional chunk of potato and cabbage. Some prisoners were so ravenous they foraged in the dust outside the kitchens for peelings and leaves. For a time, Anne's medical credentials shielded her. As a medical student, she intended to make herself indispensable and ride out Ravensbrück until the war's end.

In April 1944, Heinrich Himmler signed papers authorizing the transport of 870 Ravensbrück prisoners to the town of Svatava in Czechoslovakia. Anne was included in this transport. In mid-May, she arrived at Svatava, renamed Zwodau by the German occupiers. It was one of seventy sub-camps critical to the Reich in its last-ditch struggle to halt the Allied advance. With much of Berlin destroyed by bombs, Siemens had relocated critical war-related factories to inconspicuous targets far from the capital. In Zwodau it had repurposed a cotton mill into a factory to manufacture electronic components for Germany's V2 rocket. For two months, Anne worked on its production line by day and, by night, cared for the ailing workforce as long as she was able to stay awake.

◄○►

In mid-July 1944, when Anne returned to Ravensbrück, now chronically overcrowded, she was, by her account, emaciated and ill. As a cost-saving measure, the camp's commandant, Fritz Suhren, had given up on the practice of quarantining the sick. Now infected prisoners mingled freely with the healthy. With no medical role to play, Anne was assigned Block 15, where she was just another prisoner, at risk, like others, of infection and capricious execution. Every day she endured the daily spectacle of "death transport" drivers jettisoning their human cargoes into the crematorium. Executions by the firing squad were often revenge killings in retaliation for perceived affronts. Germaine Tillion's own mother was gassed because a guard did not care for her white hair.

Late in July, Anne's luck turned. Out of more than twenty-six thousand Ravensbrück prisoners, she walked into the *Revier* (infirmary) and rediscovered prisoner number 5749. Carmen Mory was recovering from pleurisy after her most recent stint in the punishment block. Anne was so captivated by the woman, twelve years her senior, with raven eyes and sonorous, theatrical voice, she set aside thoughts of the purloined rosary and sweater. Transfixed by this prisoner with a fund of epic stories and ready alibis, Anne volunteered to care for her. It took only two weeks in the *Revier* for the medical student from Mulhouse to become, in her own words, "bewitched" by Carmen Mory.

During these last two weeks of August 1944 in the *Revier*, Carmen Mory talked nonstop, campaigning for Anne's esteem. As the medical student recovered her strength and helped the older woman convalesce from pleurisy, she was introduced to her topsy-turvy world of mixed principles, exotic allegiances, easy ethics. As both recovered their health, Carmen became Anne's shining star, rising through society, snubbing institutions, seducing the powerful, cheating death. In her telling, betrayal, disloyalty, and duplicity were passports to success.

Much later, in testimony, Anne admitted her intoxication for Mory. Others who witnessed her conversion verified this concession, explaining that the young medical student from Mulhouse and Männedorf was needy and gullible—an awestruck ingenue in the hands of a wily seductress.

With Anne's help, Mory recovered and was able to resume her role as *Blockova* (block elder), in Block 10, dedicated to prisoners suffering from tuberculosis. It also contained a room for the insane—or those deemed insane. In her senior role, Mory was given instructions to report prisoner activities and conversations to the prison authority. While some *Blockovas* earned their positions through leadership skills, most won the privilege by promising to inform against fellow prisoners. Carmen Mory was already known to be close to Gestapo chief Ludwig Ramdohr. Because she was an "honorary prisoner," even SS guards feared her for her reputation of informing against all, including guards.

Late in August 1944, *Blockova* Carmen Mory dismissed Block 10's sole prisoner doctor, a certified pulmonary specialist from Poland, and replaced her with an unproven medical student. Mory's power to banish anyone at will was a measure of her influence. As soon as Anne Spoerry was installed in Block 10, Mory instructed all prisoners and guards to address Anne Spoerry as "doctor," even though most knew by now she was a medical student.

So began a star-crossed friendship between Ravensbrück's most powerful prisoner, nicknamed *Vulgaris* (common wolf), *Schwarzer Engel* (Black Angel), and "the Witch," and a panicked twenty-six-year-old about to make the most calamitous error of her life.

On the surface, Anne might be excused her wonder, for everything about Carmen Maria Mory spoke of the exotic. The *Blockova* claimed she inherited her striking looks from her mother, Leona, born in the Philippines, of "royal Spanish blood." In Carmen's account, her mother was lovely, innocent, and blameless. She had fallen prey to the conniving Emil Mory, who, she claimed, had cunningly seduced young Leona von Kauffmann-Bischoff and persuaded her to divorce her English husband, abandoning their two sons. Compliant to Emil's demands, Leona married him, took the name Frau Mory, and settled into his house in Adelboden in the heart of Switzerland's Bernese Alps. And in 1906, Leona gave birth to Carmen Maria, the youngest of three girls.

Officially, Emil Mory was Adelboden's doctor. Unofficially, he was the town's publicist and nag, exhorting citizens to whitewash their homes and shovel horse manure from the streets. An unapologetic snob, Emil compulsively ingratiated himself to wealthy Germans and grandees, whom he saw as kindred spirits. He desired the village to turn out the welcome mat for all aristocrats. On the other hand, Jews and Frenchmen would not be welcome. The latter Emil Mory termed "ignorant hypocrites and drunkards."

In time, Emil Mory's wife, Leona, felt so uncomfortable in his ostentatious home she moved to a nearby boardinghouse. As the marriage failed, Leona focused her attention on her children, especially Carmen, but one morning when she was four, Carmen awoke to learn that her mother had left Adelboden, with no plans of returning. Her father provided no explanation for Carmen's mother's departure. The puzzled little girl was left to her own despair.

In later years, Carmen would learn that her mother had not deserted the family but had drowned in a bathtub—not by accident, but perhaps by her father's hand. Because Emil was not just Adelboden's doctor but also its coroner, he had free rein to sign autopsies. He cited that his wife's death had been caused by sudden heart arrest. With no other coroner present, the death certificate was not questioned, though for years rumors swirled through Adelboden that Emil had murdered Leona.

When she turned fourteen, Carmen began rebelling against her father and his social ambitions. When assigned the morning chore of buying bread for the household, she was said to have entered the bakery, barefoot, in only a thin nightgown. Captivating the throng of customers, she lifted her nightgown to give them a full view of her nubile body.

At night, with Emil Mory believing his young daughter to be safe in bed, she climbed out a window to barhop with British, German, and French visitors. Her final gesture of defiance was to drop out of school after nine years, before her sixteenth birthday. She told her father she had better ways to spend her time. Emil was livid.

When Carmen turned twenty, Emil's patience was exhausted. He described his daughter as "a liar, intriguer, and schemer," with a "defective sense of ethics." Carmen might well have said the same about him, so convinced was she that he had murdered her mother. Young Carmen now lit out for a succession of big cities. Fluent in six languages and said to possess an appealing singing voice, she told friends she intended to enjoy the company of men—not one, but many. She would hold to only one rule: no Jews. While there is little evidence she had ever met one, she appeared to share her father's bigotry from an early age.

◄○►

When Anne, child of conformist bourgeois parents, listened to the tales of the maverick Carmen, she was transported into a world of make-believe. As the two recovered from their separate maladies, Mory filled her with stories of her many romantic escapades in England, France, Italy, and Spain. At one juncture, Mory settled in Holland with a steady boyfriend, but when he turned possessive, she broke off the arrangement, boasting to him of a wild affair she was having with an Englishman. Her motto, she told Anne, was *"Tu was du dir lassen kannst"*—"Do whatever you can get away with."

After a succession of conquests, Carmen moved to Munich, where, declaring she held degrees in journalism and art history, she landed freelance newspaper assignments. Her desire now was to be acclaimed as a chanteuse and actress—in the mold of Marlene Dietrich. At parties she regularly gave impromptu bel canto performances of Cole Porter, Yip Harburg, and Richard Whiting. She told Anne that she had everyone on the edges of their seats, that women were riven by jealousy and men insatiable. Fritz Erler, from a prominent political family, was one such admirer. He followed her to Berlin, and soon they were an item, living together, and, as Carmen boasted, the city's most celebrated couple.

As the Nazi Party grew to power in the early 1930s, Carmen and Fritz sought out its rising stars. Carmen told Anne she enjoyed an intimate friendship with Joseph Goebbels in advance of the 1933 Nazi seizure of power and his appointment as the Reich's minister of propaganda by Adolf Hitler. She also claimed to be friendly with Colonel General Ernst Udet, the World War I flying ace and architect of the Luftwaffe, as well as with Alfred Rosenberg, central to Hitler's rise to power.

Because Carmen and Fritz were living the high life beyond their means, their only stipend being modest checks from the publisher Ullstein, she sought other forms of income. The easiest was to borrow money from friends, then deny there had ever been a transaction and, when pressed by creditors, denounce them as Jews, homosexuals, or money launderers. In most cases, her victims preferred writing off the loans to facing Carmen's public slander.

Between a succession of trysts, which she did little to conceal, Carmen's life with Fritz Erler was anything but dull. In 2010, a woman living in Manchester, England, offered details recounted by her mother, who, in 1936, had shared a Berlin boardinghouse with Mory and Erler. Because the young woman was a music student, she and Mory (who "possessed a fine alto voice") regularly sang together. The story might have ended there had it not been for the boardinghouse's thin walls. Living next door to Carmen and Fritz, the music student soon established that the two enjoyed vigorous sex, with Carmen taunting Fritz while slapping chains against his thighs. After a few months, the pair vanished, skipping out on their rent. The furious landlady invited the music student to observe the state of their vacated room. Coating the wallpaper were gobs of dried blood—evidence, the young woman concluded, that Mory and Erler had enjoyed a "sadomasochistic life."

Carmen Mory's astounding life comes into bold relief, in large part, thanks to Caterina Abbati's biography, *Ich, Carmen Mory*. She recounts that at Nazi political functions, Carmen and Fritz mingled with high Nazi officials, including Bormann, Himmler, Goebbels, and Göring. At one gathering, according to Abbati, Mory succeeded in capturing everyone's attention when she spontaneously burst into what some recall was Cole Porter. With all eyes glued to her, she started flinging off clothes. One by one they went—fur, gloves, dress, nylons, bra. Mory adroitly executed these maneuvers in time to the lyrics "And even the palms seem to be swaying, when they begin the beguine." By the last stanza, Mory was buck naked. To the enthusiastic applause of bedazzled men, she took a deep bow, while scandalized wives hurried their men from the room.

The next time Carmen performed her singing striptease, she leaned back so far a stray candle ignited her hair. Generals merrily rushed to her side to douse the flames, while the mortified Fritz passively waited on the side, incapable of reining in Carmen's exuberance.

When accounts of Carmen's exploits reached Adelboden, the shamed Emil Mory wrote to his daughter in a rage. Fritz penned this response: "Carmencita can be difficult and is not an easy character to understand, but . . . she is the only woman with whom I can be happy, and it is my greatest wish to be everything to her. I know her faults so well as we have been together for 2 years. Her generous, big heart and intelligence have made me recognize the partner with whom I want to spend my life. Her brutal openness and honesty can be overwhelming, yet I know she will change for me and some characteristics of a personality can only be battled as a pair."

Fritz was not the only one to suspend common sense in the company of Carmen Mory. Gestapo boss Bruno Sattler also fell for her. She visited his office frequently, eager to pass on intelligence about the politics, ethnicity, sexual orientation, and secrets of her Berlin circle of friends. So captivated was he by the information she provided that in 1934 he appointed her Gestapo agent, number S11.

Every time Mory visited Sattler, her narrative improved. Soon she was fabricating stories about her friends, even denouncing her boyfriend, Fritz, as a homosexual. While the besotted Gestapo boss caught her in more than one lie, he still found her irresistible and in 1938 rewarded her loyalty by sending her and Fritz to Paris to spy on a certain Max Braun to determine whether he ran a secret underground railway for the purposes of secreting Jews out of Germany. Using a publishing house as cover, Mory charmed Braun's housekeeper and gained access to his apartment and private office to read his mail. She then slipped across the hall to install a microphone in the apartment of a neighbor. Returning unexpectedly, the stranger found Mory rifling through his files. He shouted at her to leave. Instead, piece by piece, she removed her clothes. Again, another stranger found her irresistible.

During her time in Paris, the chronically indebted Carmen Mory implored the Swiss embassy for a loan. Normally, the tightfisted Swiss would have denied such a request, but Mory was so persuasive the ambassador gave in, providing enough for her and Fritz to enjoy Paris, in style, for the next two months.

On Sattler's orders, Mory explored fortifications and assessed troop movements along France's Maginot Line. After she handed in a report, she and Fritz, now her "fiancé," were instructed to infiltrate an anti-German newspaper and to murder its editor. Carmen and Fritz botched the assignment when they confronted him in his office. Now, planning to shoot Braun on the street, they staked out his route from office to home. In the midst of the plot, they decided to take a break at the George V bar for a bottle of Dom Pérignon. Unknown to them, they were under observation by two French secret policemen seated at a corner table. As Fritz and Carmen clinked glasses, the two men approached and, after several questions, charged the couple with espionage against France. Carmen Mory and Fritz Erler were now under arrest.

For eighteen months, Carmen endured La Petite Roquette Prison. On April 28, 1940, she and Fritz were found guilty of espionage against La République and were sentenced to death by firing squad. Upon learning of the sentence, Mory demanded a meeting with her captors. Behind closed doors she begged for clemency in exchange for changing sides and spying for the French. Her proposal was passed on to President Albert François Lebrun, who agreed to pardon her in exchange for her loyalty. Somehow, Mory never requested the same generous terms for her fiancé, Fritz Erler. On June 6, 1940, a week before the Germans entered Paris, Fritz was executed by a firing squad. On learning of her fiancé's death, Carmen Mory never expressed a word of regret.

Mory's career as a French spy was short-lived. On the eighteenth day of her new assignment, she submitted a complaint about her salary, calling the French "unpleasant and ungrateful." When they did not deign a response, she decided to terminate her agreement with France and to return to the German side, but before she executed the volte-face, she was captured in Tours by an advance party of the Wehrmacht. For two weeks, Carmen was detained in Fresnes Prison (coincidentally, not far from the cell Anne would occupy in 1944). After two weeks, the German High Command transported her to Berlin and interned her in Alexanderplatz Prison. Once again she fell back on her powers of persuasion to gain her freedom. Within a few weeks she was on the streets of Berlin.

The city she once adored had now turned on her. After a career denouncing friends, she was viewed by many as a pariah. One described her as "the . . . international swindler and thief." Recognizing that she was persona non grata, Mory decided she needed to bolt. She applied for a German "Aryan" passport, with the intention of returning to Switzerland, where, she hoped, few would know her past. Almost immediately, she was caught and brought to Bruno Sattler. Embarrassed by her betrayal, incensed by her disloyalty, he finally cut off all ties. Undaunted, Mory set off for the office of Sattler's boss, the feared SS *Obergruppenführer* Reinhard Heydrich. Once highly suspicious of Mory, he allowed her to close the door to his office. Pinch-lipped, condor-nosed, and famously sadistic, the man who, at the 1942 Wannsee Conference, had helped forge the "Final Solution" for the extermination of Jews, the man who even Hitler thought was heartless, in the end, proved seducible. When Carmen Mory assured him she would never again flee Germany, he believed her and granted her freedom.

Four months later, Carmen Mory walked into the Swiss embassy and, in a voice heard by all, demanded a Swiss passport. Gestapo agents, lying in wait, captured her on the spot. Still fuming over her unpaid debts to its Paris embassy, the Swiss did not come to her defense. As the Gestapo hauled her off, she yelled insults at both the Gestapo and the Swiss. Witnesses said Mory appeared unhinged.

One month into her prison term, a vigilant guard caught Carmen Mory in the act of cutting her wrist. He reported the suicide attempt to Bruno Sattler and Reinhard Heydrich, who exploded. Determined that she would never escape again and would die by his rules, Heydrich issued orders for her transfer. On February 26, 1941, thirty-four-year-old Carmen Mory found herself assigned prisoner number 5749 in the only concentration camp for women—Ravensbrück.

—◦—

"From the first day that I arrived," Carmen Mory later recounted, "I realized that only utter discipline would save my life." This was one of the few statements she ever made that rings unequivocally true. During her four years in Ravensbrück, her fortunes ran to every extreme, from "honorary prisoner," to *Strafblock* inmate, under the watchful eye of her soon-to-be archenemy, SS-*Oberaufseherin* warden Dorothea Binz.

From her cell, Mory saw Binz dispatch prisoners to the hospital for random medical "experiments" without anesthesia. Often a victim was tied to a table, where her calf was incised, then injected with gangrenous offal. On one occasion, Mory saw "La Binz" (the nickname Mory conferred on her) kick a woman in the stomach so hard she fell down a flight of stairs and broke her neck. Other prisoners testified that meticulously coiffed "arch sadist" Binz never went anywhere without a whip and an attack dog. When she attended a flogging, her lover, fellow SS guard Edmund Bräuning, often accompanied her. On these occasions, the two were said to hold hands and laugh at the victim's distress.

Mory's first term in the *Strafblock* stretched to fifteen months. In May 1942, midway into her punishment, the German High Command had her transported to Berlin to provide testimony against Dr. Helmut Klotz, Max Braun's partner. Like Braun, Klotz was accused of having enabled Jews to escape Germany. Now Göring's office wanted the court to convict Klotz and sentence him to death. Mory complied by fabricating a long list of alleged crimes. The witness stand on Prinz-Albrecht-Strasse became Carmen Mory's theater. After running out of incriminations against Klotz, she turned the court's attention to herself, boasting that she had been so vital to all that she had once spied for France against the Germans. Her claim was, in effect, her conviction. If there had once been sympathy in the courtroom for Mory, it now vaporized. Mory was trucked back to Ravensbrück, with instructions she be executed by firing squad, with a date set for November 19, 1943.

As always, Mory used her wiles for a stay of execution. With only a few weeks to live, she introduced herself to the doctor presiding over the *Revier* (infirmary) and congratulated him on his recent appointment. Mory followed the meeting with a letter, drawing his attention to the squalid living conditions of Block 10. Born to an English mother, Dr. Percival Treite read the letter and recognized the surname, Mory, from a family visit to Switzerland. Wondering if there was a connection, he went to Block 10 and asked whether Carmen was, by chance, related to a certain Dr. Emil Mory of Adelboden. Intuiting that Treite was about to shower admiration on her father, Mory responded with counterfeit pride. Treite explained that because Emil had saved his mother's life, he was indebted to her family. Seizing the opportunity, Carmen gushed over her father's medical prowess. Treite was so impressed he canceled Mory's execution.

Few other Block 10 inmates shared Carmen Mory's admiration for the doctor. Most knew Treite sterilized Gypsy girls without anesthesia and made random injections into the uteruses and Fallopian tubes of Polish girls. Nearly sixty years later Block 10 prisoner Dr. Louise Le Porz was still outraged: "He was totally contemptible for what he did as a doctor. One day, a patient was brought in the main *Revier,* and this patient was in such a bad shape that she was lying on the floor of the hallway. Treite did not bend down to examine her. He pushed her with the tip of his boot, not wanting to dirty his hands. And this was the one so admired by Carmen Mory. She did not hide it. She used to say he was an intelligent man, with such a good education, and very distinguished. Her remarks were surreal."

Mory's friendship with Dr. Percy Treite did not keep her from the punishment block. During her March 1944 sentence for attempting to bribe guards with goods purloined from prisoners (including Anne Spoerry), she was incarcerated in the *Strafblock* for nearly six months. During this period, she gained a reputation for colorful storytelling and shameless self-promotion. From her cell, fellow internees called her "a great source of information," with her voice, carrying up and down the cell block, telling "wonderful stories."

Isa Vermehren, a Dutch prisoner two cells away, nicknamed her "Beromünster," after the outlawed Swiss radio station Radio Beromünster, "because of her very uninhibited way of expressing her opinions." Mory's verbosity met with consequences. On April 16, 1944, when "La Binz" overheard Mory sounding off about one of the guards, she horsewhipped her thirty times until she lay unconscious in a pool of blood.

◄○►

No one else in Block 10 shared Anne Spoerry's attraction to the *Blockova*. Most, watching Carmen Mory's daily excursions to the office of Ludwig Ramdohr, the political head of the prison administration, to inform on her fellow prisoners, saw her as enemy. Those who witnessed her finger fellow prisoners for death convoys did all to avoid her. According to historian Sarah Helm, she was the most dangerous prisoner in all Ravensbrück.

In her memoir, Polish countess Karolina Lanckoronska, once an inmate of Block 10, saw Carmen Mory as a feral animal: "Hair and eyes as black as a raven, a very wide, thin-lipped mouth and a heavy jaw. At first sight, the expression on that face—neither human nor animal—gave me such a surprise that I could not recall where I had seen it before. It was only later that I retrieved the prototype from my memory of the she-devils painted by Hieronymus Bosch."

All who were with Carmen Mory during the last months of 1944 would have agreed with Countess Lanckoronska. All, that is, except Anne Spoerry.

CHAPTER 11

DR. CLAUDE

> *Or do we know, as we have always known,*
> *that evil walks among us; that no monster*
> *(or his friends and lovers) thinks himself*
> *monstrous, no madman thinks himself*
> *mad; and that, as the filmmaker Jean*
> *Renoir once said: "The terrible thing is*
> *that everyone has his reasons."*

—from Dorothy Gallagher's New York Times
review of Heike B. Görtemaker's *Eva Braun:*
Life with Hitler

After the war, few Ravensbrück survivors were as doggedly silent as Anne. Some talked as soon as they were free. Others opened up in time. Most survivors spoke out, believing that silence was surrender and the vilest of tyrannies. Single-minded in their belief there would never be another Ravensbrück, they wrote memoirs, granted interviews, and broadcast to the entire world accounts of their hell. There are now said to be over sixteen thousand memoirs of the Holocaust and concentration camps.

I had the good fortune to meet three women who had known Anne in Ravensbrück. None had any hesitation recounting their Ravensbrück stories. Even in their eighth and ninth decades, these women all admitted they still suffered from anguish related to their incarcerations. When I informed them that, quite the opposite, Anne called Ravensbrück "inconsequential" and refused to speak out, one (Violette Rougier-Lecoq) expressed outrage, another (Odette Allaire Walling) shook her head in dismay, and the third (Dr. Louise Le Porz) gave a Gallic shrug, saying she knew why.

In May 2002, I called Odette in Paris. When I brought up the name Carmen Mory, she fired back with one word: *ordure,* "garbage." I was startled. When could I fly to Paris to take her to lunch? Odette responded, *"Ce n'est pas possible,"* explaining that she never ventured out. Instead, she would receive me at her home. Her son, Christopher, later clarified that even fifty-seven years after her release from Ravensbrück, wounds were so fresh she refused to go out in public. Her psychiatrist diagnosed her condition as extreme agoraphobia. Christopher told me that throughout his childhood his mother recited the camp's name every day to him. For a time, he even believed that "concentration camp" was spelled as one word.

I met Odette in her penthouse on the Rue de Mondovi. The elegant drawing room was alive with spring light and the fragrance of lilies of the valley, carried in by the maid from the terrace in my honor. Odette's eyes were bright, her silver hair studiously in place, and a set of gold earrings and a string of pearls sparkled over her black turtleneck.

The moment I uttered the name Ravensbrück, I saw Odette tense. During my two hours with her, she smiled only once, when Zoe, her Jack Russell, went into a barking frenzy, affronted by the sight of pigeons alighting on her terrace. Otherwise, Madame Walling remained somber and frail. Condemned for life to the memory of a place in Germany, she seemed to endure steady pangs of anguish verging on anger. Three times she recited the number "47,321" as her long finger, turned inward by age, circled the tattoo on her arm. The gesture was emblematic of her descent from Paris haute couture model of the 1930s to Ravensbrück prisoner for life.

She intoned the numerals as if they were a prayer. As I rose to leave after two hours, when she wished to reprise the gravity of her incarceration one final time, she repeated the number "47,321," this time adding, "Ravensbrück destroyed my life."

Promptly at noon, the maid brought Madame Walling a martini. With its arrival our conversation turned to Anne. Odette recalled how in April 1945 she and Anne were among the first prisoners the Swedish Red Cross liberated from Ravensbrück. "The Nazis chose us because they didn't want cadavers to be seen by the outside world. They selected the ones who looked reasonably well. I had lost forty kilos, but I was still pretty. Anne was unchanged because she had been able to eat potatoes at will and had been able to live so well each day—clean clothes and comfortable shoes, while all of us had frozen feet."

In stark contrast to Anne's silence after the war, Odette opened up about Ravensbrück almost from day one after her release. In 1947, two years after she joined the Red Cross convoy, *Vogue* interviewed her. The maid brought me the vintage magazine. Nestled between an advertisement for silk lingerie and a feature on fur coats, the article began, "Nothing has stirred Paris more than the return of the women deportees from Ravensbrück prison camp." The first to be interviewed was "the beautiful Odette Allaire, age 24," imprisoned, it said, for her work in the French Resistance. *Vogue* noted her "transparently pale face, dilated, tragic eyes."

Odette and Anne had been friends long before the war, having sailed together as little girls offshore the Spoerry family seat in Männedorf. Both served in the Resistance in occupied Paris. In unrelated incidents both were caught and imprisoned. When she arrived in Ravensbrück in July 1944, about the time of Anne's return from Zwodau, Odette was thrown in with tens of thousands of "political prisoners, criminals, prostitutes, moral degenerates, religious fanatics. We slept head to foot, five in a bed, on wood shavings ... There was always someone screaming, and all night long women stumbled through the dark to the latrines for we all had dysentery.

"We worked twelve hours a day, did factory work, cut trees in the forest, filled up marshes, cut ice, shoveled sand, mended roads, unloaded coal wagons and baggage cars. At noon we ate the only food of the day: three fourths of a liter of rutabaga soup, and 165 grams of bad bread."

One memory still pained Odette. It was her punishment for talking with two other prisoners: the sewer detail. She explained: "I had to separate shit, and there were tons and tons of it coming out of the camp. I walked barefoot through pits of it, I swam in shit, with the temperature at forty-five degrees centigrade and I was not allowed to clean myself and I had to work with criminals and lesbians all fighting for pieces of bread. It was the only time I ever thought about killing myself.

"Ravensbrück made us passive beasts, corpses—or it made us superhuman."

With the arrival of a second martini, Odette told me of her horror when she encountered *"les lapins,"* the guinea pigs, Polish girls whose eyes and muscles had been removed by Nazi doctors for "scientific research." She remembered having to restrain herself from lashing out at the Germans on more than one occasion: "One evening a woman was too tired to keep her place in line, and the SS guard gave her such a blow that he broke her spine and she died a few hours later. The worst of the SS men was a crazy drunkard ... who would fly into a mad rage, beating, kicking, finally clubbing ... to death with a wooden stool. While I was at Ravensbrück, he killed nineteen Russian girls that way."

Odette returned to her cocktail while I held my breath, searching out those "dilated, tragic eyes" noted by *Vogue* in 1947. When I adjusted the conversation to Anne, Odette appeared to regain focus, taking a long pull on her cigarette. Perhaps she was deliberating how far to go—whether or not to protect the sensibilities of someone whose veneration for Anne was no secret.

Finally, she began, "Anne's time in the camp was altogether different from mine, because of that horror, Carmen Mory." Odette deliberated again. Anne was dead, after all: "Let her lie in peace." But soon she relented, believing that greater good lay in talking than in silence. With Ravensbrück's wounds still raw after all these years, even a childhood friend of "a very good family" had to be held to account.

Odette explained that while never in the same block as Anne she saw her at least twice in the camp. The first time was late in 1944, when she spotted her moving between blocks. Odette had heard rumors of Anne's Block 10 activities and needed to confront her. She touched her elbow and begged her to "get out of it." Anne brushed off the hand, saying, "I know what I'm doing," and stormed off. Odette had lost. "Don't you see," Odette explained to me, "Anne was weak."

On slippered feet, the maid floated through the drawing room, shooing Zoe out onto the terrace, as Odette's eyes kept track of all goings-on. She took another sip from the stemmed glass: "I can't make up your mind for you. Speak to others." I nodded, not ready to tell Odette that I was already deep in court testimony and in conversation with two other Ravensbrück survivors and that I had begun to fear the worst.

—◦—

In September 1944, when Carmen Mory introduced Anne Spoerry to Block 10, instantly promoting her to doctor, she incensed three fellow prisoners, all seasoned nurses. These were Violette Rougier-Lecoq, Jacqueline Héreil, and Janine Ceyrolles. Soon, Louise "Loulou" Le Porz, a fully accredited pulmonary specialist from Bordeaux, would join them. That they were better qualified than the medical student little mattered to Mory. In the autumn of 1944, young Anne was her protégée, and no one could talk her out of her decision.

Block 10 had been designed exclusively for tuberculosis patients as well as "idiots." It was conveniently situated near the *Revier,* and its floor plan reflected the somber hierarchy of the incurable. At one end of the rectangular structure lay the tubercular ward, with thirty-seven beds (at the time of Anne's arrival occupied by five hundred patients). Nearby washrooms and toilets were flanked by an enclosed space called the *Dienstzimmer* or *Idiotenstübchen*—a room for those who were thought to have lost their minds. It measured fifteen by seventeen feet (twenty-five square meters). Between the TB ward and the ablution areas a small space was allocated to "nurse personnel" and furnished with three bunk beds, occupied by Violette Rougier-Lecoq on the bottom and in time, Louise Le Porz in the middle and Jacqueline Héreil on top. Adjoining the cubicle was a more spacious alcove, with a privacy curtain at the entryway. Furnished with a square table and a large hair mattress, this alcove was designated for the *Blockova.* Beginning in September 1944, its sole bed accommodated one other—"Dr. Claude."

When Anne arrived in Block 10, she exchanged her given name for the androgynous "Dr. Claude." Whether this conversion was Anne's idea or Mory's is not clear. What is known is that Mory required that in future all prisoners and guards address Anne as "Dr. Claude."

In more than one postwar account of Block 10, fellow prisoners claimed Anne never hesitated in using her alias. They believed she did so to ingratiate herself with Carmen Mory and, through association, Mory's protectors, two SS officers dreaded by almost every prisoner—Dr. Percy Treite and political chief Ludwig Ramdohr.

In the *Blockova* alcove, Carmen and "Dr. Claude" enjoyed privacy denied all others. After the war, Anne reported that when they were together in their room, they engaged in food talk, with Mory reciting ingredients to favorite Swiss dishes. Almost certainly, Mory led the conversation. Glib, multilingual (French, Italian, English, Spanish, German, and Dutch), she possessed opinions on many subjects and recounted intimacies in the lives of Himmler, Rosenberg, and Hitler. Her monologues were often enlivened by song. In her own testimony Anne said that their friendship was based on shared "intellectual" values and a mutual longing for Switzerland.

Most times when she emerged from her alcove to visit the infirmary, "honorable prisoner" Mory made her rounds, armed with a whip. According to historian Sarah Helm, she "would lash out at the sick with her whip or her fists." Once satisfied with what she had seen, Mory went straight to the camp's administrative offices. Noting that she often took along "Dr. Claude" for regular meetings with Ludwig Ramdohr, Block 10 prisoners drew the conclusion the two were informing against their fellow prisoners. Few other *Blockovas* held such power. SS guards let her pass freely into their headquarters, fearing Mory's avowed friendships with Nazi elite, including Alfred Rosenberg. In November, when *Reichsführer* Himmler visited and directed the camp's two crematoriums to work nonstop, Mory supported his cause by agreeing to dispatch on death transports all "undesirables"—Mory's euphemism for the insane.

As Block 10's *Blockova*, Carmen Mory was in charge of the Idiot (sometimes known as the Lunatic) Room. During the glacially cold autumn and winter of 1944, this minute space was occupied by as many as seventy women, dressed in thin, filthy chemises. Sanitation was limited to one bucket in the center of the room with a solitary barred window affording the only ventilation. The frozen women slept curled against each other, much like a pack of dogs. Not all *Idiotenstübehen* inmates were insane. Some had been confined there as punishment—which Dr. Percy Treite euphemistically termed "for observation." On several occasions, Mory invited

Dorothea Binz, her former tormentor, and Binz's SS boyfriend to join her to taunt the insane as an amusement.

By late October, Mory was said to be showing signs of psychosis. In court testimony, a fellow *Blockova*, a Pole, testified that while boasting of her unchallenged authority in the "Idiot Room," Mory said, "Let me show you something . . . You should know all these roaches will die. I'm human, instead of the syringe they deserve, they die the human way." (Presumably, Mory meant that rather than execute them, she let them die of starvation.) "They are warm because their own stench keeps them warm . . . Sometimes I throw a slice of bread into the crowd, then you should see the action. I most enjoy watching them eat their feces. They think it is chocolate and I reassure them it is. You always give them water after such a feast."

On visits to the "Idiot Room," Mory instructed Anne to throw buckets of cold water on "troublemakers." Later in court, Carmen Mory verified this report when she admitted treating inmates with little care for their well-being. Incredulously, she testified that she shackled "idiots" until "foam came from the ears and nose."

One morning Mory discovered that four women had been strangled overnight. With instructions from Dr. Percy Treite, she "disciplined" those she believed had been the killers. The ten "most insane" were thereupon dispatched to the gas chamber. On another occasion, Mory was heard complaining that screams coming from the "Idiot Room" were keeping her from sleep. She ordered a nurse and "a medical student" ("Dr. Claude") to join her to quell the disturbance. When the three burst into the room, they found a Russian and one other fighting. Mory whipped them both with a leather strap and then sent "the medical student" to fetch syringes of Evipan, a barbiturate that, taken in excess, caused death. Mory and "Dr. Claude" took turns injecting them. The following morning Violette Rougier-Lecoq and Jacqueline Héreil entered the "Idiot Room" and found two corpses.

Accounts of Carmen and Anne's vigilante justice were not confined to the *Idiotenstübchen*. Violette Lecoq testified she witnessed a Polish girl, recovering from surgery, being "dragged by Carmen Mory and Anne Spoerry to the toilets. There, they hit her, and splashed her with cold water—all of which advanced her death." On another occasion, Lecoq witnessed Anne, on Mory's orders, standing over a hunchback and administering a lethal injection into her heart. In other testimony, "Dr. Claude" injected a German dwarf with "10 cubic centimeters of air into her heart which provoked her almost instant death." Trynte (sometimes spelled Trijntje) Duvivier de Beer testified in Birmingham after the war that she saw Anne inject up to sixty "lunatics" in one night, on Mory's instructions. "I suspect the cause of death was the injection because after the injections the room became empty." One other, Elsa Schütz, testifying from Basel, Switzerland, maintained that "Claude" has "got hundreds of human lives on her conscience with the injections she administered." Duvivier de Beer's and Schütz's astonishing numbers were never verified by other witnesses.

One very credible witness was Block 10 doctor Louise Le Porz. After the war she testified at the Hamburg war crimes trial, and years later I was privileged to visit her in Bordeaux four times— twice in 2001, once in 2009, and two years before her death, aged ninety-eight, on April 1, 2013. Throughout my time with her, Dr. Le Porz made clear that try as she might to like Anne, she could not find it within her because of Anne's "blind" and "unhesitating" submission to Mory. To Dr. Le Porz, the vengeful, double-dealing, amoral *Blockova* found Anne weak and easy prey. Over the course of our interviews, Dr. Le Porz regularly returned to one event that to her captured Anne Spoerry's "black heart." It involved Paulina, an exquisite but disturbed Polish woman: "She had a beautiful voice and I believe she had trained professionally, as a girl. Carmen could not stand her singing. She had asked me to administer the injection. I refused.

"Claude . . . took the syringe. Yes. She did not hesitate . . . I was dumbfounded. Her expression told me nothing. She seemed to be in favor of doing it. This was a discovery for me. That anyone who is a medical doctor or wants to become one could deliberately execute a patient . . . I can only explain it by her fear of reprisals . . . I felt sorry for Claude, I felt sorry for her for the manifestation of a larger problem, which is not for us to judge. She had a black hole in her heart."

Even after the Polish girl stopped breathing, Dr. Le Porz saw no signs of remorse on "Dr. Claude's" face. I asked the doctor whether there might have been mitigating circumstances with the killing—a mercy killing perhaps. My question made Dr. Le Porz's jaw stiffen: "As a doctor, I was never trained to kill patients—even when mortally ill. We saw tens and tens of our friends die—remarkable women of astonishing character as well as simple women with no pretensions—all with the same generosity of spirit and courage. You kept women alive as long as you could and then you allowed them to die—on death's schedule. Our job was not to make a decision about when and how it was their moment to die. Ours was to make the end as painless and as comfortable as possible and never, never to execute. That is all."

It was a puzzle to Dr. Le Porz that Anne adopted Mory's virulent bigotry. "To the patients, she [Mory] only held contempt. Everything that was not German, everything that was not Nazi was, to her, loathsome. As for the Jews, she was not kind, although we could not understand why, since Jews had never harmed her."

By November, almost all in Block 10 had grown deeply suspicious of Anne, trailing after Mory. Dr. Le Porz and her roommates, nurses Jacqueline Héreil and Violette Lecoq, were convinced "Claude" reported all conversations to Mory, who, in turn, conveyed them to Treite in the infirmary or to Ramdohr in the political department. The latter, said to be Treite's rival for power, was responsible for camp interrogations. He also was credited with vicious methods of torture. One was to bind women, plunge their heads into pails of water, and simulate drowning—a technique that, years later, would become known as waterboarding.

Two witnesses testified that late in October 1944 Mory and "Dr. Claude" co-signed a document pledging their loyalty to Ludwig Ramdohr by "fighting Bolshevism," "cleaning up" Block 10, and punishing all those who did not share his views on "hygiene, tidiness, morals and ethics." Fräulein Lambrecht, Ramdohr's clerk, witnessed Mory and "Dr. Claude" sign the document, pledging their support for the Nazi cause.

The block elder and her accomplice's written resolution had immediate implications in Block 10. In no time, Mory and "Dr. Claude" started accusing fellow prisoners of "smuggling of food, abortions, lesbian relationships, communist underground work and other criminality." Fellow prisoners claimed the pair helped make death transport selections for SS guards: when standing at *Appell*, the two were seen identifying prisoners they wished to have executed. (Half a century later, a Dutch woman, visiting Kenya, requested that, under no circumstance, was she to cross paths with Anne Spoerry, for she would never forgive her ill-disguised hand signals that led to the killing of many of her friends.)

—◦—

Were Anne and Carmen lovers? In testimony after the war, Anne denied a lesbian relationship. She claimed their friendship was altogether innocent, born out of common heritage and shared intellectual interests. Later, several Block 10 prisoners challenged her claim. Under oath in 1946 and 1947, six former Block 10 inmates insisted that the *Blockova* and the medical student were romantically involved. While no one had witnessed them "in the act," they all believed the two were lovers because they exchanged presents and shared the same bed.

Fifty-six years after the war I visited the nurse Violette Rougier-

Lecoq in her fin de siècle Paris apartment. Physically ailing, she riffled the pages of *Témoignages,* a book of thirty-six Ravensbrück drawings she had had privately published first in 1948 and later in 1982. When I uttered Anne's name, she lay the book down and shook her head in seeming disdain. The bunk beds Violette shared with two others, she said, were up against the thin wall separating them from "Claude" and Carmen. They heard much. "The little one, Claude, Dr. Claude, followed her [Mory] around. It was so troubling. They were lovers. Lesbians. Dr. Claude would do everything Carmen Mory asked."

Block 10's doctor Louise Le Porz, separated by the same thin wall, also confirmed "Claude" and Mory slept together. She could not verify with absolute certainty they were lovers. She was analytic: "Their room was obscured by a curtain. I did not see them together making love. I don't know . . . In the camp there were many accusations . . . Still, Claude . . . was completely besotted by Carmen Mory."

Sitting in her elegant Paris penthouse, Odette Allaire Walling told me that it was common knowledge Anne was in a lesbian relationship. After her first encounter with Anne outside Block 10 late in 1944, when Anne walked off, saying, "Don't worry," Odette called after her, "But I do worry." It was no use. Odette explained, "Anne, you see, was vulnerable. She wanted love so much. She wanted recognition."

Dr. Louise Le Porz had an explanation for Anne's submission to Mory: "You see, I always thought I was condemned to death, so I did not care. I was going to die. Not Anne. I think she suffered from incredible fear. Fear explains her attitude. Anne was intelligent, but she was scared about being badly treated or by being executed. I don't think she had the ability to see beyond this and to realize Carmen Mory was fundamentally evil. There were many I knew, like her, overcome by fear, but none of them I knew was willing to do what Anne did to delay her own death. She must have been very scared, very scared."

It is possible that in other concentration camps there were prisoners whose actions mirrored Anne's. Auschwitz survivor and Holocaust chronicler Primo Levi wrote about the phenomenon in *The Drowned and the Saved*. He called these Nazi sympathizers "gray, ambiguous persons, ready to compromise," and he asked his readers not to be shocked by their easy duplicity. Yet Dr. Louise Le Porz continued to be shocked half a century after being with Anne.

In the last days of 1944, truckloads of Polish and Jewish women from Auschwitz-Birkenau added to the misery of Block 10. Dr. Le Porz called Christmas Day "lamentable," with SS doctors engaged in a campaign to sterilize Roma girls. Meanwhile, prison guards were erecting a Christmas tree, with decorations, beside one of the blockhouses. For most, the sight of the tree was an insult. At *Appell* that morning, Le Porz herself came close to being executed: "A guard passed me and for absolutely no reason landed a huge blow to my face. The prostitute behind me—such an intelligent woman—grabbed my arm as I was about to take a swing at the guard in self-protection. The prostitute said, 'Don't do anything.' She spoke good German and had heard the guard say I wore too proud a look on my face. Without that woman I would have been sent off to my death."

Later on Christmas Day, Block 10 received another cargo of prisoners, many wounded by Allied bombing. Dr. Le Porz worked through the night caring for them, flaunting Carmen Mory's orders to let them die. Even under her care, 108 perished that night, adding to the 811 deaths Le Porz had already witnessed in Block 10 in December. She recalled one patient in particular—a pregnant Dutch girl, her lungs perforated by tuberculosis. As she lay dying on the floor beside a terminally ill Russian woman, Dr. Le Porz provided the only medicine at her disposal that night. She sat on the floor between them, holding their hands until they stopped breathing "in their own time."

On that tragic Christmas Day, Dr. Le Porz was surprised to find an envelope awaiting her on her bunk. In it was a Christmas card addressed to her as "Loulou" in red crayon. In French, it wished her "Merry Christmas 1944" and was signed "Carmen Maria" and "Claude," their names entwined. "I don't know why they sent it to me," recalled Dr. Le Porz. On one side was a jolly snowman holding a broom. On the other, a coiled snake, referencing Asclepius, mythological father of medicine, said to have killed a snake only to see another snake revive it with an elixir of herbs. Anne had painted both.

Dr. Le Porz kept the Ravensbrück Christmas card stored away in a file cabinet for the rest of her life. Nearly sixty-five years after receiving it, she was still stupefied. How could Carmen Mory and Anne Spoerry, she pondered, have conceived such a gesture, while hundreds of women lay wounded and dying to either side of them?

Even more astonishing to Dr. Le Porz was the exchange she overheard between the *Blockova* and the medical student a week later on New Year's Eve 1944. While Le Porz and Lecoq lay on their bunks, listening to the firing squad executing "undesirables," through the thin wall they heard what sounded like the pleasurable cooings of two people, enjoying a good meal. It seemed to her Carmen Mory and Anne Spoerry were celebrating New Year's Eve with food they had appropriated. When their meal was done, Le Porz heard Carmen break into "Begin the Beguine."

◄o►

On January 2, 1945, Ravensbrück's political head, Ludwig Ramdohr, had Carmen Mory removed from Block 10 and replaced by Erika Buchmann, a German Communist. Some claimed Mory's ouster was punishment for having crossed Dr. Percy Treite. Others asserted that Ludwig Ramdohr had orchestrated the move, wishing to conceal his "honorary prisoner" from the justice of approaching Allied armies. On January 27, 1945, the day Soviet troops liberated Auschwitz, Mory was posted to Barth, a forced labor camp that supplied slave workers for Heinkel Aircraft Works to aid in the manufacture of cockpits and wings for Germany's HE 111 warplane. Mory had asked permission for "Claude" to join her, but Percy Treite, who had once called Anne "an incapable medical student," denied the request.

Ludwig Ramdohr needed Mory in Barth to continue working on his Nazi campaign against "bribery, dissipation, guards' intimate relations with prisoners and abortions." Mory set to immediately, and in March she delivered her report, enumerating a succession of crimes against hygiene, tidiness, morals, and ethics, as well as incidents of smuggling, abortions, Communist underground work, and lesbian relationships.

When Mory was demoted as *Blockova* of Block 10, Anne was an immediate target of fellow prisoners seeking revenge, and SS guards justice. In desperation, Anne ran to her former patron, Ludwig Ramdohr, and begged to be transferred out of Block 10. On January 6, 1945, she was assigned to Block 6, for women with typhus and dysentery. Unrecognized, Anne could now circulate without fear of reprisal. In a postwar affidavit, she claimed that in Block 6 she set to vaccinating several thousand women. Her evolution from Carmen Mory's accomplice to high-minded caregiver was solemnized by a name change: henceforth she wished to be known as Anne Spoerry, not "Dr. Claude."

In February 1945, Anne fell sick with "infected swollen glands" and was transferred to Block 11. During her convalescence, one of the first Red Cross shipments to penetrate Axis lines reached Ravensbrück. Sent by Anne's aunt, working for the International Red Cross, it contained a supply of precious medications. According to her postwar affidavit, even in ill health Anne distributed her medications to all.

By March, Anne had convalesced enough to return to Block 6. Her rehabilitation was nothing short of miraculous. Within days she was forging patients' medical records to help them escape death (or "black") transports. Anne also mixed with prisoners in Block 8, designated for Jews. One was Odette Fabius, who testified Anne saved her life by bringing her a daily bowl of soup while tending to her wounds and plaiting her hair. When Fabius was liberated, she wrote that she would never have survived Ravensbrück without Anne.

In her 1986 memoir, *Un lever de soleil sur le Mecklembourg,* Fabius was not so kind. In it she made allegations about misconduct in Block 10 without disclosing names: "Of course, homosexuality existed, and no one bothered to prevent its existence. Couples formed, separated, exchanged partners between themselves . . . One case more pitiable than the others was that of . . . a medical student, from an old Mulhouse family . . . On arrival at the camp, she pretended to be a doctor and became friendly with the hospital doctor. She soon became madly taken with this doctor who was a lesbian, and the two lived together as a couple. This chief medical practitioner was charged with the lethal injection of women who had, in camp, gone insane and she included our compatriot in responsibility for this inhuman work."

There were others equally astonished by Anne's 1945 transformation. Madame Courtaud, who had known "Claude" in her Block 10 days, helping guards select prisoners for the gas chamber, testified that in Block 6 Anne treated the sick "admirably." Another one to witness Anne's conversion was Trynte Duvivier de Beer who, in Block 10, had seen the medical student and Carmen Mory administer lethal injections. She explained, "Away from Carmen Mory, Anne was quite different. She was good and kind, a devoted helper for all."

On a Sunday in March 1945, during an SS guard witch hunt for Jews, Anne again demonstrated her reformation. On learning that SS guards were hunting down six Hungarian Jews in Block 8 for a "death transport," she set off at a run to alert them. She spirited them through the blockhouse, out a window, and to safety. Later, when guards confronted her, she shrugged: "How would I know?"

A year after the war, as Antoinette Lenoir lay on her deathbed in a Swiss tuberculosis asylum, she asked a friend to blow Anne a kiss, for "it is thanks to the continuous and devoted care which she lavished on me that I was able to return alive to France and that I had the pleasure of seeing my mother and my little child again. Tell her I am eternally grateful to her."

In March 1945, Odette Allaire again encountered her childhood friend Anne in Ravensbrück. This time Anne did not dismiss her friendship with Carmen Mory by asserting she knew what she was doing. This time she confessed, telling Odette, "I was bewitched, I was mad, I think, but all that's finished."

In spite of commendable behavior throughout 1945, Anne's previous Block 10 legacy must still have weighed on her, for on April 23, 1945, two days before the arrival of Ravensbrück's first liberators, she stormed into the office of political chief Ludwig Ramdohr and demanded his clerk, Fräulein Lambrecht, turn over the document she had co-signed with Carmen Mory. Anne needed to destroy all proof of her Nazi complicity evidenced by her pledge of loyalty to Ramdohr and his political agenda. Under Fräulein Lambrecht's gaze, Anne Spoerry ripped the incriminating document to shreds.

As the Russian Red Army advanced on Ravensbrück, the air grew thick with smoke from the crematoriums, belching death on an industrial scale, while the adjacent gas chamber was put to use day and night to eradicate evidence of Ravensbrück's wholesale executions.

During the camp's final days, SS guards ordered Anne's friend Odette Allaire to shower in a room beside the crematoriums. She looked around, certain it was a gas chamber. Inexplicably, the guards did not turn on the jets. Nearly seventy years later, describing what she perceived as her final moments of life, Odette recalled, "I have never been so frightened in all my life. I was banging on the door to be let out. That's why I still need psychotherapy to this day."

On April 25, 1945, surprise visitors arrived at Ravensbrück. Dr. Louise Le Porz recalled the precise moment of abject incomprehension when she saw a team of men, wearing white uniforms, jumping from a convoy of matching white trucks. What struck her was their reaction to the prisoners. When their eyes fell on her and others, they burst into tears. Puzzled by the spectacle of grown men bawling uncontrollably, she looked down at herself and understood: after a year in Ravensbrück, she was nothing more than "a filthy, proto-human skeleton."

The men in white belonged to the Swedish Red Cross. In the war's final days, diplomat Count Folke Bernadotte had negotiated the rescue of some six hundred Ravensbrück survivors. Among the lucky ones admitted to the convoy were Dr. Louise Le Porz, Odette Allaire, and Anne Spoerry, formerly "Dr. Claude."

For four days, the band traveled by truck, skirting the smoking wreckage of Berlin, bouncing along potholed roads, overnighting in a school gymnasium and, later, inside a marble cemetery mausoleum. As the convoy negotiated its way through the devastation of war, Odette studied Anne, stupefied that she was the sole prisoner not suffering from malnutrition.

On the fourth day, the party reached Lake Constance, where Germany, Austria, and Switzerland converge. Along its shore strutted curlews and dunlins. Offshore loons broke the still surface. Overhead soared a golden eagle. These were the first birds the women had bothered to notice in two years. The eagle wheeled past the Alps, still fringed in snow.

In front of bemused onlookers, the medical student and the

emaciated Paris haute couture model stripped off their "horrible dresses and filthy sandals" and, buck naked, plunged into the lake's clear waters. The two accomplished swimmers made for deep waters, where, in the reflection of snow and under the wings of an eagle, they washed themselves clean for the first time in years.

The next day the two separated. Odette would travel to Geneva, then on to Paris and finally into the pages of *Vogue* magazine. Anne would make her way to various Spoerry family estates, then through several jurisdictions, before settling in Kenya.

For the rest of her life, Odette and a preponderance of survivors felt a responsibility to inform the world about Ravensbrück. Not Anne. The whippings, the injections, the death convoys, the regrets, and, not least of all, personal reflections on human frailty—these were memories she would keep bottled up, defying the imperatives of her fellow prisoners and the lessons of history, until the end.

CHAPTER 12

NO. 40 FLAT HEELS

Who needs a heart when a heart can be broken?

—Tina Turner, "What's Love Got to Do with It"

Anne arrived in Männedorf on the day wirelesses around the world crackled with news of Adolf Hitler's suicide. Nothing could dampen Henry and Jeanne's jubilation with the return of their daughter, after two years of anxiety. The war had weighed heavily on Spoerry prosperity, with materials in short supply, factories shut, and food rationed. Topping all that, the disappearance of two of their four children had been a near-insuperable burden. For Jeanne the anguish had fueled existential doubts—whether or not her children's work in the Resistance had been worth the cost. In 1944, she expressed her misgivings to François's Resistance colleague the scientist (and later member of the Académie Française) Jean Bernard. In his memoirs, he recalled their encounter:

Madame Spoerry handled her burden with dignity and courage, but circumstances didn't prevent her from asking, "Is this all for a purpose?" I responded with many encouraging but hollow words . . . A bit later, I reflected on her question and came up with a more precise answer. Yes, the Resistance has worked. We've given our lives, our liberties; at the least we have sacrificed a cozy existence. We have rejected slavery and now . . . France is no longer naked . . . Insecurity, aggression, sabotage, have greatly bothered the Germans. At the same time we have provided information for the Allies . . . But if it has been shown that the annoyance was modest, that the safety it brought France slim, I still hold the Resistance was justified. When we accomplished difficult tasks, the warmth that filled us was not ours alone. A little flame raced through many countries. It flickered. It burst forth. It was never extinguished.

With Anne's arrival, Jeanne, the doting mother, cast aside all qualms and treated her daughter as a verifiable French heroine. For the last two years, Anne had been anticipating a triumphant return. But once reunited with sisters, mother, father, and the household staff, Anne seemed awkward with praise. While she glibly recounted her experiences in Fresnes and Zwodau, she dismissed Ravensbrück with bromides. Innocent Jeanne pressed her for more, but Henry knew his daughter well enough not to probe.

On May 7, Germany surrendered unconditionally. The next day Anne's face registered its first smile when she heard the sound of a truck reversing on the gravel drive. Seconds later François burst through the door, after his two years of imprisonment. Once again there was a joyous reunion. This time, there was no end to stories, and the returning hero talked without restraint. After Fresnes, François was transported to Neue Bremm, then Buchenwald. Following an interval in Dora (where he dug tunnels to house V2 rockets for Germany), he was transferred to Struthof, then Erzingen. His final camp was Dachau. Just the mention of those hideous place-names made the two young Spoerry girls squirm.

Anne was especially attentive to François's tale because, after Fresnes, she had had no idea of his whereabouts or condition. In large measure, her will to survive had been fueled by a dream of reuniting with her brother. Now she could compare their various ordeals and evaluate whether he too had struck a Faustian deal. Instead, she would learn that François had survived Dachau by volunteering to work as a cook. In his preface to his reflections on his life's work, *A Gentle Architecture*, published in 1991 (with a foreword by the Prince of Wales), François opened up about his time in the concentration camp. He wrote that the camps "showed me the true dimensions of the human condition in both its greatness and its misery. This also helped me to change my personal opinions and to make different evaluations . . . I forced myself to forget the horror of my present situation and to think only of the future. With makeshift drawing materials I tried to sustain my companions by sketching the houses of their dreams, the homes in which they would live as free men after the war . . . Deportation made me differentiate clearly and forever between matters that are essential and those of secondary importance." François's survival strategy was so heroic, so creative, it would make its way into the fabric of Spoerry family legend. The same could not be said of his sister's.

How did Anne view her brother's stratagem? Did she ever consider that she, too, might have survived more gracefully if she had followed a different path? In their first days of freedom, François and Anne talked, one more volubly than the other. Whenever his little sister lapsed into imprecisions, François was quick to fill in the gaps. While he had never met Carmen, he recognized the type: in Dachau, he had encountered several such prisoners—impressive, versatile, manipulative, with flexible principles. Knowing his sister so well, François could offer palliatives—that all would be well if she completed her studies, and that now she should cast her mind to the future. Shattered France had had enough of war. Who wanted to waste energy over Ravensbrück?

By June, Anne was back on the Rue de Sundgau in the house of memories. Servants greeted her with red eyes, and when she raced upstairs, her bedroom was just as she left it, even with wooden soldiers arrayed in formation. A few days later, she took the train to Paris. While parts of the city were unrecognizable, Anne's apartment on Quai Voltaire had escaped serious damage; it still boasted a radiant view of the Seine and the Louvre, now happily stripped of swastikas. Striding around the apartment, she peered into the closet where once she had concealed Roger. Over the last years of war, her parents had stayed at Quai Voltaire as they sought to locate her and François. Her mother's touches stood out: the bureau neatly arranged, a flower vase waiting to be filled.

Anne returned to the site where the Gestapo had marched her off. Her old station at Hérold Hospital was still drab, as if the life-changing event it once witnessed had not occurred. Walls were filthy, medical stations unattended, and colleagues seemingly vaporized, their positions now occupied by strangers, indifferent to the past. She was now more intent than ever on completing her studies and becoming an accredited doctor. In Ravensbrück, medicine had saved her life. Maybe in another place, in a better time, it would again.

Most troubling of all were Anne's encounters with old acquaintances. According to her friend Odette, on her return to Paris she was ostracized. Anne wondered what they knew. How had rumors of Ravensbrück circulated so far, so fast? Anne sat alone in cafés, studying faces. A friend, upon spotting her, hurriedly looked away while attempting to dissolve back into the seventh arrondissement.

◄o►

As Anne endured the silent treatment, some five hundred miles away Carmen prospered. In late April, when the Russian Red Army liberated Barth, the former *Blockälteste* of Block 10 embarked on a campaign to dazzle its commanding officers with her language skills and commitment to Bolshevism. The Russians soon signed her up as an interpreter. The arrangement was brief, because Mory grew exasperated with her new allies. She wrote to a friend, saying she found the Russians' politics loathsome and their manners boorish. After six weeks, she made for the British liberation zone in Plön, Germany. There she presented herself to its officers as an ardent devotee of all things British, even claiming to be of English stock herself. Once again, she could not resist the temptation of self-aggrandizement. In a letter to the commanding officer she wrote, "I have important information which I want to give at once." Mory's intelligence, she explained, involved Gestapo operations in Berlin and Munich, insights into "concentration camp matters," and privileged knowledge of the lives of "party criminals," such as "Hermann Göring, Dr. Kaltenbrunner and Martin Bormann"—all of whom she claimed as friends. Her love for England was incontestable because her two English half brothers had served in the British navy (Mory failed to mention she had never met them). She added that she "had done some important work" for the "German Movement of Resistance Against the Nazi Regime . . . My part in German Politics is not without importance." For verification of the above, she recommended contacting "Dr. Anne Spoerry . . . in the service of the British Services in the French Movement of Resistance."

So dazzled were the British by Carmen's razor-sharp memory, protean medical feats, command of languages, and eagerness to hunt down Nazis they hired her on the spot without bothering to consult Anne Spoerry. The occasion called for Carmen to write a celebratory letter to her friend in Paris: "Dear Annisch, Alive, safe and absolutely O.K.!! ... Don't tell my family yet—they waited 7 years so they can wait another few weeks. After 6 weeks in the Russian zone I joined the British."

Carmen must have already had presentiments: "I am looking for Percy [Treite]. Will you try and find out where he is?" Her concerns were brief for she ended on a fashion note: "Let me have a decent tailored suit and a pair of shoes No. 40 flat heels. Well, you know how I like them! Hug you to my heart and lots of love, Carmen."

◄o►

Carmen's letter arrived the same week Anne passed a critical medical exam, bringing her ever closer to a medical degree. There is no record of whether she responded or satisfied Carmen's fashion needs. During the university break in August 1945, Anne traveled to Mulhouse and Switzerland to visit her family. Under other circumstances, she would have vacationed with them in the South of France, but the retreating Germans had left La Bastide, the Spoerry villa, in rubble. Instead, François and Anne rented a cottage for a week on a large estate of friends in Montmorency, north of Paris.

In the French countryside, Anne confided in François, sharing her sense of unease over a recent incident in Männedorf, when in the town center she had chanced upon a woman she had known in Ravensbrück. Instead of embracing each other as fellow sufferers might, the woman fixed her eyes on Anne with steely menace and refused to return the wave. Anne hurried after her, rummaging through her purse for a present. She found a scarf and gave it to her. The woman looked at it in disdain, returned it, and strode away. What did she know, and what might Anne expect next?

At the end of August 1945, Anne failed an exam that would have earned her a hospital internship. She now had to delay her departure from Paris. To fill the interval between October 1945 and April

1946, Anne worked as a part-time extern for Professor Heuvier at the Cochin Hospital, a public assistance facility in Paris.

◄o►

Meanwhile, as Anne kept to herself, Carmen, now a uniformed member of Field Security 1001 in the British zone, was busy making friends. As late as August no one in Plön knew much of her Ravensbrück past. The British were so awestruck by her zeal in hunting down war criminals they had dubbed her "Nazi-hunter"—a title she appeared to wear with pride. Once, in collaboration with two British officers, she staged an automobile accident that led to the capture of Dr. Fritz Fischer, formerly of the Waffen-SS. Mory thereupon provided the British with much apparently privileged information, saying she had known Fischer in Ravensbrück, where, as surgical assistant to Karl Gebhardt, she had observed him performing medical experiments on Polish women. Thanks to Mory's damning claims, the British arrested Fischer. Later at his hearing at the American military tribunal in Nuremberg, he was condemned to life imprisonment. (Like those of many other former Nazis found guilty of war crimes, his sentence was later commuted first to fifteen years, then to seven, and finally, in 1954, it was lifted altogether, at which time Fischer resumed his medical career in Germany.)

Sometime late in August, at a British officers' casino, Carmen met the intelligence officer Carlos Clarke. There appears to have been instant chemistry, for a few weeks later they were engaged. Clarke was besotted by Carmen, indulging her with clothes and perfume. Once he had exhausted his resources, Carmen introduced him to her old dodge—attending parties, gathering up their hosts' belongings, and then denouncing them for having stolen Jewish property. In Plön, their new acquaintances were so bewildered by the unprovoked charges that they allowed Carmen and Carlos to steal away with clothes, soap, perfume, and money.

Carmen, the former Nazi anti-Semite, had now morphed into archfoe of the Nazis and, wondrously, champion of the Jewish people. Once in an office typing pool, overhearing a British secretary utter the word "Jew," Carmen called the secretary a "damn anti-Semite," then lunged across the desk and pummeled the bewildered woman until shocked onlookers regained their composure and separated them.

Mory's rabid zealotry met first with concern and then with suspicion. A week later, the British command began to investigate her past. In early September, when Mory got wind that intelligence officers were focusing on accounts of her role as Block 10's *Blockova,* she wrote to Colonel Bradshaw asking to be transferred from the British sector to the United Nations Relief and Rehabilitation Administration (UNRRA). Her overarching aim, she claimed, was "World's Peace." As she prepared to take up her new role, the British had made progress, trying to understand her role in Block 10. Toward the end of September, when Mory learned the British sector was calling in survivors of Block 10 for questioning, she wrote to the Swiss consul. Her letter sounds a note of desperation: "My situation at present is not quite clear . . . They are all very nice and I am treated as one of them wearing the Uniform which is less pleasant to me, but which I need for my work . . . It would still be much better, if you would be able to have Anne Spoerry over here. It would make things so much easier. I am really fed up for being Mata Hari and I already think it is bad enough to have a name like Carmen Mory, unfortunately I have been born with it."

At the end of September, the British informed UNRRA that their interviews with former Ravensbrück prisoners had uncovered intelligence incriminating Mory. The UN agency instantly returned her to the British. Investigators in Field Security 1001 were now learning that those whom Mory had once denounced as Nazi sympathizers had, in fact, been quite the opposite—vocal critics of their German captors. Unable to contest the newly uncovered testimony, Mory frantically wrote to Anne. In the letter she enclosed a snapshot of herself, with urgent instructions to take it to the Swiss embassy to obtain a passport. The letter's tone was commanding—perhaps an echo of the dominant/submissive relationship that had once characterized their life together in Block 10.

Bewilderingly, as Mory was entreating Anne for help, she was also informing against her, telling the British that the medical student had been the real Block 10 murderer. Mory embellished her allegations by adding that in March 1945 Anne had sanctioned the extermination of three hundred prisoners—a particularly dubious claim because in March Mory was away in Barth, out of contact with Anne.

Mory's desperate maneuvers backfired. On October 5, 1945, British Field Security 1001 arrested her and remanded her to Camp 030 in Plön. Even in a jail cell, Carmen Mory could not be stilled. In a letter she complained about living conditions, claiming she had been "put in a cell in the cellar without heating—nor windows—a bed on the stone floor." By now, the British were so irritated by their prisoner they invited the French to take over her case: "Mory is a most undesirable person and she proved a considerable nuisance in this Corps District." When the French declined, British military investigators set to work, charging their ward with the deaths of more than sixty Ravensbrück prisoners and also with having engaged in gas chamber selections. When informed of the accusations, Mory wrote to Major Russel-Ross, "If any of them were true I would kill myself at once." She argued, how could a hunter of war criminals be one herself? Soon, she asserted, the truth would win out, and she would be acquitted when she called up her most reliable witness—Anne Spoerry. By now, the British were in no mood to believe anything she said, including accusations against a medical student.

◄o►

Unknown to Mory at the time, throughout the late spring, Anne Spoerry was having troubles of her own. In Paris on May 10, 1946, she had attended a private gathering, billed as a reunion of fellow Resistance fighters. Upon arrival in the large drawing room of an apartment belonging to a former Resistance fighter, she found herself facing a court of honor, described to her as a tribunal, convened on short notice and without official designation, to respond to allegations that she had brought dishonor on France in Ravensbrück. Anne now faced a jury composed of veterans of the Free French Forces—eight men and two women, both fellow Ravensbrück survivors. The judge presiding over the court was the much-decorated Lieutenant Colonel Michel Hollard. Anne knew many of her jurors for their gallant reputations in occupied France.

To its members, the Resistance tribunal was officially the Cour d'Honneur de la France Combattante. In time, it would answer to the Association Nationale des Anciennes Déportées et Internées de la Résistance (ADIR), a collegial organization whose stated purpose was to sustain bonds between camp survivors and to honor those who perished during imprisonment. A few years after the war, the ADIR also pursued and attempted to bring to justice Nazi camp criminals, like Fritz Suhren, the Ravensbrück commandant. To that end, Germaine Tillion (author of *Ravensbrück,* the book singled out by Anne in her memoir as the definitive work on the subject) attended the Hamburg war crimes trial, representing ADIR as observer. There are no records of any other courts of honor convened to try former prisoners in Ravensbrück, apart from the one questioning Anne's conduct. While the jury she faced in May and June 1946 possessed no official standing with the French government, for Anne there was no telling whether or not the court's findings would circulate outside the walls of the apartment in the sixth arrondissement. These men and women might talk.

After two days of testimony, the third and final Court of Honor hearing was convened on June 7, 1946. Anne stood before the jury as Hollard read out the court's judgment. She was charged with impersonating a doctor while in Block 10 and with having administered injections of Evipan and of air, leading to the death of at least one patient. The court's final charge was that Anne had engaged in "anti-French and anti-patriotic behavior."

While minutes of the trial have not survived, two members of the jury testifying independently the following year at the Hamburg war crimes trial (the British military tribunal standing judgment over Ravensbrück officials and prisoners) provided accounts of the Paris proceedings. Anne, they said, first refuted the Court of Honor charges, then burst into tears and confessed. After Colonel Hollard asked her to speak up, Anne admitted that she was glad to acknowledge guilt. She had indeed given an injection, but Carmen Mory had ordered it. When one of her jurors asked why she blindly followed Mory, Anne responded that Mory held a privileged position in the camp. Before Block 10, Anne contended, her prison record was admirable. In Mory's orb, she was "spellbound." Anne begged the court and her "companions" who had shared her "captivity to forgive her and she asked us to help her lead a good life. She wanted us to keep her from Mory's influence and then she said, 'the woman is a devil.'"

After charging Anne with three crimes against the Resistance, Colonel Hollard and the Court of Honor jury declared that Anne could no longer claim membership in the Free French Forces. In spite of "spotless, efficient" work before her imprisonment, her records in the Resistance were to be "downgraded." Worse, her final sentence was exile from France for twenty-five (one witness recalled forty) years.

Anne left behind no record of her state of mind after the Court of Honor's judgment. On François's advice, she left Paris and made herself scarce by traveling to Pontresina, near St. Moritz, Switzerland. She had much on her mind, not merely the Court of Honor, but the possibility she would be officially charged in French and Swiss jurisdictions.

Following a healthy routine of hikes through pine and larch forests, Anne chose not to risk a return to Paris. Instead, she settled in Männedorf, enrolling in a course in pediatric medicine and general psychiatry at the University of Zurich. Throughout the autumn of 1946, every weekday she caught the train from Männedorf for the city. By December she was bundling herself in scarves to stave off the cold and to avoid chance encounters.

December was a critical time for Anne, because the Hamburg war crimes tribunal had convened on the fifth of the month, and already its proceedings were being reported in newspapers across Europe. This military tribunal, made up of five British officers acting as judges, and one lawyer, sat in judgment over war crimes alleged to have been committed by Ravensbrück officials and prisoners. While the hearings ran more or less simultaneously with the higher-profile Doctors Trial in the U.S. occupation zone in Nuremberg, there was no shortage of reporters filling the Hamburg courtroom. In Anne's third-class railroad carriage, she devoured German, French, and English newspapers, reading out the names of the tribunal's first sixteen defendants. She knew them all— Ludwig Ramdohr, Dorothea Binz, Percy Treite, and, of course, Carmen Mory.

In a letter dated November 29, 1946, Dr. Otto Zippel, Carmen Mory's defense counsel in Hamburg, instructed Anne to respond to charges, made by seven women, who had claimed that Carmen Mory, the *Blockova* or *Blockälteste*, had enjoyed a privileged position as an "Honorable Prisoner" in the eyes of the prison command, that she spied on prisoners, that she sold and bartered medicine, that she sent prisoners to their deaths, and that she personally killed some through injections of Evipan. Dr. Zippel ended his letter with a plea: "It is possible that the fate of Mrs. Mory depends upon your statement, and I therefore beg of you, to appear without regard for your own interest as Defense-Witness for Mrs. Mory before the War Crimes Court in Hamburg."

Anne knew enough not to appear in Hamburg. Instead, she chose to defend her friend by letter, in response to Dr. Zippel. Writing under the watchful eye of a Winterthur notary, Anne denied any wrongdoing by Mory, in blatant contradiction of her confession before the Court of Honor in Paris. She testified that the *Blockova* had never enjoyed special privileges in Block 10, nor had she spied for the SS, hurt the sick, selected prisoners for the gas chamber, or killed anyone. Carmen Mory's worst faults, Anne allowed, were her anti-French sentiments and her penchant for getting "very excited."

Four days after Anne wrote her defense, Carmen Mory betrayed her. While Anne was defending the *Blockälteste,* Mory was testifying that "Claude," not she, had done the killing of the insane in Block 10. Before six judges in Hamburg, Mory claimed that Anne was, in fact, the true Block 10 mass murderer. More than a week would pass before Anne learned of Carmen's treachery.

—◁○▷—

With Hamburg enduring one of its coldest winters on record, 120 spectators crowded the gallery of the unheated courtroom located in the Curio-Haus in Hamburg's Rotherbaum quarter. Dorothea Binz was everyone's perfect villain, and according to *Atrocities on Trial* one observer in the balcony commented, "I have followed the Ravensbrück Trial and I am satisfied the witch, Binz, is kaput. Now her angel's head will begin to rot."

The British press came out in force, with the *Daily Mail,* the *Sunday Dispatch,* and the *Daily Express* sending special correspondents. National and local newspapers depicted Carmen Mory as "the monster," the "third-rate Mata Hari," the "Bella Donna." *Le Petit Parisien* unearthed Carmen Mory and Fritz Erler's 1940 espionage conviction in France and supplied its readers with a blistering opinion. After President Lebrun commuted her death sentence in 1940, it reported, Mory exhibited "her gratitude toward this act of mercy in full Nazi fashion by torturing helpless and innocent Frenchwomen . . . until they die." The editorial ended, "I hope that even the biggest opponents of the death penalty will hold back in this case so that justice can run its course, which does not want monsters like her to live among us any longer."

Carmen Mory seemed immune to public censure. She arrived in court kitted out in a red fox fur jacket, a gift from her former fiancé Carlos Clarke. The courtroom was now her theater. Here she could challenge prosecutors, heap scorn on witnesses, and draw attention to her central role in Ravensbrück. Enhancing her performance, she screamed, cried, and called anyone who dared challenge her testimony a "liar." The press found her rants a continuous source of first-class entertainment.

Miss Mary O'Shaughnessy was asked to appear in Hamburg to describe her impressions of Block 10, even though she never set foot in it: "I have heard the name Carmen Mory and I believe that it was her who was concerned in the incarceration of some sixty women who were more or less demented and who were confined in one small room without clothes, bedding or any other amenities.

"Although I have never got near enough to this Block to see inside one could continuously hear the screams and shouts of those unfortunate women who, I am practically certain, were subsequently removed from the camp and gassed."

Among other witnesses testifying against Mory in December were two of the three Block 10 nurses, Jacqueline Héreil and Violette Lecoq, as well as Dr. Louise Le Porz. In brutal detail, each described

Mory's cruelty toward patients in the *Dienstzimmer* (*Idiotenstübchen*).

In her response, Carmen Mory agreed with the Block 10 nurses that *Dienstzimmer* patients were eliminated en masse. But they had made one error: she was not the culprit. Someone else, she claimed, had done the killing by injecting Evipan and air into the women's arms, legs, buttocks, and hearts. That person was "Dr. Claude," "the Idiot Room murderess."

Anne's notarized defense of Mory, written from Winterthur, Switzerland, was entered into evidence as Exhibit 23. Because Anne did not deliver it in person, it had little impact in its defense of Mory. Thwarted, Carmen Mory treated Anne to a combination of condemnation and enticement by letter: "I read all the nice declarations," but "I still do not believe you are not coming to give evidence in a British Court. My lawyer will let you know what Hereil, LeCoq, LePorz . . . gave as evidence against me, Anne! Anything . . . from ill treatment to selection, to pilling, to injections, etc. of course with you as my accomplice. One Polish woman died in three different ways at quite different times by a bucket of cold water! Useless to tell you all perjury, which they gave. Hereil exposed her jewels." In the next paragraph, Mory turned on the charm: "Dear Anne, I can see your kind and silent face . . . I think you will not leave me to the cats—I can't call them lions—for all beauty is missing . . . You are the only person to solve the drama of Block 10. I think a War-Crime-Court is not a playfield for spiteful women, but as the charges are so unbelievable I beg you Anne to show yourself as a fellow-prisoner as you were before."

─◄○►─

It is not certain when Anne learned that Carmen had informed against her. But after spending Christmas with her family, Anne expressed a desire to be by herself. She immediately left for Lenzerheide, in the canton of Graubünden. Her holiday was brief. Early in the New Year 1947, she received a letter from Lieutenant Colonel Michel Hollard, honorary president and magistrate presiding over the Court of Honor. It instructed Anne to meet him in Zurich. He would be traveling from Paris for one reason only: to force her to revoke her defense of Carmen Mory.

Anne was in no position to deny Hollard. She traveled from Lenzerheide to Zurich, where she met him, probably in the station restaurant. After ordering coffee, he came to the point, informing her "that her comrades, former Ravensbrück internees, did not appreciate and understand the positive statements she had given in relation to Carmen Mory." He had the full support of Major F. M. Nevinson, British representative of the Criminal War Branch. The two of them now demanded she retract her December declaration and condemn Mory for what she was. If Anne would not agree to these conditions, Hollard would release her Court of Honor confession to the press. After she accepted his terms in full, Hollard returned to Paris on the night express, while Anne awaited the local back to Lenzerheide.

Anne's run of bad luck was just beginning. On January 12, 1947, she answered a knock on the door of her hotel room. Facing her stood two Swiss police officers. Citing Article 6 of the Swiss Legal Code, they informed her she was under arrest for war crimes involving "murder and torture." If found guilty, she would be facing many years in prison. Anne said little. She packed and paid her bill, and en route to the Meilen police station for booking, she was instructed to stop in Männedorf to collect all papers related to Ravensbrück.

At the time, Anne was the only female Swiss national at large accused of war crimes. There is evidence that the Swiss were relieved that the responsibility for prosecuting Carmen Mory had fallen to the British. She was not someone they wished to have back in Switzerland.

Upon learning of his daughter's arrest, Henry Spoerry placed a call to his British cousin Godfrey Broughton Edge, barrister-at-law. He explained his urgent need for a lawyer to defend Anne against charges of crimes against humanity. While admitting he knew few details, he believed Anne had had some undetermined connection with Carmen Mory, now on trial in Hamburg. He was especially concerned that a supposed confession Anne had made before a court of honor in Paris would be used against her if she came to trial. He assured Edge he would spare no expense to defend his daughter.

Godfrey Edge immediately placed a call to a colleague, barrister David Maxwell Fyfe, soon to be famous for his nimble cross-examination of Hermann Göring at the Nuremberg Nazi war crimes trials. Maxwell Fyfe declined the offer but said he would get back soon with the names of appropriate attorneys. Shortly after, on Maxwell Fyfe's recommendation, Henry Spoerry hired Zurich attorneys Dr. Warren Niederer and Dr. Otto Erminger.

Most embarrassing for the Spoerry family at the time was Zurich and Basel newspapers' coverage of Anne's imprisonment. Drilling into Hamburg testimony, one editorial suggested there had been a provocative relationship between Carmen Mory and Anne. Almost all daily newspapers reported Anne was accused of making lethal injections. The *Neue Zürcher Zeitung* claimed the medical student had a guilty conscience and was an "escape risk." Newspapers, even including the *Sydney Morning News*, described Anne's friend Carmen Mory as unsympathetic and deranged. They recounted how, as the prosecutor, Major S. M. Stewart, was telling the court that all sixteen defendants might be found guilty of "many thousands of murders," Mory smiled broadly. "When one witness, Mrs. Sylvia Salvesen, a Norwegian, said, 'Ravensbrück was hell,' Mory laughed outright and pulled her expensive fur coat more closely around her."

Undeterred, Mory continued her denunciation of Anne as the Block 10 murderess:

MAJOR S. M. STEWART: Did your friend, the Swiss Doctor
　　Spoerry, administer lethal injections?
MORY: There was no poison in the entire camp.
STEWART: That is not an answer.
MORY: Yes, Anne Spoerry administered a lethal injection once.
　　If there was no morphine or other anesthetic available, she
　　administered 10 c.c.m. of air to the heart.

As Anne was being prosecuted by inference and implication in
Hamburg, in her Swiss prison cell she was busy at work on home-
work assigned to her by Dr. Erminger. In tight cursive script, she
wrote a twelve-page document titled "Lebenslauf" (Biography),
recounting the highlights of her life, beginning with birth and
ending with her Zurich medical studies. She distilled her Block 10
experience into one page, focusing mostly on medical conditions,
especially tuberculosis. The "Idiot Room" took up two paragraphs,
with "physiological misery" cited as the common cause of death.
She mentioned Carmen Mory only twice, as Block 10's block elder.
She never admitted a friendship or revealed that they shared the
same bed.

Anne's second assignment was to identify all individuals likely
to present favorable testimony on her behalf. The list ran to thirty-
three women. Conspicuously absent were any Block 10 prisoners.
Anne's final task was to disavow her previous defense of Carmen
Mory. Having promised Hollard a retraction and having now
learned of Mory's deceit, she was unambiguous: "In respect to the
declaration I made about Carmen Mory, I maintain that I acted
only out of a sentiment of pity for the accused Carmen Mory, in
her desperate situation. In particular, I would like to be precise in
saying that, in no way, do I contest the testimonies of three of the
following witnesses: Dr. Louise Le Porz, Jacqueline Héreil, and Violette Lecoq. I especially believe they did not incriminate Carmen
Mory out of personal revenge."

It is unclear whether Anne knew that the three women cited were incriminating her. One called her "more or less her [Mory's] accomplice." Another asserted that "Claude" was hostile toward French and foreign patients. Violette Lecoq said she saw Mory and "Claude" drag a seventeen-year-old Polish girl, recovering from surgery, to the toilets, where they hit her and splashed water on her, "thus advancing her death." Lecoq also recounted how Anne killed a hunchback by injecting air into her heart.

The most devastating testimony against Anne was delivered on January 24, when Hélène Roussel testified that in June 1946 in Paris, before a court of honor, which she served as juror, Anne had confessed to having impersonated a doctor, tortured Block 10 prisoners, and murdered at least one. Later, Violette Lecoq, also a juror at the Court of Honor, said that the presiding judge, Lieutenant Colonel Michel Hollard, had sentenced Anne to exile from France and that Anne had promised to dedicate the rest of her life to the care of lepers.

Over Hollard's reassurances, Anne's Court of Honor confession now resided in the public record. Compounding Anne's despair, in December Carmen Mory had written to Mr. G. de Rham, the Swiss consul general in Hamburg, saying, "AS [Anne Spoerry] is a young ruthless doctor who once dissected her best friend to see what she died of. I took her to me like a mother. She was young and suffered because of the camp regime, while possessing incredible physical strength. She made the deadly injection. She only told me after it had happened, that she had been seen by other inmates . . . Today any feeling ceases to exist now that I've been facing a War Court for an injection which she gave."

By fingering Anne as the one and only killer, Carmen was doing her utmost to assert moral superiority, as in this exchange:

MAJOR STEWART: There is one question which I did not ask you yesterday and that refers to the case of mercy killing which you mentioned yesterday, the injection into the heart administered by Miss Anne Spoerry. When did you hear of this woman having been killed through this injection?

CARMEN MORY: The same day, sir.

MAJOR STEWART: Before or after the injection was given?

CARMEN MORY: After the injection was given.

MAJOR STEWART: And it was Anne Spoerry who told you?

CARMEN MORY: It was Anne Spoerry who told me.

MAJOR STEWART: Did you discuss this case with her?

CARMEN MORY: Yes, I discussed this case with her.

MAJOR STEWART: Did you approve or disapprove of what she has done?

CARMEN MORY: I personally disapproved . . . I told her from the point of view of our religion it is not allowed to give anything to kill a person. I furthermore cited to her the old Hebrew law, 600 years older than Christianity and where there is one paragraph which every doctor knows.

No one was fooled. In the final days, a cluster of Ravensbrück survivors gathered outside the Hamburg courthouse, protesting they had not been given a chance to add their own charges against Carmen Mory. On January 11, 1947, one spoke to the *Hamburger Volkszeitung* correspondent: "For years, we have had to endure terrible crimes of the now accused guards and doctors, sometimes on our own bodies. We despise the beastly methods of these criminals and only have one desire, to see them get the punishment they deserve."

◄○►

After forty-two days of testimony, the Hamburg war crimes tribunal drew to a close. On January 30, 1947, prosecutor Major Stewart presented his summary against Carmen Mory: "Everyone was frightened of her, even the SS. She must be made accountable for the horrible conditions in Block 10, the special section for feeble-minded prisoners. Her role as a spy for the defendant Ramdohr was clearly documented by the witnesses. Numerous witnesses gave evidence of her cruel and horrible punishments . . . At one point she even suggested eliminating the mentally ill."

Dr. Zippel, Carmen Mory's court-appointed lawyer, defended his client by portraying her as a hapless victim of the concentration camp system. Because she was imprisoned through brutal force, she could not be held accountable for the terrible conditions of Block 10. Dr. Zippel even argued that Carmen Mory had been a force for good in Block 10, saying she did not terrorize prisoners in cooperation with the SS. "Instead," Zippel held, "she tried to help in a comradely fashion and tried everything to organize food and clothing for her patients. She cannot be put on the same level of criminality as the others who are accused."

On February 4, 1947, representatives from over ten nations sat in the unheated Hamburg courtroom gallery to hear the court's verdicts and sentences. Outside on the courthouse steps, a large crowd braved glacial winds to clutch at handwritten notes, slipped past the guards.

Before sentencing, the prisoners' defense attorneys were given an opportunity to plea-bargain. Standing before the military tribunal's five sitting judges and one lawyer, they presented their final arguments. Of the fifteen defendants facing possible death sentences (Adolf Winkelmann had died of a heart attack on February 1), seven were women. Of these, four had been guards and three prisoners, each accused of turning *Kapo*. Outside on the courthouse steps, the crowd—mostly Ravensbrück survivors—were unable to stay warm in only wool coats and tattered scarves. Promptly at 3:30, plea bargaining was terminated, and sentencing began. In the gallery and on the courthouse steps, women blew into their hands for warmth and held their breaths for silence.

Within the courtroom, a British Pathé newsreel cameraman recorded the final moments of the trial. The judges' peculiar seating arrangement amplified the tension. For sentencing, all had turned out in dress uniforms and had arranged themselves, sitting with their backs to the stand to avoid eye contact with the defendants. The only member of the law seen by the defendants was a clerk, tasked with solemnly shouting out each sentence.

Wearing stenciled numbers hanging from their necks, prisoners were marched one by one onto the stand. Once a sentence was called out, two guards rotated the defendant off the stand. Each prisoner was sentenced in less than a minute. No one was acquitted. Four received prison terms. The rest, including Carmen Mory, were condemned to death.

Carmen Mory, the most stylish of the fifteen, was the only prisoner seemingly excused from wearing a numbered sign around her neck. Dressed in her signature red fox fur jacket, she held her head high. When the clerk shouted out her sentence—death by hanging—she arched her back and performed the sign of the cross, the single most dramatic moment of the afternoon.

No sooner had she returned to her jail cell than the mercurial Mory wrote a letter to junior counsel and lawyer for the prosecution, Group Captain John W. da Cunha of the Twenty-Third Hussars, then twenty-four years old: "You are young, very young for political and deliberate murder." When da Cunha did not respond to the jailhouse appeal, Mory responded with fury, calling him, "You sly hypocritical British fox."

Before his death in 2006, John da Cunha, now a famed senior barrister, recalled his role in the Hamburg war crimes trial. He noted that even after the passage of fifty-nine years he did not regret sentencing Carmen Mory to death.

Carmen Mory spent much of February trying other maneuvers for a stay of execution. No one on the British legal team was moved to help. Even members of the Mory family were unsympathetic.

In March, Carmen's sister Leontine, nicknamed Tiny, wrote to da Cunha. She gave her full support to the verdict and the sentence and said that in her sister's case death was well deserved.

◄o►

In February 1947, from her cell in Meilen, 450 miles away, Anne was able to follow the Hamburg proceedings. By now her family knew that CROWCASS, the Central Registry of War Criminals and Security Suspects, had charged Anne with "torture." She was the only Swiss woman on its consolidated list. When Anne was lucky to have a newspaper slipped through the bars, she saw that Carmen Mory was now everyone's favorite scapegoat. Even the Germans did not have a kind word. In florid language, a *Neue Zeit* of Berlin editorial linked Mory to the now reviled SS-*Obergruppenführer* Gestapo police chief, Reinhard Heydrich: "She tasted the dark dangers and charms of the 20th century like no other, lived a restless and unbourgeois life like a demonic product of Shakespeare's fantasy and was called the 'Mata Hari of World War II' by the French press . . . She devoured the passions of the human mind." But "her nerves were greedy for bigger and bigger excitement . . . So she dedicated herself to espionage . . . But suddenly an iron curtain fell on Mory's stage and she found herself in Ravensbrück." There "she triggered commotion . . . She had her fingers everywhere and took part in brewing all kinds of threats." She was "feared by the SS because she threatened them with revelations . . . But she was smart and always knew how to gain advantages and connections in the hierarchy of terror that led her right into the middle of the bloody whirlpool."

One month before her date with the hangman, Carmen sent Anne a last letter. Dated February 23, 1947, no document better illustrates the older woman's wiles, as she marshalled conflicting sentiments—forgiveness, love, loathing, self-pity, and revenge—in one blistering last testament:

Chère petite Anne! In the middle of the trial, the prosecutor announced that you were arrested in Switzerland. Instead of seeing you as star witness in my case I had this rather upsetting news.—Your truthful and correct statement was not accepted . . . I know that in our country [Switzerland] you will be acquitted—I don't think that common sense + justice has left them altogether.

I, dearest Anne will be hanged by the neck for murder + ill-treatment of Allied Nationals and for the collective guilt of the SS staff and this in the months Sept–Jan 1944–45 when you and I worked and slaved together—when we strained our last bit of brain to save our fellow-prisoners from death . . . You will have [seen] the written statements of Le Porz, Hereil, Le Coq . . . Without hesitation, they gave perjury on the Bible in front of a British-court. The discrepancies in their statements were so evident . . . I'll spare you the details of the most outstanding case of perjury the 3 women gave—you know them better than I do and when you hear all [those] damned lies they told, you [will] know what a trial it was. I must admit that the so-called camp elite, . . . and others did not say a single nasty word about me—just stated that I had been an ordinary prisoner in Ravensbrück. I do not think that a former C.C. [concentration camp] prisoner alive can say that I have not been a perfect fighter and fellow prisoner for their cause.—Out of 28 prosecution-witnesses the 4 "Françaises" were the only ones to tell tales. I must admit, Anne, it rather amused me to hear their lies. Hereil, hysterical as ever, gave her prof [profession] as a journalist . . . Cheeky bitter liar. Well it is all the same to me, Anne. Only I am really very sorry the British Court was impressed . . .

Who on earth was the woman Roussel who gave evidence against you? Telling about some "French Court of Honor"

where you, Anne, had begged the forgiveness of the French
for your behaviour in the Camp.—That was more than I
could bear—why . . . should you be sorry working and slaving
for the sick ones? For fighting crime and corruption?—
Anyhow I believed not a word of it.

Anne, you are having an awful time and I am sorry about
it. If I had guessed the end effect of this trial I would have
taken the injection you gave to the French gipsy on me. Anyhow she was a dying woman and a transport amongst healthy
prisoners for 4–5 day with a corpse would have been awful . . .
After all, a grown up person has to take the responsibility
for her actions . . . I know in the heart of my hearts that in
France, in regard to the political situation, you were a coward
or not interested in clearing matters. Never mind, my dear. I
don't blame you . . .

I am reading Shaw's St. Joan of d'Arc and I want you to
read his preface. Not that I feel like her, but I admit that her
fate, her trial [and all the] surrounding[s] could have happened a few weeks ago! Do we have to go back to the darkest
Middle Age[s]? If I think of the expression hanging by the
neck, it revolts me, Anne. It seems that all breeding, culture,
education of the 20 Cent. [will] vanish into nothing.

So, Annisch, you know all about me and only you will
know what I suffered . . . My stay in the death cell in France in
1940 seems to me like the Palace-Hôtel . . .

This is my last letter for you, little Anne, and I even do not
know if it will reach you . . . Please do not think that I bear
any grudge in my heart, Anne. It is not everybody's doing to
be a hero. I don't even know for what reason I am sentenced
so I can't tell you if you could have saved me.—You did your
best in the camp and you were a perfect friend. As I took my
beating for you in the spring 1944 I had always hoped that you
would have done the same for me, Anne.

Do not think of me as a wretched broken woman in jail, Anne. Remember me as a happy gay creature full of imagination and sense of humour.—And don't forget death is not the end of all for me . . .

I wish I could give you some of my courage to master life, Anne. I want you to be happy. Do not drag that hysterical female atmosphere of the Concentration Camp with you. Leave it behind. There are still so many beautiful things in life in spite of that awful war. If it is only the scenery above our Swiss-lakes, a trip across our Mountains, music, books, decent company of nice men . . .

For the last time Anne, don't take this horrible event of my death sentence too much at heart. Don't let it spoil your remaining life. Don't waste yourself on useless things . . .

Until my dying hour comes, you will be my friend, Anne, and nothing will change it!

Je t'embrasse milles fois [I hug you a thousand times]. *Tout à toi* [All yours], Carmen.

◄○►

Anne received Carmen Mory's letter in her Swiss cell. There is no record she responded.

CHAPTER 13

RABBLE OF COMMUNIST FOMENTERS

The barbarities of war are seldom committed by abnormal men. The tragedy of war is that these horrors are committed by normal men in abnormal situations.

—"Major Thomas" in the film *Breaker Morant*

During the last weeks of Mory's trial in January 1947, Anne learned to her dismay that the Swiss public prosecutor was preparing his case against her, from testimony supplied by the British prosecution team based in Germany. On the very day Mory and the other fourteen Ravensbrück prisoners were bused back to their cells, the Swiss public prosecutor wrote to the British War Crimes Group requesting related testimony. "Since this office possessed the authority to prosecute Swiss Nationals in Switzerland for crimes committed abroad," the public prosecutor wrote, "it was now intending to investigate the case of Anne (Claude) Spoerry."

From Germany, the prosecuting officer, Group Captain John W. da Cunha, was quick to respond: "This office will be pleased to give you all possible assistance." He had in his possession transcripts citing Anne Spoerry as accomplice to Mory: "You are referred to those passages of the evidence given by the accused MORY which refers to Anne SPOERRY (lethal injections) which appears in the transcript of the trial. You will appreciate that, as it was not proposed to indict Anne SPOERRY, all the witnesses who mentioned her were not questioned any further on the subject." Da Cunha supplied the names and addresses of six women who might prove useful to the prosecutor's case.

On March 7, 1947, Henry Spoerry paid thirty thousand Swiss francs [approximately seven thousand dollars at the time] as bail for his daughter's release from prison. The substantial payment was sufficient to reassure Swiss authorities she would not escape their jurisdiction. At the same time, a French military tribunal had begun to assemble its case against her, also with testimony supplied by da Cunha. Unlike the Court of Honor, it was a governmental body tasked with implementing the Military Code of Justice, which, in Anne's case, involved an offense against honor or duty. Even though Anne was not a member of the military, it charged her with "deeds damaging the French national defense," including the torturing and execution of her compatriots, thus "bringing shame on France."

Once released from prison to the family estate in Männedorf *en liberté provisoire* (provisional freedom), Anne was on a short rein. She was no longer free to leave Switzerland or enter France. As early as 1945, Dean Baudouin of the Medical Faculty of the University of Paris at the Sorbonne had been receiving complaints about her "troubling" behavior in Ravensbrück. One letter, from Louise Le Porz, the only qualified doctor in Block 10 at the time, claimed Anne personally approved the execution of a fellow Frenchwoman, that she had given an injection into the heart of another prisoner, and that she had accompanied Dr. Percy Treite on his rounds, helping to eliminate those who displeased him. "Anne Spoerry habitually presented an indifferent and even hostile manner towards her patients, especially if they were French. She addressed them in German. On numerous occasions she used violence against them, slapping them and striking them with a leather whip—just as the S.S. did. In addition, upon receiving a quantity (insufficient, by the way) of medication from the French Red Cross she kept all of it for her friend [Carmen Mory] who did not need them. Instead the two of them sold the medications."

With her medical ethics under scrutiny, there were now real doubts Anne would ever be certified as a doctor in France and its jurisdictions. Even in turmoil, she was able to conceal her state of high anxiety from all, except her brother. Years later when she came to write her memoirs, *They Call Me Mama Daktari*, she was still on high alert, careful not to breathe a word about Carmen Mory, her imprisonment, or that she had been charged with crimes against humanity. Healing "spiritual wounds" was her blanket depiction of the times.

—◁o▷—

Late in February 1947, the press announced that Carmen and seven others were to be hanged in May at Hamelin. For over a month in her Plön jail cell, the great escape artist held out hope she would receive a last-minute stay of execution from the hangman's noose, but by early April all stratagems were exhausted. Now only a miracle could save her. In the adjoining cell paced her former savior and patron, half-English, half-German Dr. Percival Treite. Through the bars, they formed a pact.

On the morning of April 9, 1947, guards found Dr. Treite, convicted of crimes against humanity (including experiments on Gypsy and Polish girls), dead from a self-inflicted wound. On the night following his suicide, Carmen Mory jimmied a razor blade out from inside the heel of her shoe, and while guards slept, she slit her wrist. Shortly after dawn on April 10, they came upon her still body in a pool of blood, surrounded by a hundred items of clothing, including her signature red fox jacket. The prodigious letter writer never left behind a suicide note.

Nor did Anne ever memorialize her feelings about Carmen's death. At the time, Anne was in a panic as she redoubled her efforts at concealment, sitting out the twenty-one-minute train ride to Zurich in drab clothing, attending medical classes from the back row, and, most evenings, holing up alone at the family house in Männedorf. On May 13, when François heard she had been seen dining by herself in Zurich's *Bahnhof* restaurant, he wrote to Lieutenant Colonel Michel Hollard begging for a waiver from the Court of Honor's banishment from France so Anne could pursue her studies in Paris. Hollard's response was a flat no.

Both the Swiss tribunal and the French military court convened in December 1947. In Switzerland, a chief justice would adjudicate before the Meilen district tribunal, based in Zurich. In Paris, four military officers would decide Anne's fate. The two countries agreed to share testimony entered into evidence. In both jurisdictions, the court's decision would be final, with no right of appeal. Mindful of Anne's ill-considered confession before the Court of Honor, Dr. Erminger informed the courts that his client would not appear in her own defense.

In Zurich, the public prosecutor opened deliberations with a full frontal attack: "The gravest accusation against Mlle. Spoerry was that she assassinated a number of sick patients by means of injection. In Block 10 where there were up to 60 deaths a day she is accused of intentionally having provoked some of these deaths, in giving fellow prisoners excessive doses as well as injections of air."

The public prosecutor also charged Anne with complicity in making death camp selections and exhibiting a "deplorable attitude" toward fellow prisoners by threatening and striking them. Over the course of several days, he called to the stand six former Block 10 prisoners. Elsa Schütz, twenty-seven years Anne's senior, accused both Anne Spoerry and Carmen Mory of eliminating hundreds of prisoners. She described Anne's behavior as "horribly bestial . . . Dr. Claude gave Treite . . . lists of people who had to be suppressed. He gave approval. Dr. Claude did the rest. It didn't really matter as the TB ward was constantly overcrowded . . . Many were very ill, but others Dr. Claude and CM had found unsympathetic. These people were either gassed or else got injections . . . A few hundred female inmates were liquidated this way by Dr. Claude." Mrs. Trynte Duvivier de Beer alleged that as an "accomplice to Carmen Mory" Anne was responsible for mortal injections, maltreatment, and torture. Janine Ceyrolles testified, "I am convinced Anne Spoerry would not have acted so were it not for the influence of Carmen Mory. She appeared to me to be a young woman of bad disposition and I never understood the hatred she exhibited against the French." In addition, Ceyrolles testified she witnessed Anne kill a German dwarf with an injection of air into her heart. When the medical student realized she was being observed, she told Ceyrolles the killing had been "an act of charity."

Ceyrolles also claimed to have witnessed Mory and Spoerry conversing with German guards and gesturing with their hands to single out two healthy Frenchwomen as well as a Belgian woman suffering from Parkinson's disease. The guards took their suggestions and dispatched the prisoners onto a "death transport." The French nurse Violette Lecoq testified she witnessed Anne selecting prisoners for death transports and giving a lethal injection in November 1944 to the hunchback and another in December to a "mentally defective." Simone Loche attested that she saw Mory and "Dr. Claude" steal medicine for their personal use. The final witness for the prosecution was Dr. Louise Le Porz, who had seen Anne slapping, whipping, and throwing cold water onto prisoners. "This medical student presented a perfectly odious attitude to both French and foreign patients, injuring them and often depriving them of food." More revelations about Anne dispensing mortal injections would follow, reported the *Tages-Anzeiger* in Zurich.

Anne's counsel Dr. Otto Erminger took the stand, calling Anne's detractors "politically inspired . . . communists." He then focused on Anne's exemplary behavior after leaving Block 10. The true Anne, he asserted, was a model caregiver who, during the January 1945 typhus epidemic, "inoculated almost the entire camp . . . There exists no proof that on this occasion the accused was driven by acts of extermination." Dr. Erminger added, "My client contests any fatal injections and declares that she only dispensed normal dose injections for diagnostic purposes, for healing and to alleviate pain." Had Anne made this assertion in her own words, one suspects her case would have been stronger. During the proceedings she was not to be seen.

Next, Dr. Erminger called to the stand witnesses who testified to Anne's good behavior: Hildegard Paechtel, Odette Allaire (later Walling), Dorothy de Ripper, Odette Fabius, Allene Zerling, Jean Fabien Courtaud, Dr. Zimmet, Sima Zepchi, and Nicky Poirier. Numerically, the prosecution's witnesses outdid the defense's by a ratio of two to one. Notably, not one of these defense witnesses had known Anne in Block 10. They could only testify to her activities during 1945 in Blocks 6 and 11 when, removed from Mory's influence, she had been an exemplary caregiver. Antoinette Lenoir declared Anne had saved her from the gas chamber. Sima Zepchi told the story how Anne had concealed six Jewish prisoners from the SS guards and a "death transport." Madame G. F. L. Brandt, seventeen years older than Anne, said that while she had never met Anne, she believed she was undergoing "her Calvary" against "this rabble of Communist fomenters." In her summary, she asked the court to acquit Anne of all charges as a matter of "sacred honor."

Four women who had never known Anne in Ravensbrück—Kate

Mangold, Mirz'l Steinhage, Claire Wohl, Auguste Gérard Besier—made the case that anyone bearing a resemblance to the monster described by the prosecution would have been instantly recognizable everywhere in the camp. Because they had never even heard her name, they concluded she had been unjustly charged. Martha Soboll (later van Och), a German living in Holland, was Anne's most vigorous champion. While she had never known her in Block 10, she had seen Anne elsewhere and believed "in her heart" that she was guiltless. Martha also maintained Carmen Mory's innocence. While ignorant of the charges brought against her in Hamburg, she was certain Mory's death sentence had been a miscarriage of justice.

Dr. Erminger agreed. He claimed that Carmen Mory's death sentence had been ill-considered and unjust, even though handed down by six judges. Mory, he argued, had been a victim of the concentration camp system. As *Blockova,* she had been forced to follow the orders of SS guards Binz and a nurse, Elisabeth Marschall. The Hamburg war crimes tribunal had "misunderstood" her and had erred in finding her guilty. Even in death, Mory should be retried, and if proven innocent, "then Anne Spoerry is just as innocent."

Under Swiss law, challenging the decision of another judiciary was permissible. It is reasonable to suppose Dr. Erminger was playing to pro-German sentiments in his country, especially in Swiss German–speaking cantons. For a while, his strategy even appealed to the chief justice, who told the court that Anne's failure to intervene to save an individual from gas chamber selections did not rise to a crime. "Swiss law," he observed, "does not recognize war crimes or crimes of 'collective fault.'" Buoyed by this finding, on December 23, 1947, Dr. Erminger approached the bench to ask that the case against Anne be dismissed. His request was instantly rejected on the grounds that the court had yet to consider other outstanding charges against his client.

In January 1948, Dr. Erminger gave up some ground by admitting that Anne Spoerry's manner might have been "brusque and sometimes combative" especially in the case of the "Lunatic Room." But such harsh measures, he argued, were essential to calm the insane. Erminger argued that even if his client had, at times, deferred to Carmen Mory, Anne should be excused from all charges because she was simply following a "blameless" woman, unjustly prosecuted by politically motivated women.

Might there be some credibility to assertions that Carmen and Anne had been victims of a Communist conspiracy? First in Hamburg, then in Zurich, later in the French military court, defense counsels argued that French Communists had vilified Mory and Spoerry because they were unrepentant "anti-Bolsheviks." In 2011, this question was raised with Dr. Louise Le Porz in her home in Bordeaux. She did not pause to respond: "I was not a Communist, either before or after the war . . . Nor Lecoq, Héreil, and Ceyrolles. The only one who was a Communist was Simone Loche. It was too simple to dismiss us as part of some Communist conspiracy. That was not our interest in any way."

While others used the Communist argument to shield Anne, she never availed herself of it. In her notarized declaration rebuking her earlier defense of Mory, she publicly declared she would "in no way contest the testimonies of . . . Dr. Louise Le Porz, Jacqueline Héreil and Violette Le Coq." Responding to her four French military justices, in respect to her actions in Block 10, she described her relationship with Carmen Mory in these words: "On my return from the work camp of Zwodau, I was called before her, sick in the infirmary [pleurisy] . . . Once recovered, she took up her post as chief of the Block and there in September, I joined her as a doctor. I had the weakness to be led by this woman of remarkable intelligence to the point that I found myself, so to speak, 'spellbound' by the seduction of her intelligence."

Later the permanent military tribunal dispatched a "judicial inspector" to Switzerland to verify her astonishing admission. He reported, "Mademoiselle Spoerry has quite frankly accepted having been wrong to have allowed herself to be influenced and that she compromised her duties of being a French doctor in Block 10. Anne Spoerry admits that her activities hurt the health of her companions."

Why did Anne freely admit wrongdoing to the French military tribunal? Either she believed the evidence against her was so damning that her best defense was to come clean and await the sympathy of her judges, or after many painful deliberations she had simply given up and was willing to accept French military justice.

It is reasonable to assume Anne Spoerry made these honest declarations before the French military court without her lawyers' consent. By now, they were well aware of their client's impulsive, self-destructive streak. While awaiting the court's judgment, she had returned to Paris, violating the Court of Honor sentence and risking an encounter with Lieutenant Colonel Hollard or other Court of Honor jurors. This willful action had the effect of undermining her case while upsetting the equanimity of her family. The final straw was confessing to France's judicial inspector, effectively discounting the heavy financial and psychic burden borne by her father in her legal defense.

In September 1948, François and Henry told Anne to meet them in Mulhouse. Henry reported that Dr. Erminger was of the opinion she would be acquitted in Switzerland. The outcome of the French military tribunal, however, was not as certain. No member of the legal team was willing to wager odds how it would be decided. Meanwhile, new accusations were emerging at the disciplinary board at the Université de Paris School of Medicine. After Dean Baudouin had reported receiving multiple letters urging him not to matriculate Anne on account of her Block 10 behavior, the board had taken up the case. To Simone Loche, Baudouin had responded, "It is sadly obvious that the person in question, Anne S., is no more than a criminal."

With few other remedies, François, Henry, and François's father-in-law, Anto Besse, had settled on an escape plan, which Anne embraced the moment she was told. Within the month, she would sail on *El Hak* for Aden with Monsieur and Madame Besse. There she would find work and, with luck, a future. During the few weeks remaining before *El Hak* sailed, she was sworn to secrecy. If the permanent military judges got wind of her intentions, they would surely instruct the police to intercept her.

For a month, Anne prepared in secret, hurrying to complete all remaining university requirements. She said good-bye only to her mother, François, and her sisters, Thérèse and Martine. Until her final day in Europe, she lived in dread that her passport would be confiscated and she taken into custody.

On October 10, 1948, Henry Spoerry traveled to Marseille to see his daughter off on the *El Hak*. His plan was for her to slip all traces of her past for a far-off land where great distances would confound memory. Somewhere in a jurisdiction far from France, she would find her way, escape revenge, and, in some still-to-be-contrived way, live up to the honor of the Spoerry name.

CHAPTER 14   *THE SCORECARD*

For half a century in Africa, Anne's fearful reign of silence served her as disguise. She had chosen an inspired strategem to keep all Africa in the dark about her true identity. Who would know that beneath her bravery and self-confidence she was masking ruinous lapses of character, had bent cherished family principles, subverted the Hippocratic oath, all for love? Anne's inspired African camouflage of silence and temper bought her time. If pressed, she might have reasoned that her offenses were mere foibles, the petty misjudgments of youth, and, in time, would be dismissed. But that seems implausible. In Ravensbrück while Anne was not evil incarnate on the order of Heydrich, Bormann, Eichmann, Mengele, and Binz, she did indeed turn *Kapo* against her own people. The Nazi pledge she signed was not just to please Carmen, master of expediency, but to save her life.

One tries to imagine Anne's response had someone in Africa discovered the truth and brought her to account. How would she have defended herself? Might she have said, "Total rubbish. I was acquitted both in France and in Switzerland"? If so, why then did she institute a lifetime embargo on the subject of war? Why did she flee France? What about her public confession at the Court of Honor and her secretive admission to the permanent French military court?

East Africa, far from Europe, was Anne Spoerry's flag of convenience. "Never explain, never complain," she once said to me on another matter. While she had no difficulty hushing all journalists, could she control her own dark thoughts when she was alone? In the loneliness of the African night did she ever hear howls coming from the "Idiot Room" or recall the hunchback or the Polish girl with the beautiful voice or relive the pleasure of Carmen's special ways?

—◇—

By the early 1970s, Anne had grown confident her problems were over. Having lost Miss Mary, the keeper of all secrets, she had grown in wisdom and perfected her vow of secrecy. By now, she might have felt that she had outrun all postwar traps and that her long years exiled from Europe had rendered her reborn. Now it was time to emerge from up-country isolation. In Nairobi, she began availing herself more and more of the Muthaiga Club, which offered inexpensive accommodation whenever friends' guest rooms were occupied. The ocher-red muddle of buildings comforted her with its colonial eccentricities and the fellowship of its membership—mostly men, some titled, a few filthy rich, many young, and a fair number, like her, compulsive adventurers. Farmers and ranchers made Muthaiga their base on visits to Nairobi whenever they needed to buy spare parts or to enjoy a "hooley." It was a rare occasion when Anne failed to encounter a familiar face in the reading room or lounge. Rarely did she have to dine alone. More often she joined other tables or made up her own party with friends from the north or abroad. Muthaiga served a dependable curry and decent claret and was more discreet than Nairobi restaurants. Anne had no issue with its monastic accommodations—lumpy mattress on squeaky springs and a sink against the wall. From her bedroom window, in the mornings, the sight of sacred ibis patrolling the club's verdant lawns and rambling gardens was restorative. Anne was often the first at breakfast in the courtyard, radiant with Africa's dawn. With her bulging briefcase by her feet and her notebook beside the fruit basket, she was already mapping out her day's flight plan.

◄○►

Anne's grueling flying routine provided distraction from memory. In her early Flying Doctors days, much of her work was centered on Kenya's southwest, in Masailand and around Lake Victoria. Later she extended her range, first into the Northern Frontier, to include ten mission clinics and hospitals, from the Uaso Nyiro River north to the Ethiopian and Somali frontiers. After Miss Mary's death, Anne also began a regular flight east, along a strip of coastline from Lamu north to the Somali frontier. By the 1980s, her empire had grown to a territory as large as England, Scotland, and Wales combined.

When she first began with the Flying Doctors Service in 1964 Anne often flew five safaris a month. By the 1970s she had trimmed these to three, each one four or five days. Once a month she gave 5Y-AZT a week off for maintenance while she attended to bookkeeping.

Anne depended on personal income to survive. From her own notes, AMREF paid her an annual salary of 600,000 shillings (about $10,000) and reimbursed her for her flying time at the rate of 3,500 shillings ($60) an hour, amounting to about 644,000 shillings, or about $11,000 a year. In addition to the payment of all aircraft maintenance and fuel expenses, her take-home pay for the year was a paltry $21,000, including vacation time. Like most French, Anne took August off for *congé*, joining her family in the South of France.

The rest of the year was all work. In Masailand, Anne teamed up with British nursing sisters Winifred Robinson and Rosemary Sandercock, affectionately known within AMREF as "Robbie and Rosemary." Working in concert with the Mobile Medical Unit, Anne flew in supplies for one medical student, one dresser, one driver-mechanic, and two camp attendants whose jobs were to operate a one-ton truck, Land Rover, ambulance, water trailer, and safari trailer. In the early years, the Anne, Robbie, and Rosemary trifecta was the principal medical lifeline for the Masai. In one year alone, the team treated ailments among 12,329 adults while vaccinating 30,496 children against tuberculosis, smallpox, and polio. Anne's productivity was nothing short of astonishing.

After all the disappointments of Ol Kalou, the Flying Doctors Service was Anne's last African stand. With each passing year, she drove herself harder, finding comfort and oblivion in herculean numbers. At the end of 1972, she proudly noted she had flown 11,249 miles and her team had vaccinated over 120,000 patients. In one Northern Frontier mission, Marsabit, she personally attended to 1,093 patients. Seven years later at the same dispensary, she cared for 1,783. By 1981, she was running sixty-four clinics in all, attending to 17,722 patients, and immunizing 47,957—all noted in scrupulously detailed records.

During Anne's three and a half decades with the Flying Doctors, she logged over eight thousand hours of flight time, much of it alone at the controls. Those many flying hours worked out to more than 250 lifetime weeks spent in the Northern Frontier, 225 in Masailand and Rusinga Island on Lake Victoria, and at least 300 with the coastal peoples between Lamu and the Somali frontier.

Even today, Nicky Blundell Brown, AMREF's historian, believes Anne's record will never be broken.

Anne's official reports of her Flying Doctors work made for colorful reading. In 1971, as an example, she noted how while tending to 3,770 patients in Masailand, she built one airstrip, renovated another, and extended yet another to make it safe for others to land there. In that same year, she hosted an Italian photographer, two American doctors with their families, one French doctor, five guests, and three medical students. On one occasion she barely averted a catastrophe: "A sudden storm ripped our tent and for half an hour we clung to the tables and held to the drugs in the driving rain to keep them from being blown away by a 50 knot wind." Anne's breezy style could not disguise her pleasure in besting adversity.

After my profile of Anne was published in January 1981, our friendship grew, and I made a point of seeing her every time I visited Nairobi. When we dined together, she invariably entertained me with tales of derring-do. "In Dukana," she once told me, "I landed in the desert. I was thinking how beautiful it looked with so many flowers after the rain. So I landed on the old runway, only to discover that when I tried to turn, my wheels sunk into the wet sand. It was quite unpleasant. Thirty policemen helped us push. Then we unloaded, treated people for two hours, then loaded and just managed to take off."

Anne usually assumed that I, a bit of an adventurer in my own right, required tales of near-death experiences to stay interested. "In Illeret," she continued, with sangfroid, "we had a serious epidemic. I saw ten—all paralyzed and suffering from bedsores. At first I thought it was meningitis, but it turned out to be brucellosis—a blood parasite they got from drinking milk. That's why I now insist on having my tea with boiled milk."

"Pass the coffee," Anne said. Then, changing her mind, she instead poured herself a glass of red wine while continuing the monologue: "I had lots of TB and hyena bites. One child had his skull crushed in, with his cheekbone, eyelids, and nose all gone. I brought him to Michael Wood, who did a splendid job reconstructing him. That same year in North Horr we had lion bites. One chap lost both buttocks. I treated him with masses of antibiotics, and he made a fine recovery."

Whenever I interrupted with a story of my own, Anne usually found a way of returning the conversation to her preferred zones, non sequiturs be damned. One evening at the Muthaiga Club, she lost her train altogether: "I never wanted to practice in Europe, since I have never had to think about money. I came to Africa after *the interesting thing.*" When I asked her to define "interesting thing," she responded with another detour: "I don't know whether I would feel the same about it. West Africa? No. Nor am I drawn to South America. I've been to India, and while it's a fascinating place, I have no interest in settling there. Australia would be my second choice, were it not for Australians. Africa simply is *gripping.*"

To make her point, she recounted what happened on August 1, 1982, a Sunday when she was at Sabukia with a young French doctor as guest. At breakfast she happened to turn on the wireless for the news and, to her astonishment, learned there had been a coup d'état in Nairobi. She immediately called a neighbor for details: the air force had taken up arms against the central government, and in response President Daniel arap Moi had declared a state of emergency, shut down the capital, and forbidden all civilian air traffic. Anne now turned on her single-sideband radio to see if AMREF had any comment. No sign of life, except that over the crackle she heard an SOS from a hospital on Rusinga Island in Lake Victoria, some 250 miles away. There, the medical officer was explaining to anyone on the emergency band that two girls had had their faces bitten by a rabid dog. Anne scrambled for supplies, rushed to her Peugeot with the young doctor in tow, and reached the Sabukia airstrip in record time. "I was the only doctor available, and by sheer good luck I had a supply of antirabies vaccine in my paraffin-powered fridge."

Immediately Zulu Tango was airborne, heading due west, climbing through heavy cloud cover to avoid detection by Nairobi radar. At nearly twenty thousand feet Anne attained the plane's serviceable ceiling limit—an uncomfortable altitude when, without oxygen, pilot and passenger become short of breath and light-headed. Because there were no other voices on the aviation bands, she believed hers was the only plane airborne over Kenya at the time. Above Lake Victoria, she spotted Rusinga Island. Her descent was ear popping and her landing fast and hard. She jammed on the brakes when she saw an old man approaching on a bicycle and, through the open door, handed off the vaccine. After instructing him how to administer the shots, she pressed the throttle to the firewall and, once airborne, climbed like a fighter pilot. Never daring to use the radio, she went unnoticed by anyone in the Kenyan air ministry. Once arrived back in Sabukia, the two doctors jumped from the plane and let out a war whoop. They had successfully outsmarted the authorities and helped save the lives of two children.

At one of our regular Nairobi dinners, Anne told me how, in the bush, she had learned much from local witch doctors and had no intention of "stopping the practitioners of traditional African medicine . . . They are our allies." Anne said she owed a debt to traditional medicine, having learned from herbalists the efficacy and power of plants.

Anne's lifelong fascination with tribal Africa comes to life in her field notes. This one is from 1983: "My unit went to the Uasso Kedong where an important Masai ceremony was being held. It occurs only at the beginning of a new age grade and is called 'The Horn of the Bull.' Uncircumcised young men have to show their skill in catching a fierce bull out of a herd of heifers and take it away. The youngster who first catches the right horn of the bull is the hero of the day. The ceremony attracts a great number of Masai from distant areas." Anne, Robbie, and Rosemary used the occasion to treat every Masai *moran* (warrior) they encountered. For Anne it was another record-setting day.

Six years after beginning work with the Flying Doctors, Anne accepted a Nairobi lecture engagement when in 1970 she spoke to the Caledonian Society of Kenya (Ladies Branch). Her speech was disappointing, with an embarrassingly small turnout. She concluded that she had no future engaging in motivational lecture circuits. Five years later, in September 1975, she relented, accepting an invitation from the Norwegian Association of Nairobi. This time her subject was witchcraft, and turnout was impressive. Her message was arresting: because 85 percent of Kenyans live far from modern medical centers, they have no choice but to turn to sorcerers and witch doctors for medical care. These local caregivers believe all diseases derive from four causes: revenge of neglected ancestral spirits, ill will of another person, malicious preparations of a sorcerer, or "the evil eye of a witch." Such beliefs, according to Anne, were fine. Traditional healers were not a threat to her and should not be to any other Western medical caregiver. On more than one occasion, she even teamed up with witch doctors, sorcerers, and herbalists. They were, after all, the ancestors of modern doctors: "We must make use of all good types of traditional healers . . . The ultimate goal is to eliminate evil witchcraft and upgrade ancient healing traditions to integrate modern and traditional medicine." Witch doctors are "often very good at psychiatry. I don't worry if my patients, who are in need of confidence and tranquillity, use them." Anne held to a belief that tribalism, in all its brutality, was better than the alternative—urban slums, unemployment, and crime. Her job was to treat patients effectively, not to reengineer society.

Anne's outspoken embrace of witchcraft ensured her popularity as a speaker before white audiences. During the Q&A session at a breakfast meeting of the Kenya Museum Society, a member in the rear of the audience—a small woman, not known to Anne—asked her if she would care to speak about her experiences during the war. Anne paused long enough to close her notebook. "Another time," she said. She then thanked her host and walked off the stage.

Anne gave her last presentation in September 1995, before the Norfolk hotel's Women's Group. Her words displayed a change of mind about traditional medicine. Some tribal customs now met with her absolute disapprobation. She reserved her indignation for the practice of clitoridectomy (surgical removal of the clitoris) and infibulation (removal of the inner and outer labia and the suturing of the vulva). She paused gravely and then, much to the horror of her listeners, parted the flap of a ragged envelope and removed a finely whittled tree branch at whose end was sewn a broken razor blade. "This is a Pokot surgical instrument," she announced solemnly. Waving it before her awed listeners, she urged, "Study it. It has many applications—on the lighter side, for one, uvulectomies—to stop snoring. Its primary function, however, is not going down the mouths of old men but somewhere else with young girls. I leave all this to your imagination." Anne then handed the tool to a prim lady on her right and watched it, still bloodied, make its way around rows of aghast women. Her show-and-tell brought the presentation to a close amid thunderous applause.

Following her inexpert answers to Barry Wynne's cross-examination in 1967, when she blurted out that she had once encountered the famous Carmen Mory, Anne begged off all requests for further interviews. But in the early 1970s she began to relax this self-imposed rule. In the future, she would stick to a well-rehearsed script, painting herself as the young adventurous ingenue who, after an ocean voyage, found her calling in Africa, practicing medicine, farming, flying, and chalking up one adventure after another. Even with her blanket exclusion of most of the 1940s, journalists were still able to piece together lustrous profiles of the one-of-a-kind flying doctor.

With each article, Anne's legend grew. In 1992, Annie Kouchner wrote "In the Good Hands of Mama Daktari" for the magazine *Destins*. In it, she predicted that the moment Anne stopped doing her work, she would die: "For thirty years A.M.R.E.F. has been her reason for life, and the service of the Flying Doctors, the most beautiful finial in this non-profit, her cherished child. The Flying Doctors undertake 400 missions each year. But times are changing. More and more specialists prefer to work in large western hospitals. Not Anne . . . who maintains the great tradition of the bush. The indefatigable *Mama Daktari*."

By 1995, Dr. Tom Rees, the Flying Doctors' co-founder, claimed that smallpox had nearly been eradicated in Kenya, in large part because of Anne. He also was convinced she would achieve similar results with polio vaccines. He calculated that on the Kenyan coast alone Anne had, so far, inoculated over 100,000 children. On average, every year across Kenya, she treated more than 10,000 patients and vaccinated 30,000. In Rees's opinion, Dr. Anne Spoerry single-handedly performed the work of a hospital. Applying conservative estimates, and distilling her lifetime work into thirty active Africa years, he estimated that she had already cared for no fewer than 1.2 million patients—for any other doctor, an unimaginable feat.

Flying her own plane and setting her own schedule partially explain Anne's achievement. Dr. Rees added that it would never have been possible without her military efficiency, gift for diagnosis, and knack for making on-the-spot medical judgments. He explained Anne's staggering output through her exceptionalism, calling her "one in a million." Neither he nor other colleagues knew the dark truth: that, above all, Anne was driven by a lifetime of unmet obligations.

CHAPTER 15

THE WRONG SIDE OF THE
BINOCULARS

After Anne's father's death late in 1966, fortune grew alongside fame. With characteristic Spoerry restraint, Anne disguised her wealth, preferring to be viewed by her Kenyan neighbors as a pennypincher. She drove a battered Peugeot and wore faded bush jackets and old denim jeans. Whenever it was necessary to wear a dress, she appeared in her only one, suitable for all formal occasions. Her nephew Yves described it as "Margaret Thatcher blue."

In the late 1960s, Anne had defied fiduciary wisdom by placing a large chunk of her inheritance into one investment. The venture consisted of a French seaside tract of land, selected by her architect brother. François's plan was to transform a marshy river delta, four miles west of St.-Tropez on the French Riviera, into a yachting community. He envisioned each villa with an individual jetty for its owner's yacht, all polished brightwork, spotless teak, and neatly folded spinnaker. A forerunner of the European Urban Renaissance movement, François wanted his Venice-like community to reflect the soft palette and classic lines of a timeless Mediterranean village. With little prompting, Anne turned over much of her inheritance to him.

Almost from day one, Port Grimaud was a success; and, for Anne, it was an inspired investment. In the 1970s and again in the 1990s, she redoubled her commitment by investing in the construction of more canals and villas. With each outlay, Anne's equity and dividends grew. Her nephew Bernard declared that in her mid-fifties, "Anne began swimming in cash."

Anne never made a show of her financial acumen. Quietly, she used some of her windfall to speculate in Kenyan real estate. One investment was a property in the Nairobi suburb of Langata. While it would not become her home, many of her friends purchased parcels in it and built homes of their own. Her real estate intuition proved prescient, and the value of Langata land doubled and then redoubled.

Early in the 1990s, François chastised his sister for living *beneath* her means in Nairobi. He urged her to ease her situation by buying Jack and Doria Block's sprawling mansion, not far from the Muthaiga Club. Jack and his brother, Tubby, had been the city's most prominent tycoons, their family fortune derived from a landmark Kenyan hotel chain that included the Norfolk, the New Stanley, Keekorok Lodge, and the Mount Kenya Safari Club. Now, after Jack's tragic death in a fishing accident and with Doria in failing health, François urged Anne to purchase the mock-Tudor, mullion-windowed manor house where the glamorous Blocks had once entertained Stewart Granger, Jonathan Kenworthy, Peter Beard, Christie Brinkley, and Veruschka.

At first, Anne balked, claiming she was far too busy to care for an estate with so many guest rooms. As for its pool, she would never be caught dead in a bathing suit. In the end, François prevailed, and in 1992 Anne, survivor of Ravensbrück, became the chatelaine of a stately colonial mansion. Each evening from her terrace, she looked past the pool house into vestiges of the Karura Forest, alive with the cries of monkeys. And from the ancient kitchen came the soft murmurs of her large staff. Perhaps the grandeur of the house recalled 1 Rue du Sundgau, where Anne once played general with wooden soldiers.

Anne's buying spree did not end with Nairobi. At the time she bought the Block mansion, she was already on her way to becoming a major landholder at the coast. Anne's Indian Ocean infatuation was born in 1962 on her first visit to the remote island of Lamu. At the time, the island could only be reached by boat, and the sole hotel was Petley's Inn, a four-story walk-up on the waterfront. Its owner was the redoubtable Major Pink, who, in order to "maintain standards," barred the door of his establishment to guests he deemed beneath his station. Learning that Anne was "of good breeding," he admitted her. His approval conveyed little honor because the beds were lice infested and the ablution facilities limited to one "long drop" toilet at the end of a poky corridor.

About the time of Miss Mary's death, Anne had initiated a campaign vaccinating coastal communities north from the island of Lamu to the Somali frontier. Soon after she "discovered" Lamu, an airstrip was cleared between baobabs on the nearby island of Manda. Each evening, she flew back from her island rounds, tied down her aircraft, walked through the mangroves onto the jetty, boarded a *jahazi* (small dhow), and crossed the channel to Lamu to disembark at Petley's. Most evenings, after her shower, she sought out the company of one of the island's eccentrics—James de Vere Allen, the entertaining and erudite curator of the Lamu Museum, who lived alone in the heart of the old medieval town in a beautifully restored eighteenth-century Swahili palace. To reach it, Anne had learned to navigate Lamu's labyrinthine alleys and open sewers. Invariably, Jim met her at his door, then led her to his air-conditioned library, heavy with scholarly journals and Somali headrests. Here he held court, enchanting Anne with accounts of ancient coastal peoples who, as long ago as the tenth century, were reading learned tomes, practicing modern hygiene, and dining off Chinese porcelain. With a prestidigitator's flourish of the hand, Jim would then lead Anne into his fragrant walled garden, decorated with Tang bowls, then up narrow steps to the roof for a majestic view of oceangoing dhows, recently arrived from Basra and Al Mukalla, the port Anne had once visited east of Aden. From Lamu, these lateen-rigged wooden ships, laden with dates, would sail south in search of new cargoes in Mombasa and Zanzibar.

Jim charmed Anne so completely that soon she craved a Swahili home all her own. He introduced her to Shella, an unkempt village, two miles to the south, cluttered beneath a towering sand dune where the wind exposed human skulls left behind after a nineteenth-century battle. After wandering the remains of this forgotten civilization, she made a cash offer for a heap of ancient walls and recessed arches. Knowing that Jim scraped by on a measly museum wage, Anne hired him to do her historic restoration.

Shella possessed other attractions, especially a pristine fourteen-mile beach and the Peponi Hotel, run by a charming Danish widow who had once farmed not far from Ol Kalou. Anne suspected the hotel would supply her with a steady stream of entertaining visitors from Kenya, America, and Europe.

Anne set out to claim Shella as her own. Soon after she stood to admire her restored palace, four stories high, she began purchasing adjacent properties to protect her Indian Ocean view. Within six years, she would become the single largest landholder in Shella. Soon after she began her building campaign, wealthy and titled European sun worshippers followed. Shella went on a building spree. When Jim's health declined and as her empire grew, she passed the design work over to her nephew Bernard, an architect like his father.

A European doctor in Lamu was a most welcome addition to the small resident expat community. During leisure moments, after flying between coastal communities, Anne was available to look after her neighbors' ailments—prescribing paregoric for "dickie guts" and dispensing quinine, usually mixed with gin, to counter malaria shakes.

The woman who had once survived on rutabaga soup now threw gourmet dinner parties. As often as possible, Anne's chef served fresh crab steeped in ginger, garlic, and lime, arugula from Sabukia, and bottles of Sancerre Anne had included in her medical supplies in Nairobi, strapped down on the rear seat of Zulu Tango.

A regular guest at Anne's table at the coast was her neighbor George Fegan, a successful retired Irish varicose vein surgeon, or phlebologist. His introduction to Lamu had been even quainter than Anne's. In 1976 in London, as he was preparing to leave Ireland and sell his old masters collection at Sotheby's, he encountered my then girlfriend, Daphne, who knew Kenya through our travels. Hearing of his interest in relocating to a sunny land, she suggested he explore Lamu. When he said he would give it a look, Daphne presented him with a bottle of Tanqueray gin and a topper of Angostura bitters to take to our mutual friend, an elderly Englishman, then living in Shella. Emerging from the airport in Nairobi, George, unaware of Kenya's distances and roads, gamely hailed a taxi and instructed the driver to take him to Lamu. After a battering 290-mile drive, George took the ferry to the island, found Shella, and promptly handed over the libations to our friend Latham Leslie-Moore. George then had a look around and in no time was so enchanted by the island he chose to stay. Eventually, Dr.

Fegan would become nearly as great a landholder as Anne. Shella remained George's home the rest of his life. He claimed that his long morning beach walks, followed by a restorative "G&T" on the Peponi's veranda added a decade to his life. Visitors to the island regularly sought him out for his colorful stories; Anne called him "the Irish poet."

It surprised no one that these two aging doctors soon became fast friends. Anne and George had much in common—plentiful savings, a passion for Shella real estate, pleasure in lively conversation, and memories of war. In George, Anne found urbanity and charm. Conversely, George admired Anne's brio, tenaciousness, and no-nonsense style. Whenever he heard Zulu Tango buzz the rooftops of Shella, he followed a time-honored drill—rising from his postprandial nap, digging out his best shirt, wrapping his waist in a decorative *kikoy,* securing a bottle of Irish whiskey from the drink cabinet—to await Anne's hand-delivered invitation to dinner.

It is a possibility, but no certainty, that Anne confided in George about her wartime troubles because she knew he was discreet to a fault. If indeed she opened up, one imagines she resorted to her default style of sweeping, sanitized platitudes, with all the difficult bits left out. George was of a generation that never abused confidences of the confessional. Like so many who had lived through war, he knew when to listen, when not to ask.

The friendship between George and Anne was so enduring that on Anne's death, George presented the grave site he had purchased for himself to the Spoerry family. In return, the Spoerrys bought him an adjoining plot. Through this exchange, Anne was buried in George's grave. Later, on George's death in 2007, his heirs made the error of not checking his will before interring him. As a result, they had to dig up his grave, reopen the casket, and, next to George's body, lay a large bottle of Irish whiskey and two glasses—one for him, the other for Anne.

―◦―

In Nairobi, Anne had other great friends, almost as close. Guy and Betty Robin, a stylishly dressed French couple, liked to entertain in their Tudor-style house prominently situated not far from the Muthaiga Club. When Anne met them in September 1976, she discovered that Betty was also from Alsace. So began a long and close friendship. Bernard Spoerry, Anne's nephew, held a dim view of it, believing the Robins were drawn to Anne because her celebrity would attract Nairobi's luminaries to their parties. More likely, the alliance went both ways, with Anne needing the companionship of the Robins during her overnights in Nairobi. For nearly seven years, before Anne bought her own house, she kept a room in theirs. Betty claimed that when Anne first came to stay, she urged her to lay claim to one of their stylishly decorated guest rooms. Instead, Anne chose a small drab anteroom with one narrow bed, much like the one in her Spartan bedroom in Sabukia.

The Robins were among several of Anne's friends I sought out for insights into her time in Ravensbrück. Betty said Anne never mentioned the war to her, at least not directly. The subject arose only once, of its own accord: "One day, she was sitting here . . . and I said, 'Anne, you're putting on weight. Let me get you on a diet.'

"Anne looked at me and shouted, 'On a diet? You have no idea what it means to have nothing to eat. Never again will I not eat what I want. Do you know what it means to die because you are hungry?'

"I felt so bad. I never dared say another word. So what if she was a little bit fat." From that time forward, Betty lived in fear of Anne's temper: "You know I had to become fierce myself just to save my own life with Anne."

Betty's husband, Guy, she told me, did talk with Anne about the war. When I sat with him in their stylish drawing room, he acknowledged their conversations of war, but the substances of what they said, he sternly announced, he would take to his grave. Never would he disclose to the likes of me, or any other probing journalist, a word his friend Anne had spoken. Kitted out in a tan turtleneck and matching, tailored tweed jacket, he chose his words carefully: "So many times Anne and I have breakfast on that veranda, watching the sunrise. From those times, I keep a wonderful souvenir of an exceptional person. Anne's life in Africa was a rebirth. Don't forget that. Please take note that of all the things we discussed on that veranda only 10 percent was about the war and Anne's troubles . . . How many people from all those European countries have faced the Nazis, hmm? Why her? There are too many people looking at Anne through the wrong side of the binoculars." By now, Guy Robin had built himself to a fine rage. When I continued probing, his fury was palpable. He slammed his fist on the coffee table, rose out of the couch, and strode from the room, leaving me to make my own way out.

There were others in whom Anne might have confided. Tony Fitzjohn for one. Tony was a Kenya legend, famous for working alongside George Adamson habituating lions to the wild. Perhaps Anne looked on this young man as a kindred spirit, as an iconoclast cut from the same cloth as she was. After pondering my question, Tony recalled only one instance when Anne opened up to him. The two were sitting out a rainstorm beside their airplanes on a remote bush strip. For a few hours beside an anthill, without danger of being overheard, they talked freely. Tony began by revealing his past, much of it steamy. Watching the rain wallop their aircraft, he revealed to Anne his failures and disappointments. When he had completed his confessional, he turned to her: "How about you? Any regrets?"

"What do you mean?"

"World War II."

Anne stayed silent for a bit. Finally, she said "despairingly," according to Tony, "It was a survival thing." She did not wish to expand any further.

I also interviewed Leonora Semler, an unlikely friend of Anne's because Anne had a reputation for snubbing Germans. Leonora, once lionized for her classic Aryan good looks, recounted to me how in 1963 she had flown from Frankfurt to Kenya with a friend, a German war hero, in a Cessna 206. On arrival in Nairobi she presented the plane to AMREF as a gift from the German people. During their first office meeting, Anne made no effort to disguise her hostility toward Leonora. The German believed that her ire was fueled by an assumption she was an unrepentant Nazi—a notion she denied, even though she had once been engaged to an officer killed in the Battle of Stalingrad.

After acknowledging Leonora's extraordinary fund-raising skills, once single-handedly even saving AMREF from ruin, Anne gradually warmed to her. As the friendship grew, Leonora began spending weekends with Anne at Sabukia. Her most vivid memory was of Anne's geese strutting in and out of the sitting room. Even in the privacy of the remote house, the two steered clear of the subject of war. So secretive was Anne about her past that Leonora falsely presumed she was Jewish and that Ravensbrück was not a concentration camp but a cushy "holding area" for "special" women, almost a country club. Anne never disputed Leonora's canards.

◄○►

At the coast I ran down Ali Gabow to see whether Anne might have confided in him. Ali is a pediatric nurse and midwife, and over the last seventeen years of Anne's life he served as her assistant. If anyone were privy to secrets, it would be this gentleman, who had lived alongside her until the end.

The friendship between the doctor and the African caregiver should never have happened, for in 1982 when Ali, aged thirty, and "Mama Daktari," sixty-four, met, she began by shouting orders at him in public. He found her manner insulting and her words derogatory. "People in Africa don't stand for abuse," he told me, recalling that difficult time. After a month with "Mama Daktari," he had had enough of the abrasive lady. He decided he would work with her for only one more day before handing in his notice.

On that day, Mama Daktari piloted Zulu Tango north to a small deserted coastal airstrip with Ali silently fuming. After landing, the two set out on foot for a village. On the dirt track they encountered four men carrying a makeshift stretcher. On it lay a man with his thigh gushing blood from a crocodile attack. Ali knew straightaway that unless they closed up the wound, the man was sure to die from septicemia.

"Suture kit," bellowed Anne. Ali froze. Hanging his head, he confessed he had forgotten it. She threw down her cane in a rage and, hobbling away, ordered him to close the wound himself.

"But how?" Ali begged.

"What do you need to sew with?" she shouted back.

Ali found a needle while Anne took a *shuka* off one of the men. From it, she extracted threads, which she rolled on her knee. She disinfected the wound and then used the yarn as a suture. As she sewed up the leg, Ali held the patient down because they had no anesthesia. Whenever he screamed, Anne shouted, "Look, I can leave you here and then what? Shut up!"

Ali stayed on, and a month later, when they flew in to the airstrip in the north, they found the man walking without a limp, as if nothing had happened. "From that moment," says Ali, "I knew that Mama Daktari was my master. She does not carry bad things in her heart . . . Out of all the noise came good."

CHAPTER 16 | *I KNOW WHAT I'M DOING*

> *Memory is a great artist. For every*
> *man and for every woman it makes*
> *the recollection of his or her life a work*
> *of art and an unfaithful record.*

—André Maurois

During the 1980s and into the 1990s, I busied myself with filmmaking and writing. In 1983, I expanded my magazine profile of Anne into a chapter of a book, *No Man's Land*. In both iterations I expressed the opinion that Anne would not talk about war because she did not wish to relive the unspeakable horrors she had endured. Privately, I told friends it was almost certain she had been tortured and possibly mutilated.

In 1992, I set out to produce a PBS TV documentary, *The Africa Passion,* showcasing the lives of three individuals who had escaped Europe to live out their dreams in Africa. One was Latham Leslie-Moore, another Kuki Gallmann. The last was Anne. When I asked her to give us two days of her time making her rounds at the coast, she readily accepted. By now, the intrusion of a film crew was nothing new for her. She knew how to manage them, and she had committed to memory the script. As always, I held out hope I could breach her defenses. Perhaps, over the years, she had wearied of secrecy, and this time she would confide in me, a friend, about the war.

In 1992 the long rains of April began early, in March at the coast. While mornings were cloudless, late in the afternoons the sky crackled with lightning, and the seas turned to slate. For two days my crew and I set off early to fly with Anne on her medical rounds from Lamu along the East African coast, as far north as we could before crossing into Somali airspace. On our first day we landed on a rough strip, and by 9:00, Anne had already set up her battered card table and stacked it with plastic jars of pills. She paused long enough to tell me that one contained placebos, which she prescribed to "make them happy." For the next two hours, Anne treated a total of sixty-three patients of the Bajuni tribe. After the last patient and many packets of "happy pills" she snapped shut her Gladstone bag and instructed us to load the plane.

Before the sun reached its zenith, we were beginning another clinic on the island of Paté. There, in filigreed light, a large crowd solemnly waited. With her baseball hat matted to her hair, Anne set up her table and piled it high with containers, including "happy pills." She then fanned a stack of immunization cards, reading them methodically, in chilling silence. Apparently, the people of this island knew not to fidget, lest they ignite "Mama Daktari's" temper. By her feet lay bags of Anamix, a powdered milk supplement fortified with nutrients, which she intended to present to the villagers as a gift for the children.

Well into old age, Anne's legend had grown exponentially, and these days she was more respected than ever throughout the wild lands of Kenya. With the sound of the Indian Ocean sighing over a reef, the villagers held their breaths, watching her every move. Even I, directing my cameraman with hand signals, was jittery. At last the doctor laid down the cards, reached for a syringe, and fixed her eyes on a small boy. When he saw what was in store, he let loose a wail that drowned out the sea. This was her style—what some might call military medicine. By day's end Mama Daktari had added another ninety-four patients to her life list.

Anne was on Kenya's north coast largely to inoculate infants against polio. Whether she was delivering a jab or a diagnosis, her method was swift and muscular. She listened to every complaint—a mother suffering from epilepsy, a child's broken arm, three cases of infantile diarrhea, one of diphtheria. At her scuffed table, she made no attempt to invoke doctor-patient privilege, and the throng overheard everyone's most intimate secrets. Anne's syringe, randomly sterilized in alcohol, was a horror to children, and a baby's howls could kindle mass hysteria.

As the queue thinned, Anne resorted to theatrics. After plunging her syringe into one small bottom, she assumed a swami-like pose—perhaps from fatigue. As she danced her stethoscope over one small body, both child and mother became spellbound, staring at the wondrous instrument, certain it was a magic wand and she a sorcerer. Moments later all crying ceased, and Mama Daktari basked in the ovation of silence.

As winds skittered across the sea and thunderheads crowded the horizon, we took off to return to Manda Island. It was obvious Anne was tired from the long day. Struggling to stay awake, she "horsed" the controls to maintain straight and level and then on the landing came in low. Zulu Tango bounced three times before safely coming to a stop. Offering no apology, Anne taxied to a tie-down spot signposted MAMMA DAKTARI. She killed the engine, and a loyal assistant secured ropes as she jimmied herself onto the wing, slid to the ground, and set off at a lope down the long quay. Hauling gear, we struggled to keep up. Once onboard the Lamu-bound *jahazi*

Anne closed her eyes again. Twenty minutes later when the boat crunched against Shella's concrete jetty she awoke.

After dusk, my film crew and I, again laden with gear, set off from our hotel and followed a lantern swung by Anne's houseman. He guided us down medieval lanes and between dozing donkeys, eventually delivering us to a brass-studded door. There Anne greeted us and led us through a colonnaded courtyard and up four flights of dimly lit stairs. On the way to the roof, we passed an elegant Aegean-blue foyer and, above, two bedrooms with spindly antique Lamu beds. Standing out from the exotic decor were Anne's distinctive touches—three yellow jerricans, filled with avgas, propped onto an antique shell-inlaid dresser, while a single-sideband radio was balanced on a brass-studded captain's chest. When we emerged onto the roof, I looked to sea and saw the moon rise between mangroves and, riding at anchor, *jahazis* turn the color of old ivory. The splendor of the night was not lost on Anne. She saw my admiring look and smiled proprietarily.

Immediately, Anne got down to business, telling us where to sit, even where to set the camera. She had thrust a fragrant stem of frangipani into a buttonhole as a flourish against her blue flight shirt. Fortified by a glass of South African Pinotage, she readied herself for my questions. For a second I studied my notes and then grilled her about the future. She laughed and said, "Why should I retire? You can retire at twenty or at ninety. It all depends if you can do the job. In Africa they let you work if you are old. Not like in America. Here, it doesn't matter as long as you are effective." I asked for her recipe for gaining patients' trust. She responded by saying it helped to work alongside African witch doctors. When I turned the interview to the past, Anne grew misty-eyed as she described her lifelong attachment to her brother. Emboldened by the fluidity of her responses, I saw an opening: "Were you and your brother interned in the same concentration camp?"

I might have lobbed a hand grenade. Anne's smile evaporated. "I have half a mind of kicking you all out of my house," she barked. Her body was now all sinew, her eyes barred windows, and her face burgundy: "Don't you ever talk about war with me. Do you understand?"

—◁○▷—

Until then, Anne had carefully stage-managed the interview, dismissing her bravery as inconsequential, crediting colleagues with all the hard work, distilling Africa's allure into one nebulous word: "gripping." She was practiced at this, and I was but one of many compliant journalists. In the 1990s, a score of magazines, European as well as Japanese, New Zealand, and Brazilian, featured Anne. Some led with catchy headings like "From France, with Love," "Flying Doctor Sees Hope for Health in Africa," "Flying Doctor with a Bouncy Walk," "In the Good Care of Mama Daktari," "The African Adventure of Mama Daktari, Age 74." One article published in Kenya dubbed Anne "the Bird Doctor," explaining that locals believed she was "sent from heaven." One French journalist declared that her contributions to African medicine rivaled those of her fellow Alsatian Dr. Albert Schweitzer.

No journalist ever breached Anne's private world. Writing in the magazine *Destins*, Annie Kouchner was shut down like the rest of us: "About her incarceration in Ravensbrück, she does not want to say anything." One writer speculated, as had I, that she had been "tortured by the Germans."

In 1992, Sylva Maubec-Benardeau spent four days with Anne in Kenya's northern deserts. While she uncovered nothing new about her past, she did learn that Anne, aged seventy-four, had no intention of slowing down or giving up. After they left Nairobi, their first stop was the mission of Laisamis. Here Anne examined twenty patients and discussed their treatment with the attending Sister. When they returned to the plane, its interior temperature had risen to eighty degrees centigrade. Seemingly indifferent to discomfort—hers and Ms. Maubec-Benardeau's—Anne took off, sweat running down the steering column and into the fabric seats. By mid-afternoon, after stops in Korr and Marsabit, Anne had seen a further eighty patients. Final stop that day was on the Ethiopian frontier, at a refugee camp called Walda, then housing over thirty thousand dispossessed Somalis and Ethiopians. What captured Maubec-Benardeau's attention was Anne's knife. Intended as a surgical instrument, it now served as letter opener and screwdriver to repair a broken single-sideband radio. By night Anne slept rough on hard ground. In the morning the sleepless Maubec-Benardeau summarized: "Twenty-four hours interrupted by frequent landings in the desert, consultations given under a leaden sun, visits to missions scattered across the savanna, and hazardous landings between herds of animals." After four days of this routine, Zulu Tango had traveled over three thousand kilometers. Not once did Anne complain about discomfort or sleep deprivation. Disembarking, Maubec-Benardeau asked Anne when she planned on retiring. Anne's response was almost menacing: "Me retire? It's a dirty word. I will never retire." Maubec-Benardeau did not ask why.

With fame came honors. In 1987, before an audience of three hundred, the head of the French Senate—too young to have known the war—made Anne an honorary Citizen of the City of Paris. On the obverse side of her medal was a fitting Latin inscription: *Fluctuat nec mergitur*—"Tossed but not sunk." Two years later, in Kenya, President Daniel arap Moi presented Anne with Kenya's medal of honor. With accolades came new friendships with members of Europe's royal families. She and Princess Anne co-hosted a fundraising event in Orlando, Florida. Later she boasted she was on a first-name basis with Prince Bernhard of the Netherlands. His son Crown Prince Willem-Alexander (now king) issued a statement that Dr. Anne Spoerry was "the only real Flying Doctor."

Fame did not guarantee respect; within AMREF, Anne was increasingly sidelined for her age, with some viewing her as an anachronism and liability. In the early 1990s, with eight aircraft, five pilots, 2,587 hours of flying time annually, three hundred employees, fifteen hundred surgeries, the foundation needed to deal with Africa's monumental health emergencies in new ways. Drought, famine, and war had displaced hundreds of thousands, and AIDS was becoming Africa's most ruinous epidemic. In Kenya alone the national HIV infection rate was 5.8 percent for men and 7.1 percent for women. Feeding whole encampments of children, modifying the promiscuous behavior of long-haul lorry drivers, and providing community-based health care were now AMREF's primary objectives, and it had extended its reach beyond East Africa. This strategy left little room for an old lady, flying solo, performing medical miracles while seated at a rickety card table. In AMREF's 1992 annual report, Michael Gerber, the foundation's new director general, even failed to mention her by name. The German version of AMREF's annual report insensitively gave a full page of advertising to Siemens, the firm that had once enslaved Anne in Zwodau during the war.

According to AMREF's Nicky Blundell Brown, Anne asserted that her patients needed her and that she was not redundant. Who else wanted to care for the thousands waiting patiently in the desert or outside mission stations or in the hot coastal sun beside the strip in Kiungu? Her penciled notes from one Nairobi head office meeting showed her growing dissatisfaction with AMREF's new mission: *"Il faudra des meilleurs projets!"* (Better projects are needed), alongside doodles of the Eiffel Tower, drawn from memory. She was especially miffed that AMREF had set off on a new course without consulting her, its senior permanent flying doctor. While her co-workers were always cordial, they appeared to treat her as figurehead or mascot, and few called upon her for an opinion.

During these turbulent times, Nan Rees recalled how early one morning as Anne prepared to take off from Wilson Airport, her husband, Tom, the Flying Doctors' last living co-founder, slipped a pair of Navaho silver-turquoise earrings into Anne's bush jacket pocket as a gift. Later that evening when she returned to Nairobi and the Reeses ran into her at a dinner party, they noticed her wearing the earrings. She hurried over to hug Tom and burst into tears, saying, "This is the first time I've ever received a present from a man."

The cruelest insult came from Michael Gerber, AMREF's director general, who flatly asked Anne to retire. According to Nicky Blundell Brown, Anne was so offended she dropped AMREF from her will and soon declined all invitations to fund-raise for the cause. Two years later, in 1994, Anne was terminated at AMREF and permanently transferred to the Flying Doctor Service to reduce risk to the international charity. The foundation's board explained that the change was necessary to avoid liability, in case of an accident.

Over a weekend spent during this period at the farm in Sabukia, Leonora Semler witnessed Anne's anguish. One night, Anne opened the door to Leonora's bedroom. In floods of tears, Anne asked Leonora, "How could AMREF reject me, after all these years when I put my life on the line over and over?" Leonora hugged her, while Anne sobbed.

Admittedly, AMREF's executives had cause for concern: Anne's health was visibly in decline. Already she had undergone cataract surgery and a hip replacement. In addition, while almost completely deaf, she was too proud to wear a hearing aid. A friend tried to reason with her: Why not follow the example of other septuagenarians and hang it up? Anne cut him short. Why should she continue listening to all the "*fatina*" (gossip) when the "real people" of Africa still begged her to continue?

While she was marginalized at work, admiring letters from fellow health workers in the bush flooded Anne's mailbox. In one, David Njoroge addressed her as "Dear Mother Dr. Anne Spoerry." Father

Luke Mulayinkal wrote, "Greetings to you from the Mission of Korr and the Rendille and the Samburu people whom you love so much and help so much . . . We are praying for you." A medical assistant, Robert Kimania, wrote, "I hope you're still giving that most worthwhile services to the needy . . . they will be remembered for many years. Because they must go down in the books of history."

During this time, Anne's flying skills were causing her AMREF colleagues concern. Beginning in 1994, Colin Davis, its chief engineer, was stunned by the eccentricity of her takeoffs and landings: "When she got it going nice and fast, she'd whack on all the flaps, and the plane would jump into the air. Then she'd put the gear away as quickly as possible and hope she could get up the speed to fly over an approaching obstacle." Davis found her landings even more alarming: "Whoo, you thought, this is going to be a helluva bad landing, this is totally out of control, and then always at the last moment she'd do a greaser."

Whenever Anne complained to Colin that Zulu Tango's rudder pedals were stiff, he promised to look into the matter. The problem, he knew, was never mechanical but medical: Anne's knees were bone on bone and very painful. Rather than risk a tussle, he went along with her: "So we'd put a lot of air pressure in the front tire while removing it from the main to make the airplane sit tail down. This way she could steer."

Twice in 1995, Anne forgot to lower Zulu Tango's undercarriage prior to landing. Each time she damaged the propeller beyond repair. When emergency crews arrived at crash sites with replacement props, Anne invariably blamed the accidents on "damned warthog holes."

Colin Davis found Anne's Zulu Tango disembarkation strategy sidesplitting, because she always emerged backside first, "settling her bottom" on the wing, then swinging her legs and shimmying into the arms of a waiting attendant, who then handed her a set of walking sticks. An awed tourist once gaped at the spectacle, "wondering how a woman so old, so infirm, could pilot her own aircraft."

Narcolepsy eclipsed all other ailments. Several times, when Colin flew with Anne, she dozed off, once even tumbling into his lap. While Colin went along with her secret, Ali Gabow could not restrain his concern. He remembered one flight when she fell asleep so hard she hit the flight controls and drove the plane into a power dive. When he shook her, she exploded, "Of course I know what I'm doing."

Everyone flying alone with Anne grew alarmed. A lady passenger once made the mistake of waking her during one of her terrifying naps. "How dare you say I was asleep," she barked. Later, when she dozed off again, the woman, fearing another outburst, held her tongue even when the plane was lashed by a thunderstorm and the stall warning sounded menacingly. When Anne's eyes opened, she erupted, "Why the hell didn't you wake me?" On yet another occasion she horrified her passenger by falling asleep while on a compass heading straight into the flank of Mount Kenya. Closer and closer they flew until the seventeen-thousand-foot mountain filled the windshield. In great distress, the panicked passenger found the courage to nudge Anne. "Why did you do that?" she responded. "I know what I'm doing." Anne banked the plane, hauled back on the controls, and narrowly averted catastrophe.

—◆—

In 1994, the Flying Doctors Service ruled that an assistant pilot must, at all times, accompany Anne. She retaliated with a reign of terror. The first candidate was a Kenyan who lasted less than a month. The next was an Englishman who, seeing Anne fall asleep, took it upon himself to land the plane on his own. On touchdown, Anne awoke and accused him of landing her plane on the wrong strip. When he pointed out her error, she turned and looked out the window. Within a week, he too had left.

Benoît Wangermez, a French Africa-phile, was the only co-pilot who stayed the course. At first, he put up with Anne's outbursts because he needed to accumulate enough flying hours to satisfy the requirements of a pilot's license. After several trying months, he sensed the employer-employee relationship evolving into friendship. Benoît believed that Anne saw a kindred spirit in him, a scrappy working-class kid. She thrilled to his tales of driving heavy trucks through the Sahara and the Congo. He, in turn, found her exotic accounts of a privileged and cosseted French childhood captivating.

Whenever the tousle-haired, chain-smoking adventurer returned from France, he arrived bearing gifts. He knew what Anne loved most: caviar, foie gras, truffles, and *saucissons*. When he spread these delicacies across the dining room table, her eyes opened wide. Forgetting manners, she would devour everything as if she were in the final throes of starvation. At Sabukia, Benoît noted other quirks—the hoarding of old food, balls of string, and jars of pills. "There was aspirin everywhere. At first I thought she must have had a permanent headache."

In his early days, Benoît was no stranger to Anne's explosive temper. After one hurtful episode, he called her out, telling her she had made a terrible mistake. "And then she did what she always did when I proved her wrong: she walked off. But now I chased her and I said, 'Anne, you've just hurt me, and you're walking away. This is terribly wrong.' And she turned around and looked at me, apologizing, not with words, but 'a look.' From that day forward she never shouted at me again."

For Benoît, Anne was a contradiction of frugality and excess. Whenever she set off for France on her annual August *congé*, she flew first-class on Air France, explaining to Benoît that "appearances matter." On such occasions she was dressed in a neatly pressed bush jacket, with Ndetto, her chef, one row behind her, also in first.

To Benoît, Anne could, at times, be devastatingly stingy. While she paid her Sabukia farm staff the province's highest wages, with health care and children's school fees included, others were excluded from her benevolence. For reasons Benoît could never fathom, whenever they flew her plane to the Northern Frontier, Anne refused to pay the going wage. Her devoted night watchman, hired to protect her plane from thieves and hyenas, never earned more than twenty shillings (about twenty-five cents) for two sleepless nights of work. Benoît was perplexed: "I felt so embarrassed since I knew she had spent a thousand dollars on aviation fuel for that trip alone . . . Secretly, I always paid the guard much more . . . Anne was generally so generous, yet she was sometimes blind . . . She was this big heart armed with two big guns. Fire them, regret it, say not a word, and move on. That's how she was."

After a difficult month with Anne, Ali Gabow, at the coast, realized that beneath the bluster beat a kind heart. He had uncovered Anne's better self when in 1992 Shamsa, Ali's three-and-a-half-year-old daughter, was diagnosed with a stomach tumor. Anne flew both father and daughter from Lamu down the coast to Mombasa, where Anne took charge of the little girl's case upon admission to the hospital. Anne paid for Shamsa to have a private room. For months, Ali stayed by Shamsa's bed. Anne called him every day to check on her condition. In addition, she covered all hospital fees as well as expensive experimental drugs she had couriered out from France. Even with all her good care, after six months Shamsa's condition declined, and on the one day Ali was absent, the little girl died.

Anne was the first person to comfort Ali in his distress. She paid all funeral costs, and a few days after the Muslim ceremony she took him by the arm and said, "Feel that you are at home. Don't be afraid of me. You are most welcome at my side." Ali never forgot her words.

Today Ali lives not far from Anne's old house in Shella. In a voice that rarely rises above a whisper, he speaks solemnly of their deep friendship. One morning, mistakenly believing she had summoned him to her Shella house, he opened the door to her bedroom and discovered her naked, sitting on her bed, looking out to sea. Startled, she covered herself with bed linens. Ali, a devout Muslim, was mortified. He stumbled backward, saying "sorry" over and over. During those few embarrassing moments, he noticed a long diagonal scar across Anne's back. A few days later, he asked her about it, but "she did not want to disclose."

In 1996, the head of the Flying Doctors Service, worried by Anne's deterioration, instructed Ali to remain by her side at all times. Over the next three years, he held to his promise and treated her as if she were his patient. It was no easy task, he explained, for in her late seventies Dr. Spoerry worked harder, slept less, and pushed herself, "as if she had something troubling her." Early in that year, Anne and Ali flew to an airstrip not far from the Somali border for a clinic with Bajuni and Boni tribal people. On their return, Ali noted that Anne was exhausted. He proposed they land for lunch at Kiwayu, a remote luxurious beach lodge.

On arrival, they found its Italian owner in a liverish mood. He greeted them curtly, saying he had no time for "do-gooders," and offered Anne and Ali only bread and water. Anne stormed out of the lodge and hobbled back through half a mile of deep sand to the airstrip. Upon reaching Zulu Tango, Ali found his boss "crying" from pain in her knees. Gently, he lifted her into the pilot's seat and then, as he sat in the co-pilot's seat, followed her instructions how to operate floor pedals and hand flaps while she attended to the other controls. Throughout the twenty-minute flight, she urged him on, and above the Manda airfield she pointed out how to land the plane. After she killed the engine, Ali carried her from the wing to the end of the jetty and into a waiting *jahazi*. "The following day," he recalled, "I couldn't walk because of the backache."

On the following day Anne flew to France for the knee surgery she had been postponing for years. Immediately after the operation, she returned to Kenya for therapy. It was during her recovery that Anne finally answered Ali's questions about the scar he had seen across her back: "She was in the concentration camp in Germany. She and a friend of hers were carrying soup and she fell down and spilled the soup and then she was beaten." Embarrassed by what was to come, Ali lowered his voice to a whisper: "After that, she was done a bad thing by the men." Avoiding my stare, he uttered a word he seemed to dread: "I think maybe she hate men because she was . . . raped . . . It really bothered her a lot . . . She really felt something went wrong somewhere. It may be the Germans are not human beings, what they are doing to her, to their fellow human beings, to the Israelis."

Ali's story is a puzzle because there is no other corroborating evidence of rape. Could the incident have occurred in Zwodau, or might it have happened in 1945 after she left Mory's protection? Why did Anne not mention it in her legal defense? Why did she tell no one, not even her own family? Or might the story have been manufactured for Ali as a convenience—Anne's way of silencing him?

On one matter, Ali is resolute: during her last years Anne was consumed by thoughts of Ravensbrück. Beginning in 1997, he observed her at her desk in Nairobi, drawing scenes from memory of the concentration camp. "You are a good artist," Ali told her. "She put her finger to her lips: 'This is just between me and you. When I am finished, I will tell the whole story.'"

Anne never told him the whole story nor got around to writing the first word of the text to accompany the illustrations. The only evidence of her intentions is a collection of six large drawings, now in the hands of her nephew Yves. Ali believes that throughout Anne was "anxious about the camp." While she never revealed her approach to the story—selectively or in full—he believed she had "revenging" on her mind. I asked him to define the word. "Blaming," he responded. Blaming whom? Ali could only guess. Whenever Ali saw her concentrating on the drawings, he found her "uneasy," with "stories too awful to speak." She explained that in her book she would "release a secret."

Ali now believes that Anne's "bad days in the camp" are dwarfed by her good decades in Africa. Even fifteen years after her death, Ali tries not to imagine what really happened in Ravensbrück, concentrating instead on her conduct in Africa. "She was my friend," he explains. Even now, he sees her in his dreams. Late at night, he feels Anne shaking him awake, telling him to get dressed quickly, hurrying him out the door. They must get to the plane. They must fly to the north. The Boni people need her. Then Ali awakes.

Ali is not the only one who dreams of Anne. One raw spring Sunday in a tearoom in York, in the north of England, Prue Keigwin shared her recollections about her old friend from Ol Kalou days. Over many cups, she recounted the story of their time together. Just a teenager when they first met, Prue at first found Anne "monstrously bossy." In time she saw her for what mattered—a brave woman with a big heart. For years friendship with the famous flying doctor was one of the milestones of Prue's life.

Just before Anne's death in Africa, Prue began dreaming of Anne. Over and over she sees her gesturing, walking, waving as if from a flickering news film. Soon it merges into an episode in which the old, failing woman flies Zulu Tango out to sea, activates the autopilot, and settles the plane on a heading of ninety degrees—due east. In the dream, Anne closes her eyes and, in no time, falls fast asleep. "Far out in the Indian Ocean, Zulu Tango runs out of petrol," Prue recounts. "It glides lower and lower until it slips into the sea, without a trace. That will be that—the way she always intended to die, secrets intact."

CHAPTER 17

I'LL BE BACK

*Old age should burn and rave at close of
day;*
Rage, rage against the dying of the light.

—Dylan Thomas, "Do not go gentle into that
good night"

By 1997, there were subtle cracks in Anne's equanimity. Ali Gabow believed she was deeply troubled. In a candid moment, she had admitted to him, out of the blue, that she had been banned from practicing medicine in France. "There was something else disturbing," he recollected. He believed she "feared" someone; "she would not say who." To Ali, she appeared apprehensive.

When Anne's nephew Bernard searched through her Sabukia safe, he found files that shed light on this anxiety. Apparently, she had been holding several documents for years. The topmost one, dated 1946 and headed "CROWCASS," cited Anne Spoerry for crimes against humanity, including "torture." The other files were transcripts of postwar testimony, selected not for their impartiality but for their favorability. Bernard presumed his aunt had retained them in the event someone came calling. Although he knew no details, he supposed the war was never far from her thoughts.

On April 11, 1997, the stranger Anne had dreaded all these years did, in fact, materialize. That afternoon, a messenger delivered a parcel from the Swiss ambassador, Hans-Peter Erismann. Inside, she found a master's thesis and two letters. In the first letter, the ambassador asked Anne to respond to a request from a "cultural scientist," Hans Hübner of Berlin. Ambassador Erismann claimed that since January, Hübner had been writing to her, on a matter of some urgency. The Swiss ambassador could not understand why Dr. Spoerry had not yet responded.

Hübner's letter began innocuously: "Martha . . . your comrade and fellow sufferer in Ravensbrück asked me to write to you with affectionate and fond wishes. Martha turns 87 years old on the 5th of February this year. She fondly remembers your friendship with . . . Carmen Maria Mory . . . Maybe you remember how . . . Martha came to help you in the court proceedings?" No doubt Anne would have found these words menacing.

Anne would certainly have remembered Anna-Martha van Och–Soboll, who had provided some of the most positive testimony in her defense at her Swiss hearing in 1947. At the time, Martha's notarized statement had been delivered from Holland in the form of a letter through her attorneys. In it, Martha had heaped praise on Anne for her conduct outside Block 10. Martha's statement, as well as other favorable testimony related to her time in Blocks 6 and 11, had helped acquit Anne.

Born in Germany, Anna-Martha van Och–Soboll had dedicated much of her life to helping victims and underdogs. In 1939 she had disguised herself as a nun to lead 150 Jews and others, scheduled for extermination, out of Germany into the relative safety of Holland. She was caught, denounced, arrested, and handed over to the Gestapo. After two years in jail, Martha was deported to Ravensbrück, where she survived electric shock treatment, solitary confinement, starvation, surveillance, and a long battle with tuberculosis. In 1945, once freed, she returned to a life of freedom, eventually making her way to Holland. While other survivors would live with deep despair after their face-off with evil, Martha remained a lifelong optimist. Even after testifying at the Hamburg war crimes trials, she claimed she never lost faith in mankind's goodness. Late in life, Martha continued to find virtue in others, believing that her remarkable survival in Ravensbrück was the result of her positive outlook.

One Ravensbrück prisoner roundly praised by Martha was Carmen Mory. Martha had formed this opinion following a chance encounter in 1944 as Block 10's *Blockova* was making her way toward SS headquarters. Believing this to be her lucky day, Martha intercepted Mory to beg a favor. The woman's scarf, blouse, and warm jacket—clothes denied other prisoners—were visible proof of the high esteem in which SS guards held her. Mory paused long enough to hear Martha's account of "a grave injustice" meted out to four women, locked up in a cold unsanitary toilet. Martha was convinced that unless these women were promptly released, they would soon be dead of infection and exposure. Rushing off, Mory promised Martha she would look into the matter. True to her word, the next day guards released the women from the toilets, provided them with straw bedding, and allowed them to get on with their recuperation.

Martha never forgot Carmen Mory's good deed. In 1997 this act of mercy, saving the lives of four women, was still on her mind. When she talked with cultural scientist Hans Hübner, who had agreed to serve her as scribe, her admiration for the *Blockova* blazed like a star.

Hübner came to the point: "Martha would like, with your written support, to do something about the memory of Carmen Maria Mory—since you knew the accused and know of her fate after the Hamburg Ravensbrück War Crimes trial. Martha would like to have the accusations of misconduct that had been brought by the cellmates against Carmen Maria Mory invalidated and removed from the world. That is Martha's greatest wish . . . It would be wonderful if you could write openly and without taboo about everything that you can remember about Carmen Maria Mory of Ravensbrück."

Martha van Och–Soboll was the sole individual to come to Carmen Mory's defense following her death. For Anne to respond was to invite attention. Who, besides Martha, would benefit from a reversal of judgment? How could anyone challenge a fifty-year-old uncontested verdict? Martha's cause was sure to reignite ancient passions.

Anne never showed Martha's letter to anyone. From its condition, she might have crumpled it, with the intention of throwing it in the fire. Instead, she folded it away for storage, as a weapon to be used in her defense against the revenge of history.

Muthaiga was now Anne's fortress, its windows barred, staff loyal, night watchmen well paid, and files referencing "crimes against humanity" secure from prying eyes. In Anne's homes over the last fifty years, she had learned to depend on night sounds for measuring Africa's mood. Ever since her early days at Ol Kalou, and then during her fearsome Mau Mau years, she had developed an ear for the well-being of her African surroundings through voices. Tonight, watchmen cough, dogs bark, and hyraxes, in the high canopy, boom like old rheumy men. Were it not for the Hübner package, Anne would be at perfect ease.

One can see Anne calling for Ndetto to bring wine and *chakula*, dinner. Soon he is standing beside her, topping up her glass. Even after decades of the old man's service, she is never certain whether or not he is in his cups. Now it no longer matters.

"Ndyo, Mama," comes his raspy voice.

Weighed by silver, porcelain, and doubt, Anne casts her eyes to the rest of Hübner's parcel—a thick document, still unread, and no doubt equally troubling. Even after all the miles and all the years, there is no sanctuary, not even in Africa.

—◄○►—

By 1997, Anne's decline was evident to all. Once, to her colleagues' embarrassment, she fell asleep during a public meeting with Kenya's minister of health. On her desks in Nairobi and Sabukia, mail went unread, charitable gifts to the Flying Doctors left uncashed. Benoît noted that in Anne's Sabukia closet alone there were six new green bush jackets and twenty-five identical pairs of safari boots, all unworn.

"'Anne,'" Benoît pleaded, "'those clinics in the north: What happens if you break your leg? Who's going to carry on if you can't?' Each time she told me off with the words 'Mind your own business. They'll wait for me. I'll be back.'"

Even nearing eighty, Anne still refused to trim her work schedule to take into account her diminished health. How easy it would be, friends said, to settle into snug old age. Why did she still cling to a territory as large as the British Isles? She waved them away, arguing that if she gave every Kenyan child just one injection, 90 percent of diseases such as TB, measles, tetanus, and diphtheria would be preventable.

One of Anne's most memorable acts of courage in her last year of life was her response to an epic flood along Kenya's north coast between November 1997 and February 1998. Worried that the Boni people, stranded by high waters and with their crops all perished, were starving, Anne personally administered a helicopter airlift. Nearly eighty years old, she sat in the passenger seat dropping "bags of Anamix, antimalarial, antibiotic, and analgesic drugs as well as exercise books" to Boni settlements close to the Somali border.

In her last year, Anne left clues that she was concerned with her legacy. In September 1998, she noted in her journal that she had received telephone calls from two German television channels, each wanting to film her life as a flying doctor. Interested in accommodating both, she asked them to fax her their schedules. A few days later she discussed the publication date of her memoirs in Canada. The following week, she penciled a one-page outline for the Ravensbrück book. It began with a heading, "The Background," then continued, "start of the Résistance," and ended mid-sentence: "try to get people out of the death convoys . . . Our freedom trip."

Even late in life, Anne held to the habit of keeping rigorous household accounts. In tight penmanship, she tallied the cost of paint, as well as charitable outlays. In September, Martin Marimo received 2,000 shillings for his Alliance Française tuition, and Grace Wagechi 8,000 shillings for children's school fees. Over two months in 1998, Anne made an average of three out-of-pocket charitable gifts a day, averaging 100,000 shillings (about $1,500) a month. For each gift, no matter the size, she demanded accountability, determined not to let anyone think her a pushover. Once, when approached by Muslim elders to build them a mosque, she responded hotly, "If you want to worship, you can bloody well do it under a tree."

While the subject of Ravensbrück remained off-limits, on one occasion Anne raised it of her own accord. At a gathering of friends, she rolled a clove of garlic in her hand. Stopping short of naming Carmen Mory, she explained how she and "a friend" had grown garlic under their blockhouse. Ever since, she had depended on it for longevity: "If anything is going to kill you, it will be white bread, white sugar, and not enough garlic." In Lamu she took two cloves of it before retiring for the night.

—◦—

Sometime between April 1997 and September 1998, Anne reopened Hans Hübner's envelope and read what remained: a ninety-seven-page German master's thesis for the Department of Philosophy and History at Heidelberg University. Written by Bettina Durrer, it was titled "Portrait of a Privileged Prisoner, Block Elder Carmen Maria Mory."

In his letter, Hans Hübner requested that Anne take careful note of the thesis and respond: "Please be very open and do not conceal anything significant." While his opening was conciliatory, by the end of the letter he had struck an accusatory note. Anne underlined as she read the thesis.

Bettina Durrer had relied on a variety of primary sources including transcripts from the Hamburg war crimes trial. The court was justified, Durrer felt, in finding Carmen Mory guilty for having conspired with SS guards, doctors, and camp administrators. Mory, she wrote, "was not alone in her criminal rampage: A close friendship existed between Carmen Mory and Anne Spoerry, who may be regarded as her friend in captivity, her confidante, and—from the point of view of the former co-inmates—her accomplice."

One keen graduate student had now, fifty years after Ravensbrück, taken up the story of Anne's wartime past. From marginalia and heavy underlining of all references to "Spoerry" and "Dr. Claude," it seems reasonable to suppose Anne studied the thesis in depth, especially Durrer's assertion that she had been an accessory to Carmen Mory's rampages. This disturbing account by Durrer was heavily underlined: "Carmen Mory as a block official was angry about the disturbance at night and did not refrain from killing two 'mentally ill' prisoners after unsuccessfully trying to beat them into submission. She was interested in restoring silence so she herself would be able to sleep. The lives of the mentally ill were of comparatively lesser value to her . . . Anne Spoerry found herself confronted with the same charge. She admitted 'having hit occasionally with a leather strap in defense' . . . Anne Spoerry justified her actions . . . by pointing to the aggression of the prisoners . . .

Anne Spoerry compared this method with the 'water therapy' used in institutions for the mentally ill . . . The prisoners saw this 'treatment' as a deliberate form of harassment popular with SS-guards and prisoner-officials . . . In retrospect, Anne Spoerry's justification appears to be flawed."

Bettina Durrer took particular interest in Carmen Mory and Anne Spoerry's "central role in the 'great' selection for Schloss Hartheim"—an Austrian castle that had been converted into one of the Third Reich's premier "gassing" centers. Beneath its turrets an estimated 18,000 prisoners were purged. Durrer wrote that during the autumn of 1944 Anne and Carmen helped SS guards make multiple selections for death transports. In November the castle received a convoy of some 120 Ravensbrück prisoners, almost all originating from Block 10, under orders of Carmen Mory and, by implication, her assistant. This one party of prisoners constituted the highest single mass killing on record at Schloss Hartheim. According to Durrer, during a Hamburg cross-examination, Mory proudly admitted her participation, testifying, "I selected these women along with Dr. Spoerry."

Durrer concluded, "Anne Spoerry and Carmen Mory could have made it possible for individual prisoners to step away . . . behind the backs of the SS-doctors from those selected to die. They did not . . . despite the pleas . . . and remained passive. This failure to act weighed heavily on other prisoners because their friends were among those selected."

"Carmen Mory," began another Durrer paragraph, "claims that Anne Spoerry had worked for the camp Gestapo. A former prison-official in the political department confirmed this and stated Anne Spoerry had asked her to destroy a written declaration—similar to the one Carmen Mory had signed—shortly before liberation."

Bettina Durrer's concluding paragraphs were especially harsh: "In Block 10, Spoerry changed her behavior, by adapting to Carmen Mory's survival strategy, and she acted as hard and mercilessly as her friend. In the eyes of French prisoners, Anne Spoerry went over to Mory's side . . . In front of the honorary court in Paris, she justified her behavior in Block 10 by stating that she had only followed Carmen Mory's order and had been completely under her 'devilish spell.'

"During her time as assistant doctor in Block 10, Anne Spoerry found herself in a loyalty conflict. On the one hand, she felt close to Carmen Mory and felt that she owed her; on the other hand, she was confronted with the French prisoners' demands to protect them, which she now rejected, in most cases. The influence of Carmen Mory as a role model was stronger . . . The example of Anne Spoerry makes it clear that it was not only the system of power in the camp that favored SS-style actions but that these actions were amplified through the social network of a 'privileged prisoner.'"

There is no evidence Anne responded to Martha's request and Hübner's accusations. Shortly after reading the thesis, Anne filed it away. With a green marker, she scribbled "Ravensbrück in German" on the brown envelope and buried it deep in a battered blue tin trunk, which she hid in the storage shed outside the kitchen door of her Muthaiga house.

—◦—

On September 25, 1998, frail and unsteady Anne Spoerry made her final notebook entry. Soon she would tally household expenses for the last time, ending her five-decades-long custom. Nor would she again record the many thousands of shillings she dispensed each month from her Gladstone bag to her many dependents. Of greater significance, Ali Gabow observed that by the end of the year Anne had also shelved her Ravensbrück project. Might she have done so because of Bettina Durrer's Heidelberg University thesis?

In mid-December, Anne took the regular flight from Nairobi to spend Christmas at her house in Shella. Lars and Carol Korschen, proprietors of the Peponi Hotel, were alarmed by her decline. When George Fegan dropped by for a sundowner, he was saddened Anne could no longer climb the stairs to her roof terrace. Instead, they celebrated Christmas Eve with a bottle of champagne in her bedroom. The following morning, Christmas Day, Ali Gabow knocked on her door to wish her well and found her "feverish and angry." She had just received a call from France with news that François had been admitted to the hospital. Anne told Ali she needed to fly to Paris immediately.

Ali guided Anne onto a speedboat for Manda and then assisted her along the path to the airfield for the scheduled afternoon Nairobi flight. Two hours later, when Anne landed at Wilson Airport, Ali's brother drove her to Muthaiga, where she changed into traveling clothes for the night flight to Paris. In the morning when the exhausted Anne reached her brother's side in the hospital, she was horrified by his deterioration. Especially unsettling was the failure of other Spoerrys to attend him during this moment of need. Anne reserved much of her ire for her nephew Bernard, who had refused to interrupt his Lamu vacation to see his father. Years later, Bernard said he had rationalized his decision because he and his father had been estranged for five years, and a hospital was not the place for reconciliation. It was a choice, Bernard said, he would forever regret.

For over a year, François had been in steady decline. In 1997, he had suffered the first of several strokes, rendering him blind and depriving him of short-term memory. On Christmas Eve he suffered an additional stroke. This one silenced him forever. For over a week, Anne stayed by his side. On New Year's Day, François fell into a coma, kept alive through lifesaving tubes.

Now Anne's most trusted protector and confidant would precede her in death. She held on to his hand, watching him breathe his last. This was not the ending she had imagined.

According to his son Bernard, François's final advice to Anne was to stop writing her book about Ravensbrück, because "there would be a strong reaction by Jews and others who would object to the way she was leading her life [in Kenya]." He believed few would forgive her for escaping justice and living the good life in Africa. The publication of *They Call Me Mama Daktari* had been her first act of rebellion. Had she completed the Ravensbrück book, she would have compounded the insult and, according to François, risked losing all she had achieved.

Soon it was over. The woman who had cared for a legion of Kenyans in their final hours was now about to attend to the most excruciating death of all. On January 11, 1999, Anne called her sisters and nephews for permission. With their consent, François Spoerry was removed from life support, and within an hour he slipped away.

At the funeral, Anne's nephew Yves could not keep his eyes off her, so stunned was he by her transformation. Sitting beside the coffin and next to her sisters, Thérèse and Martine, Anne appeared tinier than ever before, as if the air that held her together had been expelled: "When they started screwing down the lid of my father's coffin, I saw Anne turn pale . . . Her world had fallen apart, and she seemed to die before my eyes."

After the reading of the will, Anne caught the first Air France flight back to Nairobi. There she arranged for Benoît to fly her upcountry. In Sabukia, Rosemary Wacharia, whom Anne had known since the age of eleven, was the first to greet her. For two days, Rosemary recalled, Anne lay in her narrow bed, crying in despair over François's death and her family's indifference. With her face bathed in equatorial light, her eyes passing back and forth over Miss Mary's suitcase, she gave Rosemary the following advice: "Don't be afraid of anybody. And learn to argue." On Sunday, January 24, 1999, Anne regained sufficient strength to return to Nairobi. Before leaving, she told Rosemary that she intended to live another ten years. "Africa," she said, "will look after me." For Rosemary these were thrilling words. She and so many others at Sabukia needed Anne.

◄o►

Back in Nairobi, Anne's first order of business was renewal of her pilot's license. To obtain it, she was required by Kenya's aviation authority to undergo a full medical checkup—seemingly an impossibility because she walked in pain and was stone-deaf, partially blind, and prone to dozing off in mid-flight. Vowing to beat the system, Anne booked an appointment with her "pet" physician, an elderly and compliant friend. On January 24, 1999, she entered his office, kissed him on both cheeks, and sat down for her checkup. The procedure took less than an hour. Instead of testing her for vital signs, the doctor reminisced about old times with his former colleague.

Anne hurried back to the Muthaiga house to greet another old friend, a French surgeon, just arrived from Paris. When Dr. Claude Layet saw Anne walk through the front door, he found her "ebullient," and "fighting fit." She announced that she had just passed her checkup "with flying colors." The news was timely because on the following day Anne planned to fly with Dr. Layet to the northern desert on her monthly medical rounds. One more journey to the far reaches of Kenya would prove she was still up to the job of flying doctor.

On that Monday evening, Dr. Layet noted that Anne wanted to set aside thoughts of her brother's death and get on with her work, caring for her African patients. As the two sipped cocktails on the veranda, she called out to Ndetto to hurry and "to spare nothing." When her ancient retainer popped his head out the door, she told him she was going to "*fanya raha*," to celebrate.

Before the evening chill drove them indoors, Anne and Dr. Layet sat in deck chairs, luxuriating in the shadows of the Karura Forest, purple, murmuring with turacos, smelling of midnight. This was one of Anne's favorite Africas—home to colobus monkeys, the odd leopard, and, increasingly, bands of thugs. Dr. Layet was amused to note Anne's excitement at the prospect of a break-in. Her Smith & Wesson .38 Service Special weighed in her bush jacket, the windows of the house were crosshatched with iron bars, and a night watchman coughed by the entrance to the kitchen door. She told Dr. Layet she had learned much during Mau Mau and was ready for a "good punch-up."

As night fell upon the forest and the two physicians enjoyed the champagne and the camaraderie, frogs boomed from the reeds near the pool. Dr. Layet recalls Anne being especially chatty. She told him about the day she poured "liters" of antibiotic into a Masai *moran*'s lion bite. Clapping her hands to signal the end of her story, she drained her glass, rose, and, leaning on Layet's elbow, conducted him to the dining room, where candlelight made the ghostly painted walls flicker with memory.

Awaiting them on the table was Anne's surprise: a one-kilo tin of caviar and a serving plate stacked with neatly sliced *foie de canard*. When Ndetto entered the candlelit room with another bottle of champagne, he glowed to see his boss in such a merry mood. When the doctors had polished off the caviar, Anne summarized the next day's itinerary—Marsabit, Moyale, Illeret, and Loiyangalani—a journey to Anne's favorite places, not far from the shores of Lake Turkana.

After dessert and coffee, Anne looked spent. Glancing at her watch, she jimmied herself to her feet, said good night, and, with two canes, mounted the stairs to her room. Dr. Layet noted her battered briefcase by the front door, ready for an early departure.

At 7:00 the following morning, Dr. Claude Layet sat up in bed and stared at his watch. He was surprised by the hour, for Anne had promised to awaken him sharply at 6:00. Dr. Layet rushed to her bedroom door and knocked. No response. He searched another bedroom. Finally, he opened the door to her bathroom. There he found Anne, standing in front of the sink, her eyes unblinking and frozen as she stared unresponsive into the reflection. She had suffered a stroke. When she failed to respond to his voice or his outstretched hand, Dr. Layet bolted downstairs to summon help.

Most mornings, from a tree opposite Anne's window, an emerald-spotted wood dove called, awaking Anne to her Africa. For the last fifty years in all her up-country houses, its four brooding notes had been a call sign, her clock in exile, her sentinel of duty. Today those desolate notes might have been the last sound Anne ever heard.

Rushed by ambulance to Nairobi Hospital, Anne underwent a series of brain scans. At first, only her eyes showed glints of life. Within a day, they too shut down. Anne's attending physician declared she had suffered a massive blockage of a carotid artery—akin to the one that felled François. Blood flowing to the left hemisphere of her brain had been occluded and her brain damaged beyond repair. Her nephew Bernard held to the theory that Anne's heavy intake of salt from the previous night's caviar caused the obstruction. Dr. Layet's explanation was less speculative: Anne suffered from a Spoerry family history of strokes. She shared with her brother a genetic predisposition for arterial blockages.

Jim Heather-Hayes, AMREF's chief pilot, and Benoît Wangermez, Anne's assistant pilot, visited Anne on the day of her admission. Years later, Jim would remember her final look: "For someone who had never considered she would ever grow old, she looked very peaceful. She may even have smiled at my jokes. To me, it was great comfort."

Ali Gabow stayed by her bedside for seven days. Anne's sisters, Thérèse and Martine, flew out from France to stand watch as well. Loving but kept at a distance, the women had always held their willful sister in the highest esteem. She was the illustrious one, the Spoerry known to the world, the one who had healed Africa.

Once again, in the space of weeks, the family would face another sickening life decision. By February 1, 1999, the pulsing ink stroke recording Anne's brain activity was as straight as a ruler. Anne's doctor weighed her chances of recovery at nil. On February 2, 1999, a few months short of her eighty-first birthday, Thérèse and Martine gave their consent. Catheters were removed, and within an hour Anne Spoerry's heart beat for the last time. Thérèse remembered the end came "peacefully," with "Anne's face radiating calm and serenity."

CHAPTER 18 | *HIDING IN FULL VIEW*

For those of Anne's friends who had watched her decline over the last few years, her death came as no surprise. From the moment François died, they contended, she lost her will to live. One friend observed that after eighty-one years she had had "a very good run."

Word of Anne's death traveled fast and far. Obituaries appeared in English, French, German, Italian, Japanese, and Swahili, some even making the front page of newspapers. All spoke glowingly of Dr. Spoerry's life's work in Africa. The *Daily Nation* called her "one in a million." In London's *Independent,* Fiammetta Rocco wrote, "No one meeting Anne Spoerry—physician, aviator and adventurer—could forget her two great attributes: a heart of gold and the Big Voice she always wrote of with capital letters and which she developed specially, as she put it, 'to get things done.'" *The Times* in London gave her four columns, ending with "But she was loved and respected even by those who did not take her advice, and at her death, 'Mama Daktari' was mourned by the thousands of those whom she had served." *Reader's Digest* called her one of the earth's most unforgettable characters: "This woman, who had survived so much death and destruction, found happiness and peace helping others to live." In Germany, *Der Spiegel* artfully omitted all reference to her time in Ravensbrück. A French headline read, "Mama Daktari, Her Heart Beat for Africa." One blogger, a surgeon, wrote, "When people mention 'women's liberation' . . . I think of Dr. Spoerry and wonder how she could have been more liberated or more saintly."

Many close friends and admirers booked flights out from America, Britain, and France to pay last respects. The Spoerry family, anticipating a crush, staged multiple ceremonies. The first, held punctually at 9:15 Saturday morning, February 6, on the front lawn of Anne's Muthaiga house, was restricted to immediate family and close friends. After the Reverend Mike Harries's closing prayer, six pallbearers lifted the casket and carried Anne's remains through her garden, bursting with bougainvillea, in and out of the house she had enjoyed all too briefly, and finally into a waiting hearse. As the cortege wound through Nairobi, onto Jomo Kenyatta Highway and the Langata Road, Nairobi's populace came to a halt to bow heads. Because of Nairobi's uncommon hush, perfect strangers assumed the deceased had been someone of great consequence, a national figure perhaps, and hung their heads as well. When word reached up-country villages via cell phone and "bush telegraph," it prompted many to set off on foot, to board buses and negotiate murram roads, for Nairobi.

When the hearse finally reached Wilson Airport, it went directly to the Flying Doctors' hangar, where already several hundred waited.

By 11:15, when the civil ceremony began, the mourners had grown to nearly one thousand. With so many, the service ran longer than expected. Jim Heather-Hayes and Benoît Wangermez then flew Anne's body over 290 miles of Kenyan bushland to Manda Island. From there, Anne's Lamu retainers reverentially carried the casket to the dhow, *Pepo,* for the short crossing to Shella and its long, empty beach beside which she was to be buried. Promptly at 4:45 on an evening tide, with many Lamu residents in attendance, a final eulogy was read, tropical garlands removed, and the casket lowered into the sand. As final resting places go, this one boasted an enviable ocean view, half a world and half a century from Ravensbrück. As Anne was interred, questions about the war paled beside accounts of her triumphs in Africa. After the Lord's Prayer was read, a flock of African skimmers, working bait in the surf, crested a roller and flew at high speed past the gathering—a flyby that satisfied many.

Even after the three African celebrations, some of Anne's friends wanted to do more. Late in March at Nairobi's French Cultural Centre before a large assembly, a member of the French embassy unveiled the Anne Spoerry Auditorium, in recognition of all she had done to advance the French language in Kenya. In June, Anne's British and Continental friends gathered at St. Mary's church on Bourne Street in London to celebrate her life. The service was followed by a reception at the Francis Holland School for Girls, where Anne, at age sixteen, had once found her way.

Only at the first service, in Anne's garden, were there allusions to her troubled past. Her friend Guy Robin told the assembled friends and relatives, "The horrors of World War II had an enormous impact on her life." Yves Spoerry, just arrived from London, quoted Teddy Roosevelt: "It is not the critic who counts; not the man who points out how the strong man stumbled . . . The credit belongs to the man who is actually in the arena, whose face is marred by dust and sweat and blood . . . who errs and . . . who knows the great enthusiasms."

Jacques Depaigne, newly appointed ambassador of France, declared, "Anne has been an honor to France." The service ended with the congregation singing a singularly apt hymn: "Rock of Ages, cleft for me, / Let me hide myself in thee; / Let the water and the blood, / From thy riven side which flow'd, / Be of sin the double cure; / Cleanse me from its guilt and pow'r."

Many in Kenya were either too poor or too far away to attend Anne's services in Nairobi. For months the residents of Sabukia mourned her death in their own way. Around her old farm, Anne Spoerry had impacted at least three generations of Kenyans. A decade after her death, I found one of Anne's protégées, Mary Ndegwa, walking down a muddy road not far from Anne's farm after heavy afternoon rains. Skipping behind her came twenty children in school uniforms, their shoes caked in red mud. Mary paused long enough to explain to me that it was because of Anne she became a schoolteacher: "Dr. Spoerry saved me." When Mary was a child, her family was so poor there was never hope of attending school. Anne stepped in and paid her school fees, with the promise to continue doing so as long as Mary maintained perfect grades. Driven by Anne's inflexible standards and sustained by her largesse, Mary flourished at primary school, then at teacher training college. After earning her degree, she returned to Sabukia to teach. Today, she is recognized as one of Kenya's outstanding teachers and has now seen many hundreds of children through to their secondary school graduation.

Another of Anne's success stories is Rosemary Wacharia, who was so eager to heap praise on Anne she rode a bus for five hours to meet me in Nairobi. She announced straightaway that thanks to Anne her life was "a miracle." While she never complained, I sensed her pain. Both Rosemary's paralyzed legs are bent at odd angles, and she walks with two canes. She told me how, at age four, she contracted polio. Not wanting to raise such a burdensome child, her parents abandoned her. For years Rosemary lived by herself, crawling in the dirt, depending on charity, and starving. Then she met Anne. Without much ado—only knowing that Rosemary faced abuse and an early death—Anne adopted her. Shortly afterward, Anne scheduled an operation to correct Rosemary's lower spine. The operation was "a miracle," allowing her to stand upright and walk, albeit with canes. Anne paid for all her schooling until the age of eighteen, when Rosemary qualified in dressmaking, first aid, and cookery. Throughout this time, Rosemary lived on Anne's farm. There she had two children (also looked after by Anne) and earned enough money to buy a plot of land to grow coffee. Even with her afflictions, Rosemary tilled fields on her own. In her book, Anne drew inspiration from Rosemary's courage: "We are, I believe, watching the birth of a new matriarchal society." Today Rosemary is a community leader and claims she owes all her success to Anne: "We never quarreled. She took me as a child, out of her heart. She was very full of heart to poor people especially . . . May God rest her soul eternal. I miss her so much."

Wherever Anne went, she changed lives. At the coast, her legacy endures after more than a decade through all the children she inoculated. In 2014, Ali Gabow declared, "The village people still talk about her . . . I say she's still awake in people's hearts. I pray for her when I am fasting in the mosque. May God bless her."

With Anne's death, the patients who had grown accustomed to her regular flight schedule were left to their own devices. Pilots who tried to replace her failed. No one could be found in possession of Anne's wealth, skills, and resourcefulness. In settlements like Saborei, Moyale, and Loiyangalani, her death created a vacuum. In 2012, when I visited the refugee community of Illeret, I found that her name and Zulu Tango were still vividly remembered and her absence deeply mourned. A researcher I interviewed told me that needs have vastly increased and today's health care, without Anne, is "at best sketchy." Anne's friend David Coulson provided the final word when he said that wherever Anne Spoerry went, she had "raised morale."

It took several years for AMREF to come to terms with Anne's enduring contributions to health care. In 2009, colleagues decided to honor her memory with a special project, addressing a lifetime concern of hers: the tragedy of over 175,000 rural African women dying each year because of pregnancies gone wrong. In an about-face, AMREF conceded a revived need for Anne's simple style of hands-on medicine, especially in remote regions. "Protect women and you will protect children" was Anne's enduring mantra. Now, years after her death, AMREF is picking up where Anne left off.

◄◦►

As Anne's death was being mourned in Kenya, among a coterie of old women across France the response was muted. When they read of Anne's vaunted African career, at least three telephoned each other to discuss what no obituaries dared report. As homages poured into AMREF headquarters in Africa, these Ravensbrück survivors could only shrug. Over the years in Bordeaux, Dr. Louise Le Porz had kept a file on her former block mate's life, chronicling her many good works in Africa. A 1989 article retained in a folder began with the headline "An Exceptional Woman." In its final paragraph, it mentioned Dr. Spoerry had worked in the French Resistance and that she "remains very discreet on this subject." Dr. Le Porz knew why.

During four visits with Dr. Le Porz, much-decorated Resistance fighter and gifted family physician, I listened to her frightening testimony. The Anne she described was altogether different from the woman I knew. On my first visit Dr. Louise Le Porz received me in her sunny conservatory overlooking a small garden. Even though she required a walker, she rose to shake my hand, her back straight, her eyes sparkling behind thick glasses. Later those same eyes turned opaque when I spoke of Anne. Dr. Le Porz and Anne had lived in Block 10 as fellow prisoners for three months, beginning in October 1944. During that time, Dr. Le Porz said, the medical student "behaved abominably." Dr. Le Porz knew all about Anne's 1946 confession before the Court of Honor and her promise she would dedicate her life to lepers, after she was banned from practicing medicine in France. To Dr. Le Porz there was no doubt Anne went to Africa "to atone for her sins." I told her that on the contrary Anne had claimed her experience in Ravensbrück was "inconsequential." Dr. Le Porz's throat quivered with rage. Unable to restrain herself, she interrupted: "Nothing could be further from the truth. No one who endured Ravensbrück ever was the same. Ravensbrück defined everyone."

On my final visit a year before her death, Dr. Le Porz's world had been reduced to her bedroom and her wheelchair. When I entered, this French heroine, called "Madame Courage" in newspaper articles, was sitting in her wheelchair before a small shelf, arrayed with medals lauding her work as a Resistance heroine. She gave them little consideration, preferring instead to talk of Ravensbrück. She said, "No one can ever forget it, especially not Claude. I think she had a very painful life. I believe she suffered from memories."

Circumstances prove Dr. Le Porz correct. At her death, Anne left behind clues to the suffering. Anne's co-pilot, Benoît, bought the Sabukia farm from Anne's estate "just to preserve Anne's spirit." When he reached down to open her two safes, he discovered someone had preceded him. He suspected that the "someone" had been members of the Spoerry family, intending to keep sensitive documents away from public scrutiny. In fact, Bernard Spoerry admitted to being the "someone." He showed me what he had found—the file comprising the 1946 CROWCASS document alleging Anne's crimes against humanity including "torture," as well as a collection of documents containing favorable transcripts of her time in

Blocks 6 and 11. Bernard speculated that his aunt had retained only files that exonerated her, "should anything go wrong in Africa."

Bernard was not altogether thorough when he swept Sabukia. Under a chest of drawers, Benoît spotted a carefully rolled-up file. Written on it in Anne's script were the words "Please Destroy." Did it relate to Block 10? Loyal friend to the end, Benoît said he "stared at the cover of the file for about an hour and then I threw it into the fire."

Apart from Bettina Durrer's thesis, Anne went fifty years without facing direct questions about her past. How would she have reacted had Africa not been so protective? How would she have described to an inquisitor the ways of brilliant, sensual, amoral Carmen Mory, Ravensbrück's most powerful prisoner? How would she have characterized her attraction to the *Blockova* and justified their torturing and murdering of the insane?

Covering up her ruinous moral lapses was Anne's lifetime preoccupation. In her decades as a flying doctor, Anne used her visibility as cover. The more interviews she gave, the more preposterous an accusation against her would seem. Who could ever doubt the goodness of a saintly flying doctor?

Laughing, storytelling, diagnosing, planning, giving—in Africa, Anne had many ways to divert her admirers from the truth. But this stratagem—a fifty-year cover-up—must have come at a price. At least one who knew her in Block 10 claimed she surely suffered a lifetime of anguish.

Anne survived through promises kept. As early as 1946, when she vowed to her Court of Honor accusers she would dedicate her life to lepers, she demonstrated a readiness to accept a life sentence. Years later, she was still holding to the pledge, keeping accounts—not for God, but for herself and for history. In the shade of thorn trees, she maintained meticulous records, inventorying pills, counting vaccinations, and assigning numbers to all who came and went without a name. As she served as her own judge, jury, and executioner, arithmetic became Anne's sacred scorecard—the measure by which she weighed those saved in Africa against those wronged in Ravensbrück.

Whenever friends asked Anne why she stitched up hyena bites by torchlight, inoculated generation after generation of children, and risked death every day, she chided them, "Why give up if you can still be helpful?" What she would never admit was that if she stopped helping others, she would perish from promises not kept.

Anne's Africa was her worldly penance. The aberrations in Block 10 could be dispelled not by one single victory but through a lifetime of caregiving. At her death, the many Kabalas would be tallied against all those exterminated, neatly arrayed in two columns, side by side in some special ledger, known only to her.

As for a spiritual life, many of Anne's friends believed she was agnostic. During the Hamburg war crimes trials, Carmen Mory testified that in Block 10 she and Anne had converted to Catholicism. If so, Anne never breathed a word of it. Raised a Calvinist, in Africa she was seen in church only for weddings and funerals. If she sought solace, at least in Africa she appeared to find it elsewhere. During Anne's last days, Rosemary Wacharia, a woman of great devotion, thrilled to the sight of her patron reading the Bible. If this new habit signaled an eleventh-hour conversion, it does not comport with the Anne others knew—the defiant lady who refused to count on divine intervention. "People should make their own luck" was Anne's frequent rejoinder to the *inshallahs*—all in God's hands—that punctuated most Muslim conversations at the coast.

Ravensbrück created Anne and Africa saved her. Had it not been for the war, one suspects Anne would have led a life of Gallic ordinariness—perhaps a benevolent aunt at family gatherings, a curer of croup and other childhood ailments, the beating heart of a village, on Sundays doling out ladles of coq au vin and *bichets* of Bordeaux, taking in stray dogs, prospering in the still air of routine.

Ravensbrück was, paradoxically, her channel of greatness. Referring to the majority of his fellow Auschwitz prisoners, Primo Levi wrote, "It is illogical to demand—and rhetorical and false to maintain—that they all and always followed the behavior expected of saints and stoic philosophers. In reality, in the vast majority of cases, their behavior was rigidly preordained." Once Anne had wrestled her dark self to the ground in Africa, she rose to exceptional heights, remarkable, given her dark past.

Thirteen years after Anne's death, one old woman was still pondering Anne's life. During my fourth and final visit to Bordeaux in August 2012, Dr. Louise Le Porz admitted a change of mind: "Sixty years ago if I had met Claude . . . Anne . . . in the street, I would have turned my back on her, walked away, and never talked. What she did in Africa was admirable. She went there for redemption. Today, if she were still alive, knowing her suffering, realizing the beauty she made of her career, and knowing how much she has done for humanity, my reaction would be different. I would embrace her."

Africa was Anne's exile and stage. Far from home, she worked hours others found inhuman, listened to people who, otherwise, had no voice, took risks few dared, and then, during the darkest of nights, slept fitfully. For Anne, days were short and dawn came late.

It was because Anne learned history never forgets that she rose to heights astonishing even for Africa. On this continent of fathomless antiquity, slapdash death, and radiant joys, many are transformed. In special cases, the great become parables. Anne rests among them. In Africa, she sought and found redemption, but not as she expected.

E ven a year after Anne's death, some of her desert patients continued to gather under thorn trees in hopes Zulu Tango would emerge from a cloud and alight nearby. When her headstone had turned patchy and brown at the coast, up-country, news traveled in fits and starts. Evidently, no one had bothered to tell these tribal people Mama Daktari had gone. Should someone have delivered the news, it is possible they would have scoffed, for they placed her on a pedestal all her own. After half a century of caring, why would someone so devoted, so steadfast, so dedicated suddenly up and abandon them?

I see them still—warriors, women, and infants—slumped in the shade of a euphorbia. The warrior's finger is caked in dried blood; two women are pregnant; one child lives with a painful burn, another a hacking cough. They all await the one person who will make them whole. Shifting with shadows, their voices flit and fade like dust devils as they recall ancestral heroes, tribal epics, and desert justice. These men and women are adroit at enduring pain and hurrying the hours of the day, holding out for miracles. At the first sound of Zulu Tango's engine, they will leap to their feet, form a queue, and then silently place their lives into the care of a frail white woman, the indomitable Mama Daktari.

Today the sky is quiet as a hawk on the hunt. Even on the sun-baked plain, marabou storks hush, like undertakers—bills half-open, eyes frozen, legs as stiff as starch. They too appear to listen for the plane.

Finally at dusk, storks declare it a day, rattling the hollow bones of their wings, while creaky men and work-worn women stretch, gather up their few things, and head for their distant *manyatta*. They are still troubled why someone who cared so greatly, who never failed three generations of them, would abandon them now, without notice. Wouldn't she leave a sign? In this land of broken promises, an empty sky can be cruel revenge. Perhaps there was a change in schedule. Perhaps her plane was *katika*—broken. Perhaps she will come tomorrow.

They may never learn the bitter truth—much less understand it—that in the last days of Dr. Anne Marie Spoerry's life, she wore a look of transcendent calm, her life sentence in Africa complete, all demands of the heart fully satisfied.

ACKNOWLEDGMENTS

I first toyed with a book about Anne during her lifetime. It was an interest fired by time spent with her, researching a magazine article. My profile was later expanded into a chapter of my book *No Man's Land.* In 1993 during the production of *The Africa Passion,* for PBS's Travels series, which I hosted, I spent several action-packed days with her, inciting me once again to consider a biography. Over the course of the film's production, Chelle Tutt Mason, Laura Trust, Jack Sameth, and George Page (the last two deceased) were invaluable partners.

It was not until after Anne's death I took up her story with gusto, first as a research project, later as a film script. Vulcan Productions supported both with expeditions to Africa, Ravensbrück, and European archives. Individually, I am greatly indebted to Richard Hutton, Paul Allen, Jody Allen, Geof Miller, Michael Caldwell, Bonnie Benjamin-Phariss, Pilar Binyon, and French line producer Ginette Mejinsky.

A few years later, Graydon Carter, Wayne Lawson, Matthew Pressman, and transcriber Carole Ludwig at *Vanity Fair* magazine came on board to support further research into the subject.

John Dizard introduced me to the *Financial Times Weekend* magazine, where Sue Norris, Emma Bowkett, and Sophie Hanscombe brought out my distillation of Anne's story in "A Legendary Flying Doctor's Dark Secret."

Throughout these fifteen years, on three continents, Anne's friends, relatives, and witnesses came up with stories, insights, confidences, and counsel. For their generous help, I am deeply grateful. For errors or oversights I alone am responsible.

For translations from German and legal French, I depended upon Gillianne Beyer, Christine Wheale, Alexandre and Françoise Manigault, Karoline Krauss, and her daughter, Liana McKelvy.

For photographs, I extend thanks to Carola Lott, Biddy Davis, Thomas Goisque, J. J. Kelley, and David Coulson. I also wish to extend my gratitude to Bernard Spoerry for use of family photographs, and to the late Violette Lecoq for the illustrations she allowed me to use from her book, *Témoignages*.

Throughout the development of this book, support came from many corners, in diverse ways. In the United States, I owe thanks to Starling Lawrence, Christopher Buckley, Scott Asen, Tony Kiser, Ellen Sabin, Shelly Wanger, Julian Hutton, Christopher Walling, Ronald Coleman of the Holocaust Memorial Museum in Washington, Don Rooken-Smith, Tom Wilson, the late Tom and Nan Rees, the late Maddie DeMott, Nan Grusin, Joan Donner, Roberta Louckx, Bryan Christy, Jay and Pam Heminway, Hilary Heminway, Alexander and Brynn Heminway, Annabel Heminway Morgan, Tobin Heminway, Ray Hannigan, George Sheanshang, Jane Hitchcock, and Maryanne Vollers.

In the United Kingdom, I am indebted to archivist Mark Andrew Pardoe; the support of staff in the Public Record Office, National Archives of England at Kew; Sophie Bridges at Churchill Archives Centre, Cambridge; Yves Spoerry, Anne's nephew; and Anne's friends and neighbors Margery Barnes, Caroline Hanbury-Bateman, Sarah Higgins, Joanna Brierley, and Beth Fey. I especially wish to single out Prue Keigwin, who remained a friend of Anne's long after Ol Kalou days.

Shortly after Anne's death, John Dyson interviewed a vast array of Anne's friends and associates. His *Reader's Digest* article was most useful; so too many unpublished notes he generously shared with me.

I also wish to thank Martin Marimo, one of Anne's protégés. My gratitude extends also to Marja Nicolson for her story, Denis O'Shaughnessy, nephew of Mary O'Shaughnessy, historian Sarah Helm, Coline Covington, Fiammetta Rocco, Henry Singer, and my friend and colleague the filmmaker Jeremy Bradshaw.

In Ireland, my thanks go to Melanie Sadleir-Reilly for reasons she will understand.

In Switzerland, I was aided by Caterina Abbati, author of *Ich, Carmen Mory;* Michael Hegglin, producer of *Hände weg von diesem Weib.* I also owe much to Hans Ulrich Pfister and the other curators of wartime archives at the Staatsarchiv des Kantons Zürich and the Schweizerisches Bundesarchiv, Bern. Many thanks also to Bettina Durrer for extensive quotes from her important Master's thesis.

In France, I thank Anne's sisters—Thérèse Pont of Aix-en-Provence (and her husband, Maurice) and Martine Gros of Mulhouse, as well as her husband, the late Jacques, and their son, Henry. Over two sessions, the Gros family provided me with wonderful recollections of Anne. Thanks also to Anne's sister-in-law, the late Ariane Besse of Monaco, and to my friend the late Marquise Sue de Brantes for wartime background.

I am grateful to Colonel Eric Lucas, *commandant des archives,* for helping waive the Dépôt Central d'Archives de la Justice Militaire's moratorium on sensitive wartime files. With his authority, I was allowed access to documents relating to Anne's French military tribunal.

I shall always be in debt to the small band of Ravensbrück survivors I had the good fortune to meet. Two remarkable Parisians—Odette Bonnat Walling (also known as Odette Allaire during the

French Resistance) and the artist and nurse Violette Lecoq—were most helpful. Jean-Marie Liard introduced me to his mother, Dr. Louise Liard Le Porz, who, over my four visits to her home in Bordeaux, did all to make me understand the horrors of Ravensbrück. My time with her shall never be forgotten.

Because all these Ravensbrück survivors are now sadly deceased, I hope this book serves as tribute to their suffering, bravery, and commitment to shedding light on one of the darkest chapters of the twentieth century.

In Germany, I extend thanks to AMREF's Leonora Semler. I also acknowledge the important help provided to me by Dr. Matthias Heyl and Christel Erler of the Internationale Jugendbegegnungsstätte Ravensbrück. Thanks also to Dermott Bailey.

In Portugal, I extend thanks to Charles Harris for memories of Mau Mau.

In the Seychelles, Mia Dunford provided me with Ol Kalou recollections of Anne.

In Kenya, I owe much to Juliet Barnes's hospitality and to her work preparing for my visit to her home in Soysambu and to Anne's former home in Ol Kalou. Through her, I met several remarkable men—Francis Muchemi, Solomon Mbura Gitau, Joseph Mwangi Muheo, Bonnys Ndetto, Ben Ngala, and two men known only as Harangu and Githaiga. Juliet also arranged a meeting with the ailing Francis Karua Thuku, Anne's "trainer."

In Nairobi, Lamu, and Paris, Bernard, the late Anita Spoerry, and their daughter, Chloe, welcomed me and supported my research, however painful to them as a family. In Kenya, I also wish to thank Gilly and Patrick Dudgeon, Maureen "Bubbles" Delap, the late Enid Grant, who left behind handwritten reminiscences of Anne, Rose Dyer, Patricia and Gilfred Powys, Biddy Davis, Hugh Cran, Judith and Edmund Hemsted, Harrow Trompenau, Joanna Brierley, Dr. Richard Leakey, Alan Root, Guy and Betty Robin, Hélène Roche,

Angela Sutton, Shel Arensen, Roland Minor, Tony Fitzjohn, Father Sylvio Prandoni, Rosemary Wacharia, Peter Wacharia, John Wacharia, Mary Ndegwa, and Astrid Clavé and Erick Letourneur. I offer special thanks to Ian Parker, formerly in Kenya, now in Australia, who did his best to set me straight about Mau Mau.

My friend Maryanne Fitzgerald generously abandoned her own plans for a biography of Anne and, at many turns, laid aside her own interest to help me with this work. In Lamu, Errol Trzebinski encouraged me greatly, while navigating me through the shoals and reefs of writing African biographies. Benoît Wangermez was a fund of information about Anne's last years. Over three visits, Ali Gabow, Anne's last assistant, generously gave me hours of his time to tell me of his days with Anne. For logistical help I thank driver Martin Karanja Mathenge and legendary film fixer Jean Hartley of Viewfinders.

Many at AMREF, parent of the Flying Doctors Service, willingly gave me of their time. During Anne's lifetime, I was honored to meet Sir Michael and Lady Wood. Later, I was lucky to interview Jim Heather-Hayes, Colin Davis, David Mutava, David Hartwright, Florence Muli-Musiime, and, in its New York office, Lisa Meadowcroft and Betsy Kovacs. The locus of all history was Nicky Blundell Brown, AMREF's coordinator of special events and heritage, as well as one of Anne's long-standing friends. Nicky provided me with numerous leads, even while saddened by some of my findings.

The filmmaker Frauke Finsterwalder, living in Lamu, drew my attention to a little-known film about the Flying Doctors, produced by Werner Herzog, who kindly responded to my e-mails.

In South Africa: Bruce Rooken-Smith, John Platter, Heather Rooken-Smith (now living in Namibia), Aggie Dunford, Richard Morgan-Grenville, Helen Hallowes (as reported by Ros Watson), Caroline Blore, Beth Fey, and John Edge.

Patrick Walsh, then a principal at Conville & Walsh, was one of the first to believe in this book. I extend great thanks to him and his colleagues, Alexandra McNicoll, Jake Smith-Bosanquet, Alex Christofi, Henna Silvennoinen, and Carrie Plitt, as well as to independent editors Gillian Stern and Martin Fletcher.

In the end, literary agent Jacques de Spoelberch took up the book. I am indebted to him for his dedication, editorial help, courtesy, and tactical thinking.

In no small way, it was thanks to Carl Hiaasen that the story first made its way to Sonny Mehta at Knopf. I am most grateful to both for their belief in the project, to Andrew Miller for his patient and thoughtful editing, to Zakiya Harris for critical suggestions and dexterous management, and to Ingrid Sterner for fastidious copy editing.

Over the years, the burden of my absences, physical and emotional, on the Anne Spoerry trail has been borne by my wife, Kathryn, and our daughter, Lucia. Both have lived through endless layers and multiple revelations of this story. If either uttered a word of complaint, I cannot recall. I hope this volume serves as testament to my gratitude and love.

NOTES

PROLOGUE: THE END

For eyewitness details of Anne's funeral, I consulted with Tom Rees, Nicky Blundell Brown, and AMREF's chief pilot, Jim Heather-Hayes. Color was enriched by Tom's memoir, *Daktari: A Surgeon's Adventures with the Flying Doctors of East Africa.*

After her funeral Dr. Richard Leakey told me of his unquestioning admiration for Anne: "Anne always went the extra mile for people in trouble. She really put her heart and soul and herself in quite considerable danger to help people. She'd fly into strips that weren't flyable, and she'd fly through weather that, frankly, nobody should be flying through in a single-engine plane . . . She probably saved more lives than anyone else in the history of Africa . . .

"I found her as she was, I took her as she was, I liked her for what she was. I never asked about her past."

CHAPTER ONE: THAT'S ALL I'LL SAY

I first wrote about Anne, in "Desert Doctor," for *Quest* magazine. Later the profile was republished and expanded in *No Man's Land,* my book about the lives of colorful expatriates. My original notes have been used to supplement this chapter.

Before she published her own memoirs, Anne was known to show *No Man's Land,* with its chapter about her, to friends and acquaintances. She said it was the best account of her life yet. Notably, it provided misinformation about her imprisonment during World War II.

CHAPTER TWO: IF

Apart from Anne's autobiography, I relied on a succession of interviews with her over a period of twelve years. The best material, by far, was her handwritten journal, inscribed (presumably by someone else) "Journal d'Anne débutant le 10 Octobre 1948 se terminant le 10 Avril 1949—Voyage Marseille–Aden." It was stored away in a blue tin trunk in a storage shed.

In 2011, Ariane Besse, Anne's former sister-in-law, told me about her father, Anto Besse, and his career in Aden. After his death she visited Anne in Africa on more than one occasion. She admitted she was so scared of her she never dared probe her wartime past. All she knew was that Anne "got out to Aden through my parents. My father felt sorry for her after she got out of prison . . . She was at loose ends."

CHAPTER THREE: *LA COQUILLE*

Apart from Anne's own account in *They Call Me Mama Daktari,* I filled the gaps in with material provided by interviews with Anne's sisters and nephews. Photographs and accounts of Anne's time as *cheftaine* at Camp du Ventron were found at the Sabukia farmhouse.

Barry Wynne's book *Angels on Runway Zero 7* was helpful as a supplement. My visit to Mulhouse allowed me to get a feeling of the Spoerry mansion, now under new ownership, from beyond brick walls. When Martine, Anne's sister, took me on her daily walk, we circuited the walled garden, which she said had been formative during Anne's adolescence.

CHAPTER FOUR: WE ARE FINISHED

Details relating to Anne's farm came from my 1980 notes, from her files, and from a trip I made in 2012 to revisit Sabukia.

Many of the gaps Anne failed to fill in about World War II in her memoirs have been filled in by Barry Wynne's *Angels on Runway Zero 7* as well as her own short autobiography, titled "Lebenslauf," written for her attorneys following the war. Anne's nephews and sisters supplied further details.

CHAPTER FIVE: A PUKKA PLACE

For texture not supplied by Anne in conversation and in her writings, I have leaned heavily on the memories of former Ol Kalou residents. Almost all were younger than Anne. One was Prue Keigwin, who met her when she was about sixteen. She referred to Anne as a "terrific go-getter . . . Anne was no different from anyone else out there." Prue also made these commentaries:

"Anne would say if you cannot give good opinions don't offer them.

"People in Kenya who were nonentities simply vaporized.

"She [Anne] had a fiery temper. And then it was over and done with."

For further details of 1950 Kenya, I relied on an array of colonial-era memoirs. One was Heather Rooken-Smith's privately printed *Daisy's Daughter*.

CHAPTER SIX: THE EMERGENCY

Six decades after Mau Mau, when I visited Anne's Ol Kalou house, the outline of her safe, bought to store sensitive papers related to World War II and firearms, was still visible on the paint against a back wall of an interior room. In my notebook I wrote: "The safe that once had been her security from vengeance of the past then protected her from fears of the future."

Caroline Hanbury-Bateman, now living in Somerset, once told me about her troubled Ol Kalou adolescence, sharing a house with her highly artistic but indifferent mother. She found escape in Anne, who was a breath of fresh air because "she could talk with children." Hanbury-Bateman also remembered how Anne dressed and walked like a man and, during Mau Mau, "refused to leave the valley when all other women were ordered to find safety elsewhere."

Hanbury-Bateman made the following astonishing claim about Anne: "On her farm, when the Mau Mau were recruiting terrorists, she would march down (to the staff quarters), kick open the door, and anyone she did not know she would shoot. She was quite famous for it. It was considered a bit odd. But it (life) was dog eat dog."

Heather Rooken-Smith, now living in Namibia's Caprivi Strip, was another fund of information, especially about the Hovmand affair. "It was absolutely accidental. There were many accidents during that time—all due to carelessness. I presume, feel pretty certain, Anne paid all costs of drs/hospital etc. Maybe she even paid them a lump sum . . . I do remember how fed up the Pair [Hovmands] were about the accidental shooting. I cannot recall seeing them once he was out of hospital . . . I feel certain they did not press charges."

John Platter, who would go on to become a renowned authority on South African wines, saw much of Anne in Ol Kalou on boarding school breaks when the Hovmand affair was a hot topic: "I remember people wondering why Anne simply didn't call the usual 'Who goes there?' before letting loose in the dark, when she heard movement in the bushes ahead, with fellow settlers swarming about in the operation . . . I do know Hovmand took absolutely ages to recover; not sure he did completely. The incident wasn't raised publicly in later years, as far as I can recall. By then Mama Daktari was the growing legend and we all rather admired her hot-tempered gusto; her bombast was treated with a kind of amused fondness for someone doing good deeds."

Maureen "Bubbles" Delap recalled her husband, Bill Delap, "walked out on the KPR [Kenya Police Reserve]. He told me he couldn't handle the shocking cruelty as they tried to get information out of the Mau Mau . . . Bill hated the gassing of suspected Mau Mau terrorists. They [the KPR] had meetings somewhere in the middle of Ol Kalou. Anne was a party to this. There were other settlers [like Bill] who didn't approve and refused to get involved."

In 2011, I visited Ol Kalou—Anne's first African beachhead and once a hotbed where the great drama of Mau Mau played out. Anne's house was modest, today nearly completely concealed from the main road, off a rough track. The aga-panthus, rosemary hedge, mountain pawpaws, and avocado tree had gone feral, and the house was now in the grip of strangling bougainvillea that blocked light to the windows, as well as a view of the Aberdares. Were Anne to return today, she might not be overly dismayed, for, according to Heather Rooken-Smith, she "had not the least interest in housekeeping or even the state of the place."

Down the road, trimmed by settler-planted Kei apple and cypress hedges, lived Harangu, once Anne's carpenter. Baring a toothless mouth, he laughed almost continuously as he recalled Anne. His career with the "kali daktari" (ferocious doctor) seemed one big joke. For over thirty years, he hammered and sawed to make additions to her many houses, even in Lamu. Well into the 1980s he, as a member of the outdoor staff, was still not allowed indoors. Most puz-zling to Harangu was the doctor's reverse approach to dogs, no matter how fero-cious. With a friendly pat of encouragement from their master, they were given free rein to all her dwellings.

As I left Harangu's house, my guide, Solomon, took me aside to say that all the men and women I had been interviewing were "holding back." He contin-ued, "They are not telling you all, because they want you to hear what they think you want to hear."

Next stop was the site of Anne's Ol Kalou dispensary. Today all that remains is an empty lot, a jumble of flinty shards of concrete, once its floor. Beside the site sits the office of the Ol Kalou County Council, occupied by its secretary, Mr. Ben Ngala. He rose from his seat with the aid of a bent cane to recount to me how in 1959, at age five, he contracted polio and was treated by Dr. Spoerry. She was "very good" to him, but there was nothing she could do to reverse his condition.

To explain why the dispensary was gone, he looked to Solomon for direction. Apparently, I was touching on a sensitive matter. After a nod, Ben whispered,

"Because there were ghosts here." After independence, he explained, the next-door Indian duka was reborn as an all-day bar. At first it was a rousing success, but within weeks evening patrons began to complain of screams they heard coming from Anne's old dispensary, vacant since her departure. A decision was made to tear down the clinic. Still complaints persisted, with the clientele believing the screams to be the last cries of the dead. A few months later, having lost all its customers, the bar closed.

Not far away, Francis Karua Thuku was said to be living in a decrepit hotel he owned. Solomon explained that after Anne left her farm, Francis bought several pieces of her land, at bargain prices. With growing wealth and governmental support, he was appointed chairman of the Ol Kalou County Council, then chairman of the Nyandarua Conservation District and, finally, chairman of the local water board. These were lofty sinecures that provided an array of personal benefits. Apparently, his success was a direct consequence of the power Anne had once invested in him. Through her inadvertent help, he had, in effect, became one of Africa's "big men."

After transiting through a dusty reception area, we opened a door to a court-yard of beaten earth, bathed in midday sun. Francis Karua Thuku sat in the only shade, at a square table, dining on a bowl of rice. Two guards stood to either side. Francis's face was pocked and gray. He stared at my extended hand with what seemed to be suspicion, even though I came bearing gifts. Instead of shaking my hand, he rubbed his knuckles against it and continued eating rice.

After explaining that I had been a friend of Anne's, I broached the subject of Mau Mau. Francis said nothing, his eyes fixated on the camera lens. Then, with support from one of his guards, he shuffled away, into shadows. The interview was over.

On the return drive, I asked about Francis Karua's past. Both of my guides had lived around Ol Kalou all their lives. One was a postmaster, the other Solomon, a carpenter, who claimed that during Mau Mau, as a young man, he had heard that at night Francis opened Anne's dispensary to other members of the Home Guard. Here they interrogated Mau Mau suspects. Those who did not confess were gassed, poisoned, or castrated.

"How many castrated?" I ask.

The postmaster pointed to the sky.

"Fifty?"

He shook his head.

"A hundred?"

"Higher," responded Solomon.

"Francis is famous for killing everyone," rejoined the postmaster. "After independence, he ran for election as an MP [member of Parliament]. Hundreds of women attended the rallies. They were shouting at him and waving socks filled with stones . . . in memory of the husbands he castrated." Francis lost the election by a wide margin and never ran again. The people of Ol Kalou took further revenge by boycotting his hotel. In time, he became its sole occupant.

After dropping off Solomon and the postmaster at their homes, my host, Juliet Barnes, and I drove in silence. Later that evening, back at her house in Soysambu, we heard disturbing news. Just before dusk, a Land Rover had pulled up at Solomon's home. Two of Francis's "guards" approached him to deliver this warning: he was never to mix with or talk with whites again and under no circumstances was he to help me.

Heather Rooken-Smith, who apprenticed to Anne for several months in 1953 and who came to know Francis, had this commentary: "I did . . . appreciate that Anne had to employ someone who could speak the lingua franca." But, she continued, Francis became Anne's "pet." She added, "The more I think of Francis, the more I see how unreliable and unbelievable he is. Anne spoilt him rotten and trusted him . . . Having thought long and hard, I have come to the conclusion that Francis was what was known as an 'informer' . . . I am beginning to think he is a rat."

Juliet Barnes explained that young Anne's attitude toward Francis was no different from that of so many newcomers to Africa: "She trusted people too easily—especially Francis Karua. This often happens with expats who first arrive: they fail to understand the locals and their ways at first, going over the top by what the old colonials would describe as 'spoiling' the Africans. They then become disillusioned by a culture they've failed to understand and end up treating the Africans pretty badly . . . They [the old colonials] call it stage 1 and stage 2 of expat life."

CHAPTER SEVEN: THE PIPER

John Platter was surprised about Anne's assertion in her book that she did not get along with his father: "If there was any rancor on my father's part at Anne buying the farm . . . he never let on to me. Though an almost unfailingly mild man, he might have made an infelicitous aside during the negotiations . . . that irked Anne, who was easily irked. But I doubt it—it being generally understood that crossing our country doctor was not a good idea . . . She never showed me anything but easy friendliness."

Dermott Bailey, now residing in Germany, provided me with details of their flight to France.

During the 1980s, I used to see Maddie DeMott in Nairobi, on visits from her home in California. Shortly before Anne died, Maddie sent her a packet of their entire correspondence. This rich trove remained in Anne's possession at the time of her death. In 2003, I tracked Maddie down to a nursing home in Montecito, California, where I interviewed her. This lovely woman died in 2011 at the age of a hundred.

CHAPTER EIGHT: MISS MARY

As a young girl, Caroline Hanbury-Bateman knew Miss Mary when she worked for the Manton family. Biddy Davis was also helpful in providing Nairobi background. She said, "Mary O'Shaughnessy was one of the few people who did not mind talking about the war. [For her in Ravensbrück] it was survival of the fittest . . . Mary had no pennies and Anne nursed her throughout."

By far the richest trove of information came to light beginning with Denis O'Shaughnessy, who was justifiably very proud of his aunt. Sadly, he only became aware of his aunt's valor after her death. Through him I obtained newspaper cuttings reporting on her return from Ravensbrück as well as the account of her death witnessed by Vera Atkins.

CHAPTER NINE: *L'ENFER DES FEMMES*

I am not alone in voicing disappointment with *They Call Me Mama Daktari*. John Edge, Anne's cousin, was equally dismayed: "*They Call Me Mama Daktari* is interesting but not very revealing."

François, Anne's brother, was against the project from the start. According to his son, Bernard, he "advised her not to write her memoirs because there were many in France who hadn't forgotten, but she went ahead anyway, merely solving the problem by its avoidance."

Anne's first view of Ravensbrück must have shaken her, as it did all others. While she refused to discuss anything of her time there, she did, at the end of her life, draw the central courtyard from memory. A possible caption to that illustration might be this description from fellow prisoner Isa Vermehren (who would spend time in solitary confinement next to Carmen Mory): "The camp wall ran along close behind the commando building. Then a big iron gate opened into the camp, 10 m behind it was a second gate that leads directly into the courtyard of the camp. To the left was surrounded by barbed wire, behind which lay the barracks of the SS-canteen and the SS-Lazarett (military hospital). The bathroom and the annexed huge administration building with the camp kitchen were located next to the gate on the right, which at this lunch time were in full commotion: endless lines of prisoners stood waiting all the way down the long and wide camp street in front of the building and waited for the receipt of food. Many shaved heads, torn clothes, dusty faces. The expression of dullness and fatigue on their faces, which could be hiding both good and bad."

Anne's "Lebenslauf" provided a number of details of her time in Fresnes, as did Barry Wynne in *Angels on Runway Zero 7*. I have also relied on the growing library of Ravensbrück memoirs. One of the most notable is Germaine Tillion's *Ravensbrück*. The most recent summary is Sarah Helm's impressive *Ravensbrück: Life and Death in Hitler's Concentration Camp for Women*.

CHAPTER TEN: BEGIN THE BEGUINE

While newspaper articles reporting on the Hamburg war crimes trials and several memoirs provided thumbnail accounts of Mory's astonishing life, none were as comprehensive as Caterina Abbati's authoritatively researched *Ich, Carmen Mory*, in German, published in Switzerland. I was happy to spend time with Caterina, who helped me understand the imperfection of memory, especially regarding events that had occurred in concentration camps. Michael Hegglin's excellent documentary *Hände weg von diesem Weib* was also a useful source.

A Manchester, England, woman (wishing anonymity) whose mother had had an interesting encounter with Mory in Berlin in the early 1930s kindly provided the author with a colorful Carmen Mory story, previously unrecorded.

CHAPTER ELEVEN: DR. CLAUDE

I gathered enormous amounts of insight from interviews with Odette Walling, Violette Lecoq (who generously gave me permission to use drawings from her sketchbook, *Témoignages*), and, over several years, Dr. Louise Le Porz.

Ravensbrück floor plans, drawn in 1937, and found in the Lund archives, were vital.

Accounts of Carmen Mory and Anne Spoerry came from the Hamburg war crimes trial found in the following:

- · Public Record Office, National Archives of England, Kew
- · L'Anne Spoerry dossier, Le Dépôt Central d'Archives de la Justice Militaire, Ministère de la Défense et des Anciens Combattants, Le Blanc, France
- · Staatsarchiv des Kantons Zürich
- · Schweizerisches Bundesarchiv, Bern

Accusations against Carmen Mory derived not only from French prisoners. In the Lund University Library's Voices from Ravensbrück (in which the names of all those interviewed were deleted) are the words of a Swedish woman (no. 285, Stockholm, March 28, 1946):

Dr. Winkelmann slated every woman with gray hair or swollen legs for the crematorium, and especially liked to take tuberculosis patients from Block 10—helpful to him in making the selection was Carmen Mory, a political prisoner—a Swiss woman who would suggest people toward whom she had a negative attitude. She cooperated with the Gestapo, after all, she was at their beck and call and at the same time spied on our bosses, the SS doctors and nurses. She would send the victims to Dr. Winkelmann, if they were women who were mentally ill, in just a shirt to be loaded under SS guard into open trucks and taken straight to the crematoriums, which were next to the gas chamber.

Selected details of Anne's fourteen months in Ravensbrück come from Caterina Abbati's *Ich, Carmen Mory*. The other source was the twelve-page account Anne handwrote on January 16, 1947, for her lawyers. Titled "Lebenslauf" (Biography), it mentions Carmen Mory only twice. The Block 10 "Idiot Room" Anne describes analytically:

It was . . . Dr. Maudi who ordered the condition of the madwomen's room. It was only him who admitted patients . . . and who authorized the way out. The conditions soon became terrible due to the . . . arrival of a mass of convoys from Ukraine and Poland. The room . . . about 2 x 5 meters, was carpeted by straw mattresses. There were two big buckets for sanitation. The window, open for ventilation, was secured with wooden bars . . . The SS gave the madwomen only half the food given to other patients. In these terrible conditions (the maximum number of patients being 67) mortality was very high—1 every 3 or 4 days through physiological misery.

As far as I can remember, in the Block which held about 1,000 patients, the number of deaths each day was between 1 and 6. I remember an exceptional day when there were 8 deaths.

I stayed in the Block until January 6 or 7, 1945.

Mory's quotation about her treatment of "these roaches" in the "Idiot Room" comes from testimony of a Polish woman who was a fellow "block leader" in Ravensbrück. It was quoted in Bernhard Strebel, "Täterinnen im Konzentrationslager" (Culprits in the concentration camp), Verlängerter Arm der SS oder schützende Hand? Drei Fallbeispiele von weiblichen Functionshäftlingen in KZ Ravensbrück, *Werkstatt Geschichte* (1995).

Gillianne Beyer, translating original transcriptions, made a number of useful observations about Mory's state of mind:

The reconstruction of the real facts faces the same problems the British court faced: without more background information it is hard to know what really happened. The following conclusions, however, can be drawn: After having spent fifteen months in solitary confinement and almost "losing it," it is safe to assume that Mory lost her mental stability. Her activities as Ramdohr's informant took her into the dangerous territory or "gray zone" of finding herself in the middle of confrontations between the SS camp authorities and the Gestapo representation in the camp, as well as being culprit and victim at the same time. Sofsky describes her situation as follows: "In order to protect herself she had to present herself as the faithful assistant. In order not to be killed and stay in power she had to enforce terror to those below her. And the more she terrorized inmates, the more she was threatened to be lynched. She had to adapt upward and demonstrate even more power."

After reading many German newspaper accounts of the Hamburg trials, Gillianne Beyer added these comments:

There are contradicting statements everywhere with regards to Mory's behavior. I think it gets to her head that at one point she is the smart, well-educated girl who becomes the favorite of the Gestapo leaders and the next moment she finds herself as a prisoner in the women's camp. The thought of feeling better or more entitled than the rest somehow sticks with her, and she makes every point to establish her own role, elevated from the other inmates. She is smart enough to take actions yet seems unpredictable. That is what maybe makes her crazy in an intelligent, almost unnoticeable way and thus probably very scary to others. This might also explain why she is so good in her role as a spy. Nobody suspects the "devil" behind this friendly face. Those afraid of her may have noticed her lunatic tendencies; others may have believed her ways of pretending to want to make things better. All along she, too, is trying to survive. She manages quite well considering the described conditions she has to endure. After all, she also makes it through fifteen months of solitary confinement. I cannot imagine how one would come away without some loose screw.

Odette Fabius, who publicly applauded Anne's behavior outside Carmen Mory's influence, strongly condemned her activities in Block 10. She also discussed Anne's courtroom travails in *Un lever de soleil sur le Mecklembourg,* pages 181–82.

On her return to France, the medical student was denounced by her comrades and stopped.

Switzerland also demanded her extradition, and it was in Zurich that a trial took place, terminated by her [the medical student's] condemnation.

She was promptly denied the right to visit France, but after forty years a number of pardons have allowed the waiver of this interdiction.

In *Women in the Resistance and in the Holocaust,* Vera Laska linked Carmen Mory to Bruno Orendi, one of Ravensbrück's infamous doctors.

A new inmate supervisor was appointed in the person of Carmen Mory, a malicious pervert. Then into this space of 9x9 feet Orendi placed mentally ill women . . . First there were only ten of them. Then more were brought in, and even with their high mortality rate, their number in this den of doom reached the fantastic number of fifty and finally eighty.

Here at this den, at a safe distance of course, often stood the spoiled brat Orendi and had a ball. This was his project! His "Orendi Express," or his "Shanghai Express," as he referred to it roaring with laughter.

CHAPTER TWELVE: NO. 40 FLAT HEELS

Bernard Spoerry claimed that his father was the only member of the family in whom Anne confided.

Here are the charges filed against Anne leading to her arrest in Switzerland:

In a notarized document dated February 16, 1949, from the "Tribunal Départemental à Meilen," Switzerland, numbered P. 47/1948/Gi/b, in an "ordonnance" dated May 13, 1948, by "Le Parquet de Zurich, instruction no. 13/1947," Anne had been accused of "murder, cuts and wounds." The cost of proving her guilt was assumed by the State, while at the same time Anne was denied a request for indemnity by reason that she herself had provoked these charges "through her contemptible contact with the poor sick people of the Ravensbrück Concentration Camp."

Specific charges against Anne are inscribed in Schweizerische Bundesanwaltschaft/Ministère Public Fédéral, Justizdirektion des Kantons Zürich, January 11, 1947:

The former confirms the sending of dossier on AS received by Polizeidepartement of the Kanton of Baselland so that the necessary measure may be taken.

The documents assert AS administered deadly injections together with CM.

Also deposition of CM and AS having given lethal injections to fellow inmates, as well. This testimony was reported in almost all daily newspapers in Switzerland on January 10, 1947.

Consequence of all that was so far: AS is guilty of murder or possibly participation in murder, and thus may be held responsible for her actions according to the relevant law articles, particularly Art. 6 StGB (penal code).

Either late in 1946 or early in 1947, Zurich police were ordered "to arrest AS at once and to bring her to the Bezirksanwaltschaft in Meilen . . . Immediate because the case was already discussed by the press . . . danger of escape. Order for arrest and order for house search. Correspondence and other possible proof for involvement in KZ [concentration camp] must be confiscated."

From the Staatsanwaltschaft des Kantons Zürich:

Anne Spoerry was imprisoned from January 12, 1947, to March 7, 1948, "accused under the name Dr. Claude of repeated murder and mistreatment of people that were given into her care, several cases of lethal injections, participation in selections for extermination or participation in the actual killing, brutality like slapping, hitting with leather straps, kicking, pouring of ice water."

On January 26, 1947, Carmen Mory wrote to Mr. G. de Rham, the Swiss consul general in Hamburg, claiming that Anne was a fraud and had fooled her as well: "Is Spoerry Swiss, is she French, was she working for the British? In other words, on how many sleighs does she sleigh all around the world? Was she a certified doctor, as she told me in Ravensbrück, or was the document she showed me, which confirmed she had taken her final exams, valid?"

The British also seemed interested in Anne's incarceration, as evidenced by Public Record Office, Kew (Folio 865 Letter), with this handwritten letter from H. N. Fryer:

Subject: Dr Anne Spoerry: witness for Carman Mory
From: M.A., Berne 917/239/47 28th January 1947
To: H.Q., Hamburg District, B.A.O.R. (War Crimes)
Copy to: M.I. 4/Colonel, War Office
Ref: Telegram no A(PS4) 4105 of 26.12.46 from H.Q. Hamburg District

1. The Swiss woman, Anne Spoerry whom you informed me in your telegram referred to above was wanted as witness at the hearing of Carman Mory during the Ravensbrück trials, has been arrested by the Swiss authorities.
2. Swiss press reports state that the arrest took place on the grounds of suspected collaboration in the crimes committed in German concentration camps.
3. The reports also state Dr. Spoerry has both Swiss and French nationality and was brought up in Alsace. She entered Switzerland after the

German collapse in 1945. Since then she has been to Paris, ostensibly to complete her medical studies. She returned from Paris to Switzerland in September 1946 and since then has lived in Männedorf near Zurich.

4. The legal investigations by the Swiss authorities are still in their early stages. During the first examination, Dr. Spoerry strongly refuted the charge of having collaborated in the extermination of prisoners in Germany.

(sgd) H. N. Fryer
Colonel, GS.

Susanne Hélène Roussel and Jacqueline Héreil testified independently in Hamburg about Anne's Court of Honor trial, which they had attended as members of the court.

In the Swiss archives, there is conflicting testimony about Anne's general demeanor in Ravensbrück. In Block 10, however, the evidence is reasonably consistent. There she was accused of "having consciously provoked death occurrences by injecting overdoses of medicines . . . and by injecting air . . . and this while she worked in Block 10, where there were as many as 60 deaths every day."

The prosecution was at a loss because "there is no way to trace specific victims." There is "only individual case: a Pole, mental patient."

The selection of Hamburg testimony unfavorable to Anne during her time in Block 10 is very extensive. I include a sampling to illustrate its depth:

ELSA SCHÜTZ: He [Dr. Treite] gave approval, Dr. Claude did the rest. It didn't really matter as the TB-Block was constantly overcrowded. Mainly very ill ones, but other people too, whom Dr. Claude or CM found *unsympathisch* [didn't feel any sympathy toward]. These people partly gassed . . . or else got injections that killed the victims after 24 hrs, more often after 2–3 days. Dr. Claude usually came around midnight, accompanied by CM.

M. VON HALLE: Openly known in camp that AS was entirely *ausgeliefert* to Mory [at Mory's mercy], that they gave presents to each other, that they were lovers, and that they slept together in a small niche hidden by a curtain . . . One inmate named Max told me that AS gave CM a silky nightgown . . . I have seen AS repeatedly give injections. I don't know how many people died from it.

In the beginning, Anne defended Carmen Mory. She wrote this description of their relationship:

Between me and CM a friendship had developed, but without any sexual undertone. What tied us together was our being Swiss. We talked a lot about Switzerland. Also pity drew me close to her, because of the heavy consequences of having kept in custody objects belonging to me and others. She was an intelligent woman, spoke several languages and she had many intellectual interests. There weren't many intellectual personalities at the camp. In terms of emotions she was very versatile. She could be very nice but she could also get upset when she didn't like something. On the other hand I've never noticed any sadistic side about her. However, in the way she expressed herself she could be quite *grob* [rough]. She often threatened people with slaps and sometimes she did give slaps . . . CM talked quite often to Dr. Treite . . . something that fuelled the suspicion that she was a spy . . . People were afraid of her.

John Edge, whose paternal grandmother was born Mary Mathilde Spoerry, sister of Anne's father, wrote, "From what I remember my parents telling me, when Anne was arrested, Henry Spoerry immediately called my father and implored him to arrange the best legal defense he could. Because my father was a member of the UK Bar Assn, he managed to arrange for David Maxwell-Fyfe to head the defense team."

While it is not certain Maxwell Fyfe took an active role, it is reasonably certain he helped Henry identify the Swiss team.

Accounts of Mory's claims of privileged information came from several sources, including his own testimony. Captain Uff, O.C. 39, a G.S.I(b) Plön (PRO WO 208/3797), interviewed her on June 18, 1945, and reported her saying, "'My two halfbrothers Ernest and Fredric von Kaufmann [Mory meant *Kauffmann*] are British and served in the English navy. I am not able to give further informations, until I am completely out of the reach of the Germans and Russians and certain French authoritys who were in contact all the years with the Gestapo' . . . She wishes to give an explanation of these happenings to a Colonel of the British Intelligence and refuses to explain fully what it is all about. I gather however she wishes to denounce some high-ups in the French Govt. And also the Swiss Counsel in Berlin for espionage . . . She has volunteered . . . statements about life in Ravensbrück Con Camp which will certainly be useful to the War Crimes Commission . . . but it is not all very clearly expressed . . . She claims to have saved the lives of many . . . I do not know what to make of her altogether, but she seems very certain that she has information of the very highest order to give . . . I do not think she is altogether altruistic in her aims! Nor do I trust her at all." Catherine Abbati, *Ich, Carmen Mory*.

Another account of Mory's extravagant attempts at self-promotion comes from Hugh Trevor-Roper's introduction to the third edition (1956) of *The Last Days of Hitler*. In it he discusses events after Hitler's suicide:

> Doenitz's statement was indeed supported by a certain Dr Karl Heinz Spaeth of Stuttgart, who deposed on oath during his holiday at Illertissen in Bavaria that he had personally attended Hitler, when he was wounded in the lung by Russian shellfire at the Zoo Bunker on the afternoon of May 1st, and had pronounced him dead; but another authority, a Swiss woman journalist, Carmen Mory, deposed at Hamburg with equal pro- testations of veracity that Hitler, to her certain knowledge, was living on an estate in Bavaria with Eva Braun, her sister Gretl, and Gretl's husband Hermann Fegelein. Carmen Mory offered to investigate this matter, through numerous channels at her disposal (for having been imprisoned as a spy in a German concentration camp she was well supplied with means of information); but she warned the British authorities that any attempt to dispense with her services would be fatal; at the approach of anyone in uniform, all four would infallibly commit suicide. Since both these stories could not possibly be true, it was clear that mere affidavits could not be accepted as evidence in this matter.

More than once, Mory incriminated herself during proceedings in Hamburg. One example is this exchange with Major Stewart, January 10, 1947 (PRO, WO 235/306):

MAJOR STEWART: What sort of document did you sign for Ramdohr?

CM: It was a simple machine written chit which said that as the end of the war was coming I, as a prisoner, was willing to stand by Ramdohr to work against revolt, uproar and against crimes.

MAJOR STEWART: Mory, you are an intelligent woman; you know per- fectly well that if ever the British or the Americans were able to lay their hands on Ramdohr he would . . . find himself in the dock, as he is today.

CM: Why should I know that?

MAJOR STEWART: What was your object in signing this document with a man like Ramdohr?

CM: My object was to keep down the crimes. I wanted to keep Belsen out of Ravensbrück and cannibalism was very near.

MAJOR STEWART: Were you trying to undermine the morale of the French women in the camp?

CM: I have not undermined the morale of the French women.

MAJOR STEWART: The issue is quite a clear one between you and the French witnesses, is it not? You were, according to your story, doing all

> you could . . . and they say on the contrary you were killing and beating people.

No matter how Mory spun her story, she failed to dispute the barrage of negative testimony. The prosecution summary of its findings was damning (from Ravensbrück Archives):

> As the last defendant, Major Stewart turned to the former prisoner Carmen Maria Mory. [He said,] "Everyone was frightened of her, even the SS. She must be made accountable for the horrible conditions in Block 10, the special section for feeble-minded prisoners. Her role as a spy for the defendant Ramdohr was clearly documented by the witnesses.
>
> "Mory was a mean and cruel person who beat patients with leather straps, withheld and stole their food. She also stole many valuable items, which made it to the camp. Numerous witnesses gave evidence of her cruel and horrible punishments. The prisoners were more afraid of her than the doctors, nurses and the SS. At one point she even suggested eliminating the mentally ill."

Carmen Mory's reign of terror at its height was collaborative. After handing down sentences at the Hamburg war crimes trial, John da Cunha spelled out Anne Spoerry's complicity (from Ravensbrück Archives):

> Mory picked a young Swiss woman, Ann Sporry, as one of her assistants. Ann was a 24-year-old medical student, who was sent to Ravensbrueck for being in the French Resistance. There are very few articles mentioning Ann Sporry. She was accused by some witnesses as being a close friend of Mory's and participating in several cases of abuse towards the ill. One particular case has been mentioned by several witnesses, which happened one night in the sleeping room of the mentally ill. Two patients fought and Mory together with Skene and Sporry gave injections to both women, who subsequently died during the night.
>
> Anne Sporry was asked to be a witness at the Ravensbrueck crimes but declined and did not come to Hamburg. It was suggested that she might feel too guilty to be there.
>
> In a letter she admitted to giving injections, but only on the orders of Mory. She described Mory as a DEVIL.

Major J. M. Stewart was one of several members of the military court who actively encouraged the Swiss prosecutor to pursue a case against Anne Spoerry. The following letter is from the Public Record Office, Kew (Folio 892):

NOTE FOR GROUP CAPTAIN A. G. SOMERHOUGH, from Major S. M. STEWART:

The following information is available on Dr. Claude Anne SPOERRY

1. Cross-examination of accused Carman MORY—see excerpt from official transcript of trial.
2. Deposition sworn before Captain da CUHNA (admits having been present at Dr. WINKELMANN'S selections; admits giving injections with evipan but says they were not lethal; states that she was under the orders of MORY in Block 10).
3. Witnesses Le COQ, HEREIL, Dr Le PORZE all mentioning SPOERRY saying that she became quickly influenced by MORY and became more or less her accomplice, but they do not give any details though no doubt they could if they were asked.
4. Dorothy de RIPPER, Paris, address known, stating that SPOERRY was an agent of RAMDOHR the same as MORY and according to SPOERRY'S statement went to him to denounce her fellow prisoners.
5. Denise FRESNEL, France, address known, speaks about a Prison Doctor giving lethal injections with evipan without actually mentioning SPOERRY'S name but it is quite clear from her deposition that she means SPOERRY.
6. The three witnesses who appeared in Court (Le COQ, HEREIL and Dr Le PORZE) volunteered a number of strong allegations against SPOERRY after they had given their evidence in Court as soon as SPOERRY'S name was mentioned during the trial.

14 Feb 47. (Major S. M. STEWART)

In 1947 testimony before the Hamburg war crimes trial, Jacqueline Héreil provided the following deposition:

> The first thing I noticed was that Carmen Mory did not issue to the sick the medicine and . . . rations (in any case quite insufficient) . . . given her by the Germans. I have seen that Mory traded these articles against clothing and tinned goods and other things, which were scarce in the camp, with the Germans employed in the kitchen and the various stores . . . At the time, other French nurses arrived in the Revier [hospital] as for instance Violette Le Coq and two doctors Louise Le Porze and Claude Spoerey. Claude Spoerey was quickly influenced by Mory and became more or less her accomplice and she was completely bewitched.

Throughout her life, Dr. Louise Le Porz never wavered in her condemnation of Anne. This is her testimony in Zurich, April 14, 1947:

In the camp I was put to many tasks and in the last place I was allowed to exercise my profession as doctor, in Block 10 (for tuberculosis patients). Here I came to know Anne Spoerry who was equally employed as a doctor.

During this period when I knew her, this medical student affected a perfectly odious attitude vis a vis French and foreign patients, causing them serious injury, hitting them with a "lanière" and, in some cases, slaps and depriving them, on occasion, of food.

Anne Spoerry became brutal and lived without conscience, from the minute she fell under the influence of her friend Carmen Mory who was, at the time, the Block Elder of Block 10.

Violette Lecoq also was unforgiving of Anne in her deposition taken in Paris on June 2, 1947:

With a few exceptions, she [Anne Spoerry] always conducted herself in a brutal manner with patients. Notably, she hit foreigners with "une lanière" and blindly obeyed the orders of Carmen Mory. Toward the end of 1944, a young Polish girl, aged 17, recovering from a surgical procedure, was dragged by CM and AS to the toilets and there, having hit her, they splashed her with cold water—all of which advanced her death.

Anne Spoerry effectively administered mortal injections to the patients. Toward the end of December [1945], a hunchback having just arrived in the block by transport, was directed toward the toilets. There AS gave her an injection "intra-cardiaque," thus provoking her death later in the day. I saw the body of this victim but a comrade, Miss Janine Ceyrolles, was the one who told me what happened, having even assisted in a minor way. I affirm that this incident was described to the Court of Honor of the French combatants in June 1946 during Anne Spoerry's trial. Hélène Roussel who was on the jury of this tribunal led me to believe that Anne Spoerry acknowledged this incident and fell to her knees to obtain pardon. She was acquitted under the express condition she quit French soil indefinitely. She said she would go somewhere to care for lepers.

Having read the above, I interviewed Violette Lecoq in Paris on May 3, 2002:

VL: Loulou [Louise Le Porz] and I were in the same block. So too Dr. Claude. I was a nurse . . . I was six years older than Anne Spoerry. I was born in 1912. Carmen Mory was a horrible woman and she did terrible things to the prisoners.

JH: What was the relation between Carmen Mory and Dr. Claude?

VL: Troubling. They were lovers. Lesbians. Dr. Claude would do everything she [CM] asked her to do. I saw her [AS] give an injection to a young Polish girl.

JH: Was Dr. Claude's manner tough with the prisoners?

VL: Yes. She followed the other one. She did the same as she [CM] did . . . Carmen Mory was a horrible woman and the little one [AS] followed her . . .

I never saw AS after the war but I heard about her often . . . I was at the Hamburg trial, and it was in part because of my testimony CM was incriminated . . . We never talked at the war crimes trial about Dr. Claude's crimes . . .

I am sure CM did those awful things for her pleasure—to amuse herself.

Accusations against Anne also came from England. In a deposition, taken at Victoria Law Courts, Birmingham, England, May 29 and 30, 1947, Trynte Duvivier de Beer testified:

I knew Dr. Claude there but not by the name of AS. She was a doctor there. I didn't have much to do with her. I was never on bad terms with her. I never had any long conversation there with her. A lady doctor who was married told me never to speak to two persons in the Block. One was Dr. Claude.

I have seen Dr. Claude give injections to patients in Block 10 . . . She gave injections in the room where I slept. CM gave the instructions and Dr. Claude gave the injections.

Every day some 60 people died. Out of these were some who had been injected by Dr. Claude . . . The persons injected were only lunatics. Everyone was starved and most people there were ill from starvation. I don't know if the doses were given for curative purposes or to stop pain. I suspect the cause of death was the injection because after the injections took place the room became empty. When the room was emptied the next morning they were dead. The injections were done in the evening.

I've seen Dr. Claude give injections to women in the Tagesraum— women who had been delirious and violent in the mad-room. Max went into the room to get them out. The mad women fought with everyone. The worst had to be pulled out with leather straps. They were held by Max whilst they were injected in the arm.

It's very difficult to say that it was intended to kill the patients by the injections, but we suspected it was the case. I know nothing of Dr. Claude's work with Dr. Winkelmann, but she was on very friendly terms with the S.S. Doctors and Nurses.

Women died in the mad-room whether injections took place or not. It

would be difficult to say that it was the same women who were injected
who died the following morning. The people were so weak that it's
impossible to say anyone who died had died from the injection. On two
occasions I saw a woman who was injected was dead the next day. I don't
know what was given in the injections.

Carmen gave the orders for the women to be brought out of the mad-
room and for the injections. In Block 10 Dr. Claude was under the influence of CM. She wasn't sympathetic—she was brutal.

Later in Block 6, I myself was hidden. Dr. Claude knew I was hidden
but she didn't give me away. . . . In Block 6 she was a different person—
she was doing no harm. In Block 6 Dr. Claude was good and kind. She
was quite different from when she was in Block 10, where she was under
the influence of CM.

Trynte Duvivier de Beer met Anne after the war and had this to say about her:

I saw Dr. Claude in Männedorf about 11:30 a.m. and again after lunch at
1:30 p.m. I wasn't thinking of denouncing her to the police. It was against
my principles. We didn't speak on Ravensbrück. I didn't intend to quarrel
with her. After Block 6 I had no hard feelings against her. I was also quite
sure what she'd done in Block 10 was done under the dominance of CM.

In Block 6 she'd been a good friend and a devoted helper for all.

While informing against Anne, Carmen Mory wrote to her on several occasions
begging for her help. This letter was dated December 30, 1946:

I still do not believe that you are not coming to give evidence in a British
Court! Please come I think you are the only person to solve the drama of
Bl. 10.

Soon it was common knowledge in Hamburg that Anne had refused to attend:
"Letter from J/Comd. for Brig A/Q HQ Hamburg District to Swiss Consul-
General, 4 January, 1947 (4503/46/2/A)": "The accused MORY has been told that
DR. SPOERRY refuses to come as a defence witness to the Ravensbrück trial, but
cannot believe this is true."

Meanwhile on the stand, Mory accused Anne of the killings in Block 10 (Court
Testimony [3/306] on Friday, January 10, 1947):

Carmen Mory resumes her place in the witness stand and is further examined as follows:

MAJOR STEWART: (To the witness) There is one question which I did not ask you yesterday and that refers to the case of mercy killing which you mentioned yesterday, the injection into the heart administered by Miss Anne Spoerry. When did you hear of this woman having been killed through this injection?

A: The same day, sir.

Q: Before or after the injection was given?

A: After the injection was given.

Q: And it was Anne Spoerry who told you?

A: It was Anne Spoerry who told me.

Q: Did you discuss this case with her?

A: Yes, I discussed this case with her.

Q: Did you approve or disprove of what she has done?

A: I personally disapproved . . .

Anne's secret confession to the Paris Court of Honor was first made public by Susanne Hélène Roussel before the British Military Court, Hamburg, on January 24, 1947. Here is her account of Anne's reaction (Folios 397–400, day 38):

Q: Will you tell the court what Doctor Spurry said in her defence when she was charged with these things you have just told us?

A: She began by denying everything, then after some time and after my questions, as I had been at Ravensbruck, she broke down completely. She said that at last she was glad that she was going to confess. She confessed about one injection, but she said that she had given it because it had been ordered by Carman Mory.

Q: Did you put it to her that she, as a doctor, could not have been under Mory who was not a doctor at all?

A: She said that all we knew Carman Mory had a privileged situation in the camp.

Q: And what did she say, generally speaking, in order to defend herself against the accusations made against her as to her behaviour in Block 10?

A: She said that before she met Carman Mory she thought her behaviour had been all right, but that . . .

Q: Just to get that clear—Spurry said that her own behaviour was all right before she met Mory; is that what you said?

A: That is it. But she said that ever since she had met her she had been spellbound.

Q: Did she say that to justify her own action in Block 10 in Ravensbrück?

A: Yes.

Q: Now will you tell the court what the outcome was?

A: She asked us and her companions in captivity to forgive her, and asked us to help her to lead a good life, that is all.

Q: Did she make any promises as to her future conduct?

A: She made a definite promise and she asked us to keep her from Mory's influence.

Q: But at that time she was in France and Mory was far away, was she not?

A: That is what I said, but she said: "The woman is a devil."

MAJOR STEWART: No further questions.

When I first began seeking help from the French Ministry of Defense in 2002, I was advised, "Judicial military archives are regulated by Law no. 79-18, established on 3 January, 1979." This legislation seals these archives from public scrutiny for a hundred years from the "last act of the trial." Over the years I continued writing, requesting a waiver of the regulations. Each time my request was denied by virtue of articles L.213-1 to L.213.3 of the "code du patrimoine," which sealed the files in question for seventy-five years from the last hearing or twenty-five years from the death of the interested party.

Finally, on June 16, 2011, Éric Lucas, head of the political bureau, relented and granted me permission. My visit to the archives in Le Blanc occurred two months later, after my nine-year wait.

More than one witness claimed Anne killed more than one of her fellow prisoners, some claiming they witnessed her making injections that led "to the deaths of many." Are these credible accounts? The only one I interviewed claiming to have witnessed multiple killings was Violette Lecoq. Later, when I interviewed her friend Dr. Louise Le Porz, we engaged in this exchange (November 19, 2002, in Bordeaux):

JH: In your opinion, did Anne kill prisoners more than once to please Carmen Mory?

LLP: I was told that, but I have never seen her do it. But I was told she has executed others, but not in front of me. I think that, in fact, she has helped others to disappear . . . I remember the first time they [Mory and Spoerry] came to get patients in my room to send to the gas chamber. Among those to be taken away, there was a young Russian woman. But very young, probably twenty, and she had tuberculosis. [Gesticulating.] She has holes like this in her lungs. I had examined her with X-ray, so she was going to die since we did not have any treatment. She was very tired. She was on her straw mattress. She did not move anymore and they were going to, I knew they were going to get her to take her to the gas chamber. And, since I had received from Communist comrades some morphine vials, I gave her some morphine to numb her completely. That's exactly what happened, and when the SS came to pick her up from her straw mattress, he saw she was practically in a coma. Then she was left there. And me, I was worried because I had given her a rather strong dose. In fact, she came out of her coma; she lived for another three weeks, I think. But at least, I thought to myself, this one has not gone to the gas chamber. So, I, I have not done what Claude did, but if you want, I tried to shield her from the worst.

When faced with the public release of her confession before the Court of Honor, Anne reversed her previous position, as quoted in Berner Tagwacht, *Appenzeller Zeitung sowie andere Tageszeitungen, 25.1.1947—Am 16.1.1947 hatte Anne Spoerry bei der Bezirksanwaltschaft Meilen die folgende Erklärung abgegeben* and PRO, WO 309/420 (from Abbati, *Ich, Carmen Mory*).

The account of Michel Hollard traveling to Switzerland is from the Zurich archives: "M.H. suggests AS should explain, as a witness, that she was moved by a feeling of pity, when she made that statement for CM, but this doesn't mean she would want to question the statements of LeCoq, Hereil and LePorz."

CHAPTER THIRTEEN: RABBLE OF COMMUNIST FOMENTERS

To understand the level of outrage among Anne's loyal Kenya friends upon reading my 2010 *Financial Times Weekend* magazine, these are remarks Prue Keigwin made when I met her on that rainy Sunday in York. She described my article as "sensationalism." While not debating any individual points, she claimed being "deeply upset" that I had probed in the first place: "All those people who were in concentration camps had an aura about them. You never asked them to revisit those times. It would have been bad manners, the height of crudeness . . . It was treachery to make them go back [in the closets of their memory]. I am truly shocked by people who analyze. 'Get on with it,' I tell the young. Psychoanalysis does more damage than good."

Later, Prue appeared to reverse herself when she admitted that Ravensbrück had a devastating effect on Anne. "It probably was the making of her life. Things that go on behind the bike shed at school can have a make-or-break effect on lives . . . It's a Damocles moment. If you suddenly have to change course in whatever you are doing . . . you take different directions. I don't suppose she would have gone to Africa for a moment if she hadn't gone through the troubles in Ravensbrück . . . She learned from it . . . and I think she . . . relived it."

The Elsa Schütz testimony comes in large part from the Staatsarchiv Zürich.

After Lake Constance, Odette Walling's life took a trajectory far different from Anne's: "That night Anne took a train for—I don't know where—and I went to Geneva, where my British counterpart in the Resistance met me with twenty-four red roses." Odette was awarded the French Médaille de la Résistance. Later, British ambassador Duff Cooper bestowed on Odette the King's Medal for Courage.

On January 7, 2010, with Zoe by her bed in her apartment on the Rue de Mondovi, Odette Bonnat Allaire Walling died, aged eighty-eight. At her funeral her friend and fellow Ravensbrück survivor Denise "Miarka" Vernay said, "She was a superb heroine of a courage no trial could wear down."

François Spoerry's letter to Colonel Hollard, requesting permission for Anne to travel to Paris, was found in the French military archives, Le Blanc, France.

CHAPTER FOURTEEN: THE SCORECARD

Anne's achievements in the Flying Doctors Service come in large part from her own notes, AMREF annual reports, and interviews with former colleagues. The November 1978 edition of *The Rotarian* independently confirmed Winifred Robinson and Rosemary Sandercock's work with Anne.

Many of Anne's adventure stories are from my own notes. The contents of her speeches about rural medicine come from her speech notebook. When I first opened it, out fell an envelope containing the actual Pokot surgical instrument.

CHAPTER FIFTEEN: THE WRONG SIDE OF THE BINOCULARS

Bernard Spoerry helped me understand the source of Anne's gathering wealth and the circumstances of her purchase of the Muthaiga house.

The Lamu background comes from personal notes as well as time spent with James de Vere Allen and George Fegan, now both deceased.

CHAPTER SIXTEEN: I KNOW WHAT I'M DOING

Anne was one of three individuals included in the PBS Travels documentary *The Africa Passion,* which I wrote, directed, and presented.

Nan Rees told me the story of the Navaho earrings. The rest of the accounts of Anne's decline are from the author's interviews.

CHAPTER SEVENTEEN: I'LL BE BACK

Anne's great friend Prue Keigwin conceded that at the end of Anne's life, when she was "rubbing shoulders with a lot of prominent people, Anne became the most monumental snob."

Martin Marimo, whom the author met in London in 2009, was one of the many who benefited from Anne's "private charity." Thanks to her, he had found work as an accountant and was living well in London and able to send money back to his family in Kenya.

Martin believed that during his time with Anne he received a total of ten thousand pounds. He was absolutely convinced that she had made his success possible. When asked if he still thought of her, he responded, "All the time. She sits on the right hand of God."

While the Hans Hübner, Anna-Martha van Och–Soboll, and Bettina Durrer exchange comes from a file Anne shared with no one, she never gave instructions for it to be destroyed.

Benoît Wangermez was most helpful in filling in aspects of Anne's last days. So also Ali Gabow, Yves Spoerry, Rosemary Wacharia, Nicky Blundell Brown, Dr. Claude Layet, Jim Heather-Hayes, and Thérèse Pont.

CHAPTER EIGHTEEN: HIDING IN FULL VIEW

Bernard was one of the Spoerry family members who took files from Anne's safe. They related to the Swiss trial and had been translated from German into French. The covering document, dated February 16, 1949, from the Meilen Département Tribunal was her acquittal by six judges of charges of "murder and violence." Contained in this file was a selection of favorable statements made under oath. All the evidence Anne accumulated was thirdhand, taken from individuals outside Block 10 and in several cases from women who had never been imprisoned in Ravensbrück.

When, in April 2017, I finally made contact with Bettina Durrer (author of the University of Heidelberg master's thesis about Carmen Mory), she recounted this arresting but not surprising story about Anne: "While I was writing my master thesis 20 years ago, I discovered by accident (reading the newspaper while eating breakfast . . .), that Anne Spörri was still alive, living in Afrika (Kenya—if I remember well) and famous for being a flying doctor. This was quite a discovery! I then tried to get in contact with her, even got her on the phone one day. But she refused to talk about her experience and suffering in the concentration camp. She also didn't want to answer my written questions—unfortunately!"

When interviewing Dr. Louise Le Porz, I asked about Anne's life after the war:

> LLP: I have never seen Anne after my return to France . . . I know that
> other camp mates have run into her, by chance, on the Riviera. She

must have been coming back to France from time to time. As for me, I have never seen her again. And I had no desire to see her. I knew what she was doing, without details, but I had no desire to see her, because, at first, it hurt me so much to see her, and later I was uncomfortable for her, because I have seen what she has done. So, I had absolutely no desire to talk to her about the past. One must respect people, even if they do certain things . . .

If I were to meet Anne now, taking her life into account, I would forgive her. I would embrace her. I would not have done this sixty years ago.

JH: Why, why [would] you embrace her now?

LLP: Because she has redeemed herself, *hein,* she redeemed herself as she could, but she has done it, she has demonstrated the bottom of her heart, and I am telling you, people like that, I do respect them. So, we erase the past and we start anew with new data. Yes, I think she has suffered a lot . . . We have to be forgiving.

JH: Was she able to forget Ravensbrück in Africa?

LLP: Oh, I think that you cannot forget. I think she could not forget . . . It is the absolute truth, the sad truth, but one must always keep hope of seeing people evolve and regret their errors . . . After my return, you know, if I had met German women from Ravensbrück, I think I would have exploded, I would have attacked them. Yes.

I think that for her [Anne Spoerry] it was a great misfortune in her life to have done what she did in Germany and that she has been able to find again her inner life and her honor by doing what she did in Africa. And she had a second life that redeemed her, in my opinion, for what she did earlier. But she, she had the courage to do it. I think that we should not force people to remain in misfortune and disgrace. Yes.

I think there are always possibilities in all human beings, but that is not enough to feel obligated to congratulate them for doing what they did. But, we have to let them understand that what they did was abominable, but we should not push them deeper in misfortune and in the regrets to the end of their days. There should always be an open door to move toward good. And Anne knew how to grab the opportunity, and she certainly did a lot of good. And I think that redeems her . . . Listen, her life in Ravensbrück represents a short period of time, in the end, and she has spent decades to do good. But that does not distract from the fact that she did what she did.

Yes, for her it was a redemption. That liberated her, that took her out of her misfortune. Yes. But I think we cannot say that we want to congratulate her, give her kudos, but we have to mention all the good she has done.

I hope she died in peace . . . I think so. But, she had a beautiful life. It was her second life.

EPILOGUE: IN MEMORIAM, AFRICA

This chapter was inspired by a story circulating one year after Anne's death that in the north her patients of many years still awaited her.

BIBLIOGRAPHY

Abbati, Caterina. *Ich, Carmen Mory: Das Leben einer Berner Arzttochter und Gestapo-Agentin (1906–1947)*. Zurich: Chronos, 1999.

AMREF. Annual Reports, 1978, 1979, 1980.

Anderson, David. *Histories of the Hanged: The Dirty War in Kenya and the End of Empire*. New York: W. W. Norton, 2005.

Aubrac, Lucie. *Outwitting the Gestapo*. Lincoln: University of Nebraska Press, 1993.

Bahm, Karl. *Berlin 1945: The Final Reckoning*. St. Paul: MBI, 2001.

Bannister, Nonna. *The Secret Holocaust Diaries: The Untold Story of Nonna Bannister*. Carol Stream, Ill.: Tyndale House, 2009.

Barnes, Juliet. *The Ghosts of the Happy Valley: Searching for the Lost World of Africa's Infamous Aristocrats*. London: Aurum, 2013.

Barnett, Donald L. *Mau Mau from Within*. London: MacGibbon & Kee, 1966.

BBC online: "Mary O'Shaughnessy's Story: Heroine of World War Two." WW2 People's War: An Archive of World War II Memories—Written by the Public, Gathered by the BBC. This short memoir was written by Denis O'Shaughnessy, who used the pseudonym "Deniso." It did not at first provide the full name of his aunt.

Beevor, Antony. *D-Day: The Battle for Normandy*. New York: Penguin Books, 2010.

———. *The Second World War*. London: Weidenfeld & Nicolson, 2012.

Bergen, Doris L. *War and Genocide: A Concise History of the Holocaust*. Lanham, Md.: Rowman & Littlefield, 2009.

Bernadotte, Count Folke. *Last Days of the Reich: The Diary of Count Folke Bernadotte*. London: Frontline Books, 2009.

Bernard, Jean. *C'est de l'homme qu'il s'agit*. Paris: Odile Jacob, 1988.

Blum, Howard. *The Last Goodnight: A World War II Story of Espionage, Adventure, and Betrayal*. New York: Harper, 2016.

British Pathé. *Ravensbrück Trial Ends 1947*. http://www.britishpathe.com.

Browning, Christopher R. *Ordinary Men: Reserve Police Battalion 101 and the Final Solution in Poland*. New York: HarperPerennial, 1998.

Caplan, Jane, and Nikolaus Wachsmann. *Concentration Camps in Nazi Germany*. London: Routledge, 2010.

Carothers, John Colin. *The Psychology of Mau Mau*. Nairobi: Government Printer, 1955.

Central Registry of War Criminals and Security Suspects. Consolidated Wanted List (doc. 700), as of Oct. 25, 1947.

Chevrillon, Claire. *Code Name Christiane Clouet: A Woman in the French Resistance*. College Station: Texas A&M University Press, 1995.

Churchill, Winston S. *The Second World War: Closing the Ring*. Boston: Houghton Mifflin, 1951.

Corfield, F. D. *The Origins and Growth of Mau Mau: An Historical Survey*. Nairobi: Colony and Protectorate of Kenya, 1960.

Crane, Cynthia. *Divided Lives: The Untold Stories of Jewish-Christian Women in Nazi Germany*. New York: St. Martin's Press, 2000.

Crowdy, Terry. *French Resistance Fighter: France's Secret Army*. Oxford: Osprey, 2007.

D'Albert-Lake, Virginia. *An American Heroine in the French Resistance*. New York: Fordham University Press, 2006.

De Brantes, Sue. *Kaléidoscope*. Plume d'Éléphant, n.d.

Dederichs, Mario R. *Heydrich: The Face of Evil*. Philadelphia: Casemate, 2009.

Delbo, Charlotte. *Auschwitz and After*. New Haven, Conn.: Yale University Press, 1995.

East African Annual, 1965/66.

De Vosjoli, P. L. Thyraud. *Lamia*. Boston: Little, Brown, 1970.

Durrer, Bettina, Als Funktionshäftling im KZ-Ravensbrück: Die Blockälteste Carmen Maria Mory, Philosophisch-Historische Fakultät der Universität Heidelberg, Seminar für Mittlere Geschichte, Wintersemester 1995/96.

———. Eine Verfolgte als Täterin? Zur Geschichte der Blockältesten Carmen Maria Mory, Ravensbrück: Beitrage zur Geschichte des Frauen-konzentrationslagers, Schriftenreihe der Stiftung Brandenburgische Gedenkstätten, Band Nr. 9, Edition Henrich, 1997.

Eckler, Irene. *A Family Torn Apart by "Rassenschande": Political Persecution in the Third Reich*. Schwetzingen: Horneburg, 1998.

Elkins, Caroline. *Imperial Reckoning: The Untold Story of Britain's Gulag in Kenya*. New York: Henry Holt, 2005.

Fabius, Odette. *Un lever de soleil sur le Mecklembourg*. Paris: Albin Michel, 1986.

Fallada, Hans. *Every Man Dies Alone*. Brooklyn: Melville House, 2009.

Fest, Joachim C. *Hitler*. New York: Harcourt Brace Jovanovich, 1974.

———. *Speer: The Final Verdict*. New York: Harcourt, 1999.

Féy, Venn. *Wide Horizon: Tales of a Kenya That Has Passed into History*. New York: Vantage Press, 1982.

Forsman, Caroline. "Ravensbrück: The Women's Inferno." Bachelor's thesis, University of North Carolina at Ashville, n.d.

French Vogue Magazine. *In Paris Now*, Aug. 1945.

Freyberg, Jutta von, and Ursula Krause-Schmitt. *Moringen, Lichtenburg, Ravensbrück: Frauen im Konzentrationslager 1933–1945: Lesebuch zur Ausstellung*. Frankfurt: VAS, 1997.

Gaulle Anthonioz, Geneviève de. *The Dawn of Hope: A Memoir of Ravensbrück*. New York: Arcade, 1998.

Gildea, Robert. *Fighters in the Shadows: A New History of the French Resistance*. Cambridge, Mass.: Belknap Press of Harvard University Press, 2015.

Gille, Élisabeth. *The Mirador: Dreamed Memories of Irène Némirovsky by Her Daughter*. New York: New York Review Books, 2000.

Glass, Charles. *Americans in Paris: Life and Death Under Nazi Occupation*. New York: Penguin Press, 2010.

Goldhagen, Daniel Jonah. *Hitler's Willing Executioners: Ordinary Germans and the Holocaust*. New York: Vintage Books, 1997.

Goodman, Simon. *The Orpheus Clock: The Search for My Family's Art Treasures Stolen by the Nazis*. New York: Scribner, 2015.

Gorce, Nelly. *Journal de Ravensbrück*. Arles: Actes Sud, 1995.

Görtemaker, Heike B. *Eva Braun: Life with Hitler*. New York: Alfred A. Knopf, 2011.

Grant, Enid. "Diary of Meetings with Anne." Handwritten reflection of her friendship with Anne Spoerry, in author's collection.

Gros, Jacques Henry. *Au fil des ans*. Privately printed, n.d.

———. *Au fil du siècle: Mémoires humanistes d'un chef d'entreprise mulhousien*. Strasbourg: La Nuée Bleue, 2004.

Harding, Thomas. *Hanns and Rudolf: The German Jew and the Hunt for the Kommandant of Auschwitz*. London: William Heinemann, 2013.

Hartmann, Lukas. *Die Frau im Pelz: Leben und Tod der Carmen Mory: Roman*. Frankfurt am Main: Fischer Taschenbuch, 2001.

Hastings, Max. *Finest Years: Churchill as Warlord, 1940–45*. London: HarperPress, 2010.

Heberer, Patricia, and Jürgen Matthaus, eds. *Atrocities on Trial: Historical Perspectives on the Politics of Prosecuting War Crimes*. Lincoln: University of Nebraska Press. Published in association with the United States Holocaust Memorial Museum, 2008.

Hegglin, Michael. *Hände weg von diesem Weib: Die Schweizerin Carmen Mory vor Kriegsgericht*. A thirty-four-minute film, n.d.

Helm, Sarah. *A Life in Secrets: Vera Atkins and the Missing Agents of WWII*. New York: Anchor Books, 2007.

———. *Ravensbrück: Life and Death in Hitler's Concentration Camp for Women*. New York: Nan A. Talese, 2014. Published in the U.K. as *If This Is a Woman: Inside Ravensbrück, Hitler's Concentration Camp for Women*. London: Little, Brown, 2015.

Heminway, John. *The Africa Passion*. Film for the PBS Travels series, WNET, 1993.

———. *No Man's Land: The Last of White Africa*. New York: E. P. Dutton, 1983.

———. "Research Findings: Anne Spoerry Project." For Vulcan Productions, July 26, 2002.

Henderson, Ian, and Philip Goodhart. *Man Hunt in Kenya*. Garden City, N.Y.: Doubleday, 1958.

Herbermann, Nanda. *The Blessed Abyss: Inmate #6582 in Ravensbrück Concentration Camp for Women*. Detroit: Wayne State University Press, 2000.

Herzog, Werner. *The Flying Doctors of East Africa: Encounters in the Natural World*. Revolver Entertainment, 1969.

Holocaust: Ravensbrück and Buchenwald. Arts Magic DVD, n.d.

Humbert, Agnès. *Résistance: A Woman's Journal of Struggle and Defiance in Occupied France*. New York: Bloomsbury, 2008.

Illustrated London News. "The Nyeri Homestead Where Two Women Routed a Mau Mau Gang." Jan. 17, 1953.

———. "The Struggle Against Mau Mau Terrorism: Operation by Men of the Security Forces Carried On in Difficult Country, and Other Aspects of Conditions in Kenya Today." Dec. 18, 1954.

Isherwood, Christopher. *The Berlin Stories*. New York: New Directions, 1935, 2008.

———. *Goodbye to Berlin*. Richmond, Va.: Hogarth Press, 1939; London: Triad/Panther Books, 1977; London: Granada Publishing Ltd., 1985.

Jackson, Julian. *France: The Dark Years, 1940–1944*. Oxford: Oxford University Press, 2003.

Journal. "In Ravensbrueck Camp: Woman's Story of Nazi Torture; Miss Mary's Appeal." Oct. 12, 1945. Newspaper account of Mary O'Shaughnessy.

Kelly, Martha Hall. *Lilac Girls*. New York: Ballantine Books, 2016.

Kenyatta, Jomo. *Facing Mount Kenya*. 1938. New York: Vintage Books, 1965.

Kershaw, Greet. *Mau Mau from Below*. Oxford: James Curry, 1997.

Kluger, Ruth. *Still Alive: A Holocaust Girlhood Remembered*. New York: Feminist Press at the City University of New York, 2009.

Kohl, Christiane. *The Witness House: Nazis and Holocaust Survivors Sharing a Villa During the Nuremberg Trials*. New York: Other Press, 2010.

Kramer, Rita. *Flames in the Field: The Story of Four SOE Agents in Occupied France*. New York: Penguin, 1995.

Kurzem, Mark. *The Mascot: The Extraordinary Story of a Jewish Boy and an SS Extermination Squad*. London: Rider, 2007.

Lanckoronska, Countess Karolina. *Michelangelo in Ravensbrück: One Woman's War Against the Nazis*. Cambridge, Mass.: Da Capo Press, 2007.

Larson, Erik. *In the Garden of the Beasts: Love, Terror, and an American Family in Hitler's Berlin*. New York: Crown, 2011.

Laska, Vera, ed. *Women in the Resistance and in the Holocaust: The Voices of Eyewitnesses*. Westport, Conn.: Greenwood Press, 1983.

Leakey, L. S. B. *Defeating Mau Mau*. London: Methuen, 1954.

———. *Mau Mau and the Kikuyu*. London: Methuen, 1952.

Le Carré, John. *The Honourable Schoolboy*. New York: Alfred A. Knopf, 1977; New York: Penguin Books, 2011.

Lengyel, Olga. *Five Chimneys: A Woman Survivor's True Story of Auschwitz*. Chicago: Academy Chicago Publishers, 2000.

Levi, Primo. *The Drowned and the Saved*. New York: Vintage International, 1989.

———. *The Periodic Table*. New York: Alfred A. Knopf, 1995.

———. *Survival in Auschwitz: If This Is a Man*. New York: Orion Press, 1959.

Littell, Jonathan. *The Kindly Ones*. New York: Harper Perennial, 2009.

Lovatt Smith, David. *Kenya, the Kikuyu, and Mau Mau*. East Sussex: Mawenzi Books, 2005.

Martelli, George. *The Man Who Saved London: The Story of Michel Hollard, D.S.O., Croix de Guerre*. New York: Scholastic Book Services, 1967.

Mayer, Jane. *The Dark Side: The Inside Story of How the War on Terror Turned into a War on American Ideals*. New York: Anchor Books, 2009.

McIntosh, Elizabeth P. *Sisterhood of Spies: Women of the OSS*. Annapolis, Md.: Naval Institute Press, 1998.

Macintyre, Ben. *Double Cross: The True Story of the D-Day Spies*. New York: Crown, 2012.

Michalczyk, John J., ed. *Medicine, Ethics, and the Third Reich*. Kansas City, Mo.: Sheed & Ward, 1994.

Mills, Stephen. *Muthaiga*. Vol. 1, *1913–1963*. Nairobi: Mills, 2006.

Monfreid, Henri de. *Djalia*. Paris: Bernard Grasset, 1971.

———. *Hashish: A Smuggler's Tale*. New York: Penguin Classics, 2007.

———. *Karembo*. Paris: Bernard Grasset, 1971.

Moorehead, Caroline. *A Train in Winter: An Extraordinary Story of Women, Friendship, and Resistance in Occupied France*. New York: Harper Perennial, 2011.

———. *Village of Secrets: Defying the Nazis in Vichy France*. Toronto: Vintage Canada Editions, 2014.

Morrison, Jack G. *Ravensbrück: Everyday Life in a Woman's Concentration Camp, 1939–1945*. Princeton, N.J.: Markus Wiener, 2000.

Niederländer und Flamen in Berlin, 1940–1945. Berlin: Hentrich, 1996.

Oelhafen, Ingrid von, and Tim Tate. *Hitler's Forgotten Children*. New York: Berkley Caliber, 2016.

Osborne, Richard E. *World War II in Colonial Africa: The Death Knell of Colonialism*. Indianapolis: Riebel-Roque, 2001.

Parker, Ian. *The Last Colonial Regiment: The History of the Kenya Regiment (T.F.)*. Moray, U.K.: Librario, 2009.

Parker, R. A. C. *The Second World War: A Short History*. Oxford: Oxford University Press, 1989.

Port Grimaud. Publicity brochure, n.d.

Rees, Thomas D. *Daktari: A Surgeon's Adventures with the Flying Doctors of East Africa*. Santa Fe, N.M.: Sunstone Press, 2002.

Riding, Alan. *And the Show Went On: Cultural Life in Nazi-Occupied Paris*. New York: Alfred A. Knopf, 2010.

Rochester, Devereaux. *Full Moon to France*. New York: Harper & Row, 1977.

Rooken-Smith, Heather. *Daisy's Daughter: Our Lives for Africa*. Self-published, 2016.

Rossel, Seymour. *The Holocaust: The World and the Jews, 1933–1945*. Springfield, N.J.: Behrman House, 1992.

Ruark, Robert. *Something of Value*. Garden City, N.Y.: Doubleday, 1955.

Russell of Liverpool, Lord. *The Scourge of the Swastika: A History of Nazi War Crimes During World War II*. New York: Skyhorse, 2008.

Saidel, Rochelle G. *The Jewish Women of Ravensbrück Concentration Camp*. Madison: University of Wisconsin Press, 2006.

Sebba, Anne. *Les Parisiennes: How the Women of Paris Lived, Loved, and Died Under Nazi Occupation*. New York: St. Martin's Press, 2016.

Shakespeare, Nicholas. *Priscilla: The Hidden Life of an Englishwoman in Wartime France*. New York: HarperCollins, 2013.

Shirer, William L. *The Rise and Fall of the Third Reich: A History of Nazi Germany*. New York: Simon & Schuster, 1960.

Slater, Montagu. *The Trial of Jomo Kenyatta*. London: Mercury Books, 1955.

Sofsky, Wolfgang. *The Order of Terror: The Concentration Camp*. Princeton, N.J.: Princeton University Press, 1993.

Spoerry, Anne. *On m'appelle Mama Daktari*. Paris: Jean-Claude Lattès, 1994.

———. *They Call Me Mama Daktari*. Norval, Ont.: Moulin, 1996.

Spoerry, François. *A Gentle Architecture*. New York: Pheon Books in association with John Wiley & Sons, 1991.

Stokesbury, James L. *A Short History of World War II*. New York: William Morrow, 1980.

Stoneham, C. T. *Mau Mau*. London: Museum Press, 1953.

Talty, Stephan. *Agent Garbo: The Brilliant, Eccentric Secret Agent Who Tricked Hitler and Saved D-Day*. Boston: Houghton Mifflin Harcourt, 2012.

Tartière, Drue. *The House Near Paris*. New York: Simon and Schuster, 1946.

Tillion, Germaine. *Frauenkonzentrationslager Ravensbrück*. Frankfurt am Main: Fischer-Taschenbuch, 2001.

———. *Ravensbrück:* Éditions du Seuil, 1973.

———. *Ravensbrück: An Eyewitness Account of a Women's Concentration Camp.* Garden City, N.Y.: Anchor Books, 1975.

Ullrich, Volker. *Hitler: Ascent, 1889–1939.* New York: Alfred A. Knopf, 2016.

Vaughan, Hal. *Sleeping with the Enemy: Coco Chanel's Secret War.* New York: Alfred A. Knopf, 2012.

Wachsmann, Nikolaus. *KL: A History of the Nazi Concentration Camps.* New York: Farrar, Straus and Giroux, 2015.

Wieviorka, Olivier. *The French Resistance.* Cambridge, Mass.: Belknap Press of Harvard University Press, 2016.

Wilson, Christopher. *Kenya's Warning: The Challenge to White Supremacy in Our British Colony,* n.p., n.d.

Wood, Michael. *Go an Extra Mile: Adventures and Reflections of a Flying Doctor.* London: Collins, 1978.

Wood, Susan. *A Fly in Amber.* Nairobi: Kenway, 1997.

Wynne, Barry. *Angels on Runway Zero 7: The Story of the East African Flying Doctor Service.* London: Souvenir Press, 1968.

ARCHIVAL MATERIAL

Public Record Office, National Archives of England, Kew
WO 208/3797
WO 235/305-317
WO 235/526
WO 309/415-422

Staatsarchiv des Kantons Zürich
LS 432.111: Einsicht in die Untersuchungsakten zu Anne-Marie Spoerry (1947/1948)

Schweizerisches Bundesarchiv, Bern
E 2001 (E) 1968/78 Bd. 4: Annemarie Spoerry
E2001 (E) 1978/107 Bd. 128: Annemarie Spoerry und François Spoerry
E 2001 (E) -/1 Bd.111
E 2200 Hamburg 3 Bd. 1
E 2200 Paris 36 Bd. 19 B.32.12
E 4320 (B) 1990/266 C.16.212
E 4264 1988/2 Bd. 382 P.43658

French Military Wartime Files
L'Anne Spoerry dossier, Le Dépôt Central d'Archives de la Justice Militaire, Ministère de la Défense et des Anciens Combattants, Le Blanc, France.

Miscellaneous Wartime Files
Internationalen Jugendbegegnungsstätte Ravensbrück. Approximately thirty German newspaper accounts of Hamburg trials, Dec. 1946–Jan. 1947.

Journal d'Anne débutant le 10 Octobre 1948 se terminant le 10 Avril 1949—Voyage Marseille–Aden. Anne's personal journal.

Lund University, Lund University Library, Voices from Ravensbrück, Interview no. 285 with anonymous witness, Stockholm, March 28, 1946; Interview no. 420 with anonymous witness, Lund, July 25, 1946; Interview no. 192 with anonymous witness, Lund, Nov. 19, 1945; Interview no. 117 with anonymous witness, Malmö, Jan.13, 1946.

Spoerry, Anne. "Diary," Nairobi, Sept. 9, 1998–Nov. 7, 1998.

———. "Lebenslauf." Handwritten from Meilen prison, Jan. 1947.

Übersicht über das Frauenkonzentrationslager Ravensbrück (Masstab 1:2500). Layout of Ravensbrück with floor plans of each block.

ILLUSTRATION CREDITS

Page xi

Spoerry Family Archives, used with permission of Bernard Spoerry

Page 1

TOP, CENTER, AND BOTTOM: Spoerry Family Archives, used with permission of Bernard Spoerry

Page 2

TOP AND CENTER: Violette LeCoq

BOTTOM: Spoerry Family Archives, used with permission of Bernard Spoerry

Page 3

LEFT, TOP: L'Anne Spoerry dossier, Le Dépot Central d'Archives de la Justice Militaire, Ministère de la Défense et des Anciens Combattants, Le Blanc, France

LEFT, CENTER AND BOTTOM: Staatsarchiv Hamburg StAhh, 242 1-II/ Gefangnisverwaltung II/Abl. 12 Mory

RIGHT, TOP AND BOTTOM: ullstein bild/ullstein bild via Getty Images

Page 4

LEFT, TOP: Spoerry Family Archives, used with permission of Bernard Spoerry

LEFT, RIGHT: From MaryAnne Fitzgerald's collection

BOTTOM: Biddy Davis

Page 5

TOP: Thomas Goisque

CENTER: Carola Lott

LEFT TOP, LEFT BOTTOM, RIGHT BOTTOM: Thomas Goisque

Page 6

TOP AND BOTTOM: Spoerry Family Archives, used with permission of Bernard Spoerry

Page 7

TOP: Thomas Goisque

CENTER: David Coulson

BOTTOM: Spoerry Family Archives, used with permission of Bernard Spoerry

Page 8

TOP, CENTER, RIGHT AND BOTTOM: John Heminway

John Heminway is an author and award-winning filmmaker who has produced and written more than two hundred documentaries on subjects such as travel, brain science, evolution, and natural history. He has won two Emmys, two Peabody Awards, and a duPont–Columbia University journalism award. Most recently, he is known for his exposés of the illicit ivory trade. *In Full Flight* is his sixth book. Heminway lives in Montana.

A NOTE ON THE TYPE

This book was set in Minion, a typeface produced by the
Adobe Corporation specifically for the Macintosh personal
computer and released in 1990. Designed by Robert
Slimbach, Minion combines the classic characteristics
of old-style faces with the full complement of weights
required for modern typesetting.

Composed by North Market Street Graphics
Lancaster, Pennsylvania

Printed and bound by Berryville Graphics
Berryville, Virginia

Designed by Pei Loi Koay